The Public Money Manager's Handbook

The Public Money

Contributors

CHARLES COE, University of Georgia

FRANK DAWSON, Director of Finance, City of Cincinnati

WILLIAM DONOGHUE, Executive Director, Cash Management Institute

SUSAN HAYES, Consultant, Rousmaniere Management Associates, Inc.

PAUL LaPOINTE, Budget Director, City of Flint, Michigan

DAVID MAYNARD, Vice President for Public Funds Management, Fidelity Management and Research, Inc.

PAUL MARSHALL, Artist

CHARLES L. MOORE, New England Medical Center

THOMAS O'BRIEN, Vice President of Finance, Harvard University

JOHN ORDWAY, Consultant, Rousmaniere Management Associates, Inc.

GERALD POSMAN, Vice Chancellor, City University of New York

ROBERT SCHAEFFER, Staff, State Senate, Commonwealth of Massachusetts

DUNCAN SMITH, Partner, Peat, Marwick, Mitchell & Co.

DAVID K. STORRS, Director of Investments, Yale University

BRENT WILKES, Director of Field Services, Massachusetts Municipal Association

Manager's Handbook

General Editor and Co-Author

NATHANIEL B. GUILD
Vice President, Rousmaniere Management Associates, Inc.

Co-Authors

MICHAEL CLOWES
Editor, *Pensions and Investment Age*

WILLIAM DEANE
Vice President of Corporate Services, Shawmut Bank of Boston

PETER F. ROUSMANIERE
President, Rousmaniere Management Associates, Inc.

DAVID A. SHEPARD, JR.
Vice President, Institutional Marketing
Wells Fargo Investment Advisors

CRAIN BOOKS

740 Rush Street, Chicago, IL 60611

Special Acknowledgments

Baker Library, Harvard Business School; William Broadus; Coopers & Lybrand; Council on Economic Performance; Council on Municipal Performance; David Crocker; Deloitte Haskins & Sells; Federal Reserve Bank of Boston; Rosanne Friel; Steven Gilkenson; Grand Rapids, Michigan; James F. Lordan; John L. Lordan; Peat, Marwick, Mitchell & Co.; Marshall D. Sokol; St. Mary's County, Maryland.

The Public Money Manager's Handbook was conceived and produced by Rousmaniere Management Associates, Inc., which provides financial management consulting services to financial executives of governmental and nonprofit organizations.

Published by Crain Books
A Division of Crain Communications, Inc.
740 Rush Street
Chicago, IL 60611

84 83 82 10 9 8 7 6 5 4 3 2 1

ISBN 0-87251-065-4
Library of Congress Catalog Card Number 81-67754

Printed in the United States of America

Contents

Exhibits

Preface

The Public Money Manager's Handbook was written to help financial executives make the most effective use of cash resources and pensions endowment trust funds. Any interested reader needs no introduction to public concern over government spending and management. As tax-payers ask for lower government cost, localities can find extra revenues by making more productive use of their financial resources.

Written for Practical Management

This handbook was written for state and local governments of all sizes to make the best use of the management opportunities of the 1980s. In addition, organizations, such as educational, health, and religious institutions, will find the handbook easy to use. It includes understandable descriptions of technical subjects, which are essential for effective management of financial relationships, yet it provides necessary detail so managers may use the enclosed charts, forms, and tables as working copy for day-to-day decision making. The book is also spiced with specific techniques that we believe can add an extra bonus to better money management performance.

The Public Money Manager's Handbook is divided into four parts: Cash Management; Banks and Banking Services; Short-Term Investing; and Long-Term Investing. Each is a self-contained description of that particular subject matter. This modular design enables readers to turn directly to the particular information that is immediately useful to their current operations, so it is not necessary to plow through all chapters to reach any pertinent sections.

A Team of Experts

To write this book with the most timely and practical advice, we assembled a team of experts who are leaders in the money mangement field to write different sections. William Deane, co-author of Cash Management, Banks and Banking Services, and Short-Term Investing, is Vice President of Corporate Services at the Shawmut Bank of Boston, and for years has been instructing organizations of all types and sizes on cash management policy and practices. Peter F. Rousmaniere, who contributed to the sections on cash management and short-term investing, has written widely on issues concerning nonprofit and government finance, and has aided numerous governmental and nonprofit organizations to improve the return on cash and other short-term resources. Likewise, Michael Clowes, Editor of *Pensions and Investment Age,* writes on current issues and events for practicing managers of long-term investment and pension funds. The final chapter on retirement funds was written by David A. Shephard, Jr., Vice President of Institutional Marketing at Wells Fargo Investment Advisors, which has been pre-eminent in the application of Modern Portfolio Theory techniques to investment management. A distinguished panel of contributors offered many valuable suggests about format and context.

We feel confident that readers will find the material in this manual understandable, timely, and immediately useful in their money management operations.

Nathaniel B. Guild
General Editor

Part 1

Cash Management

Introduction to Cash Management 1

During these times of rapid inflation, today's money has less buying power for tomorrow; for financial managers this means that those funds which are not spent today should be invested to protect their value.

An increasing number of municipal treasurers are becoming aware of the benefits of improved cash management programs. Besides inflation, several other factors have spurred greater interest in cash operations.

- Some states have set ceilings on the revenue available from local property taxes, forcing communities to exploit other sources of funds, including short-term investment income.
- The state and federal governments, as well as the financial community and private citizens, are now insisting that municipal governments become more "professional" in their financial management, and this entails the prudent investing of funds at relatively high interest rates.
- New forms of cash management services and investments are available to local governments from banks, brokerage firms, state and federal governments, and others. These new services make it easier to invest small sums of money, to keep funds available for current uses, and to earn attractive interest rates.

Because of the rapidly developing array of new cash management practices and techniques, it is sometimes difficult for a busy local treasurer to survey all offerings. It is equally difficult, on the basis of sales promotions, to evaluate the usefulness of each opportunity to his local operation. Techniques used by large organizations may not meet the needs of smaller municipalities.

This manual helps the local official assess his own community's cash management system and identify areas that need improvement. It also explains, in understandable terms, ways that local governments can streamline operations with new management services to reduce costs and provide greater investment income.

To introduce local officials to cash management, the first section in this chapter defines cash management and explains its applicability to not-for-profit organizations. The second section discusses several questions that will help a local official assess his own municipality's program. As with a patient in a doctor's office, a cash management system may show signs of ill health. For example, one common sign of opportunity for improvement is the maintenance of a large number of checking accounts. By recognizing the symptoms of lax management, the reader may identify areas in local operations that offer possibilities for substantial improvement.

Let's be more specific. How much nonrevenue income should a community expect from a professional cash management program? That question is answered in the third section. That section takes a realistic look at the expected income of improved cash management practices. It is realistic because, as exciting as cash management opportunities are, overoptimism by those promoting better management practices might lead to some frustration and disappointment. The section ends with a case of a very successful program implemented in St. Mary's County, Maryland.

The success in St. Mary's County emphasizes the need for clear goals for cash management operations. The fourth section helps local officials focus their efforts on attaining specific improvements in operating results. With the standards listed in this section, local officials may translate their goals into specific interim steps and revenue targets, as well as giving direction to cash management programs. The goals in this section will help managers evaluate their progress and rate the performance of their new efforts.

Local officials are likely to face obstacles along the path to improved cash management performance. Despite the opportunities for substantial improvement, many municipalities are slow to adopt efficient cash techniques, for reasons related to the unique problems of state and local governments. To the degree that these are shared problems, the last section identifies circumstances that prevent local officials from improving cash systems, and it suggests ways that local officials can overcome roadblocks to better cash management.

1.1 What Is Good Cash Management?

A good cash management system pools a local government's free cash, making funds available for short-term investment. Improved cash management is attractive because with little added cost it puts otherwise idle assets to work. The benefits spill over into all aspects of financial management. Cash management systems increase management's control of cash resources, often by merely reducing the number of bank accounts; they increase the accountability of cash information through improved reporting and forecasting and they increase nontax revenue by making more cash available for investment at relatively high short-term interest rates.

In the early 1970s, when money became more and more expensive because of explosive interest rates, corporations found that their idle cash was a "hidden resource." As interest rates on short-term investment opportunities rose to 12%, corporations made money from investing otherwise idle funds. This experience gave birth to a large core of management practices and techniques that found better ways of finding and investing corporate cash.

Local governments are beginning to respond to these new cash management opportunities. Since local governments operate under legal constraints different from those of corporations, their interest in cash management has seen a slower dawn than that of private sector groups. For example, some states regulate the number and amount of municipal deposits in commercial banks. States also regulate the types of allowable investments; a few prohibit municipalities from putting their money in anything other than bank instruments, and most prohibit investment in private money market mutual funds. Although states are now lifting many regulations in order to encourage better cash management, their restrictions have impeded past performance.

In addition to the many legal restrictions, municipal governments operate in entirely different management environments. In a corporation the incentive for management is to make money, whether that is measured as increased profits or sales, and top management is more likely to understand and appreciate good management techniques, and more likely to reward financial officers for improved cash performance.

In a local political environment the elected leaders, the town fathers, and the community are probably not as aware of good cash management opportunities. In some communities there is even the suspicion that the treasurer who does anything more than keep the cash in the safe or in a checking account is jeopardizing local funds. As long as town finance directors are not heard or seen, people are likely to think that they are doing a tolerable job.

Although greater motivation is required of municipal financial managers, the opportunities for good cash management exist for government, too. With rampant inflation local money managers may preserve the value of their cash resources and increase the nontax revenue for their community. In the Proposition 13 environment of the late 1970s where government management issues are becoming more important, even a modest return on cash resources may make town treasurers "hidden heroes." This manual identifies cash management opportunities and treats their application within the context of total cash systems and the practical aspects of local government operations.

Good cash management techniques enlarge the local money manager's knowledge and control of cash collections, disbursements, and bank accounts. Professional, formal banking agreements help local officials control the costs of financial services. Good cash management programs can even help local officials and citizens assess the social benefits of their cash management decisions and policies.

Does My Community Need Better Cash Management? 1.2

To assess a community's need for improved cash management practices, a local government official must first understand and then evaluate the city's present cash management systems. This assessment begins with a determination of the size and timing of receipts and disbursements, and a description of the collection and disbursement process. The process should answer the following questions. Where are funds collected? How are they collected and deposited? When does the municipality make disbursements? What kinds of collections and disbursements are routine, which are special, which account for the largest dollar volume of your cash flow? How do financial officers receive collection and disbursement information? Are they assured of its timeliness and accuracy?

Next, the cash manager finds out how much cash is on hand by a search of all bank accounts and investment accounts. Finding all the bank accounts may be half the battle for many governments! How much idle cash does the community have in all its accounts, on average? How does it compensate its banks for their services? How much does it pay for compensation? Who controls the amount of funds in each account?

After local officials have inventoried all cash accounts, the cash manager begins a detailed understanding of banking services. For each bank account maintained by the town, the cash manager identifies the purpose of the account, the bank balance, and the source and type of deposits and withdrawals. The mere consolidation of bank accounts is often a source of significant savings. Consolidation reduces the cost of maintaining many accounts and frees large amounts of cash for short-term investment. During the inventory of bank accounts, the cash manager should identify any accounts that may be legally combined. Since accounting systems may keep separate transactions and balances for each reporting unit, and interest income may be apportioned by fund, the identity of fund accounting need not be lost when cash accounts are combined.

Historically, municipalities have maintained large numbers of bank accounts for varied reasons. One is local tradition; departments have kept separate accounts from the time when they were autonomous and maintained the power to receive and disburse departmental funds. Bank accounts have also been used to retain accounting control of expenditures, although double-entry accounting systems are more effective and more uniform methods of recording the same information. They have also been used to ensure internal control of accounts; for example, separate payroll accounts have been maintained to ensure that payrolls are properly disbursed. Zero-balance accounts (see section 2.6.1) may perform the same function at a lower cost. Finally, bank accounts may be used to maintain good bank relations, or they may be required by statute.

When financial officials inventory their bank accounts, they should identify the reason for maintaining the account, the average daily balance of the account, and the type of deposits and collections made to the account.

If a municipality invests any of its funds short-term, the cash manager should understand the local investment process. How much money is invested in what kinds of instruments? When are they due? How does the town make investment decisions? On what basis?

As the cash manager develops an understanding of the town's cash management system, he should examine the symptoms of inadequate cash planning in Exhibit 1.A. If the cash manager can answer *yes* to these questions, this manual may help identify specific management problems, then help in planning their correction.

The questions in Exhibit 1.A on cash management and banking systems highlight problems that result from decentralized and scattered bank accounts and poor cash flow information. A locality that maintains a large number of accounts has an excellent opportunity to improve cash management by consolidating idle balances into a central pool.

The following list of questions should help local officials assess their communities' cash management programs. These answers will suggest areas in need of improvement.

Cash Management and Banking System. Does your community:

- Delay disbursements beyond the date of vendor discounts for early payment?
- Incur unnecessary costs or lose goodwill because of significant bank overdrafts?
- Lack an active program to ensure the timely collection of significant receipts?
- Manually deposit large dollar collections rather than have those funds wired directly to the municipal account?
- Delay deposit of regular collections?
- Decentralize the responsibility for processing cash receipts and disbursements and for maintaining banking relationships?
- Maintain a large number of bank accounts?
- Lack current data on (1) deposits sent to the bank but not recorded by the bank or on (2) amounts deposited but not collected by the bank?
- Lack complete records of individual bank accounts that specify the purpose, activity, services, and average bank balances of each account?
- Produce irrelevant or untimely accounting information on the municipality's cash position?

Banking Relationships. Does your community:

- Maintain bank balances higher than necessary to compensate banks for the services rendered?
- Lack formal banking agreements?
- Use banks that lack bank wire facilities?
- Lack the current cost to the municipality of each banking relationship?
- Make limited use of bank administrative services, such as lock boxes, depository transfer checks and financial advisory services?
- Choose depository or collection banks on a noncompetitive basis?

Cash Forecasting. Does your community:

- Rely on inaccurate and undependable revenue estimates?
- Lack estimates of expenditures on capital projects?
- Lack adequate cash reserves for unforeseen cash emergencies?
- Make numerous and unpredictable trips to financial markets to borrow funds for short-term use?

Investment Policy. Does your community:

- Lose revenue due to a noncompetitive return, compared with current money market rates, on short-term investments?
- Fail to invest a high proportion of idle cash?
- Sell investments prematurely?
- Buy and sell investments only on an overnight basis? Fail to develop a formal, usable investment policy for day-to-day investment decisions?

EXHIBIT 1.A / Symptoms of Inadequate Cash Management

Poor information on cash balances and anticipated flows means that many municipalities also lose attractive savings by ignoring trade discounts. The imputed interest rates offered by most discounts are much more attractive than current investments; for example, a 2% reduction of a bill paid in 10 days has an equivalent annual interest rate of 18%. Poor information, especially on collected funds, might lead to bank overdrafts, which cost additional bank charges and endanger good will. Most local operations have excellent opportunities to increase investable balances by accelerating cash collections and delaying disbursements until the latest acceptable date.

The *Banking Relationships* segment of Exhibit 1.A implies a need for a systematic analysis of banking services and for a simple method for reducing costs. Many local governments overcompensate banks for their services by maintaining excess bank balances. These communities usually lack a straightforward method of evaluating the value of bank balances and the price of bank services. The bank account analysis in this manual helps communities find the true price of current services, and then shows how communities can use competition for deposits to reduce these costs.

The questions on cash forecasting enable the cash manager to determine what funds will be needed for disbursement and what amounts will be available for investment. A cash forecast is an invaluable tool for predicting cash collections, disbursements, and net balances so that the cash manager can plan for anticipated short-term borrowing or arrange for investments in higher yielding securities.

The last portion of the exhibit asks about the possibilities for devising or improving a program that invests idle funds. The real investment challenge for busy local treasurers is to find investment opportunities that minimize the need to be a market technician but offer competitive returns. Most communities suffer because finding high-yielding investments requires time-consuming analysis and because such investments require large amounts of funds. The investment part of this manual describes several investment plans that are simple yet offer smaller local governments high returns.

A cash manager may, of course, answer *yes* to one or a few of these questions yet operate an efficient money management system. For example, the town may delay disbursements beyond the date of trade discounts because it is more profitable to invest those funds in higher yielding securities. Towns may also use banks that lack bank wire facilities because they are required by law to bank locally and no local banks have wire facilities.

But, if a town can answer *yes* to many of the checklist questions, its cash management system may offer significant opportunities for finding hidden income.

1.3 How Much Improvement Might Be Expected?

Once a cash manager has identified the town's cash flows, and once average cash balances are known, the cash manager may approximate the nontax income that is

	Interest Rates			
Bank Balance	**5%**	**6%**	**9%**	**12 %**
$5 million	$225,000	$270,000	$405,000	$540,000
$2 million	$90,000	$108,000	$162,000	$216,000
$1 million	$45,000	$54,000	$81,000	$108,000
$500,000	$22,500	$27,000	$40,500	$54,000
$250,000	$11,250	$13,500	$20,250	$27,000
$100,000	$4,500	$5,400	$8,100	$10,800

EXHIBIT 1.B / Approximate Annual Interest Income from Investment of Cash Balances

realistically available from an improved cash management system. Realistic expectations are important in setting reachable goals. Exhibit 1.B shows the savings that a community might expect for a given average daily cash balance.

The table assumes a modest goal of 90% efficiency, that is, that 90% of all the town's daily balances are invested daily. The other 10% might be non-interest-bearing deposits to compensate banks for their services, or cash on hand for a cash reserve, or restricted funds regulated by trust agreements.

As the table shows, the profitability of cash management decisions is sensitive to interest rates. A rise in short-term money market interest rates from 6% to 12% increases the potential return by 100%, and that increases the motivation to implement improved cash management techniques.

Even though those with bigger cash balances can realize larger gains, cash management is for any community that maintains even one bank account. The security of funds, the proper authorization for disbursements, and the containment of banking costs are the concern of any municipality. This exhibit gives governments of all sizes a realistic estimate of expected nontax revenue from aggressive cash management.

The reader might have expected a greater return than shown in the exhibit for several reasons. First, the reader may be applying the balances that appear in the municipality's checkbook, not the average collected balances actually held by the bank at any moment. A municipality may have checks that have been disbursed but not presented to its bank for payment. Thus, these actual collected balances may be up to two times the size of the balances in the town's checkbook. It is the collected balance that is available for investment. Municipalities also have sizable opportunities for increasing collected balances by accelerating collections and timing disbursements, and thus for increasing funds available for investment.

Second, some of the savings of cash management programs are not measured in extra investment income alone. A concentrated banking system, as part of an improved money management program, reduces the number of municipal bank accounts, thus reducing the need to monitor and control those accounts. Some cash management services, such as lock boxes and paying agents, shift a good deal of the internal costs of processing collections or disbursements to the financial institutions who, because of economies of scale, are able to produce services more efficiently. For example, a town that uses a bank as a paying agent for its debt payments does not have to hire staff to process payments. Municipalities squeezed by effective budget cutbacks find that farming out processing costs to banks and other institutions is an attractive option.

Finally, an efficiency rate of 90% is reasonable, but a well-run cash management system could invest 95% of its idle funds. In the town having average daily bank balances of $2 million, a rise in efficiency from 90% to 95%, at a 9% investment yield, means an additional nontax income of $9,000.

The case of St. Mary's County, Maryland, shown in Exhibit 1.C, demonstrates the real benefits of better cash management. St. Mary's County, with a population of approximately 52,000 and a fiscal year 1978 budget of $18 million, implemented new techniques in 1976 and experienced dramatic improvement. Eliminating unnecessary bank balances, establishing an accounts payable policy, planning and analyzing cash flows, and immediately buying short-term investments increased their investment income by almost 20% in spite of the fact that interest rates fell by 50% after the program started. If interest rates had remained constant, St. Mary's would have earned another $200,000. The county also demonstrated its improved management of cash flows with a 95% increase in investable cash.

Improved cash management offers attractive gains to any community. Many municipalities using new cash management techniques discover extra nontax revenues as well as better cash control, more timely cash information, and reduced operating costs.

1.4 The Goals of Good Cash Management

After identifying areas in current cash systems that offer improvement and estimating the potential benefits of better management, cash managers then design their blueprint for action. They first plan the direction of an improvement program by identifying specific goals.

Cash managers aim to increase the availability of a community's cash resources, which adds nontax revenue cash for investment. This helps preserve the value of the community's coffers. William E. Donoghue of the Cash Management Institute calls this the "cash manager's challenge," to maximize available cash, to maximize the return on investments, and to minimize the costs of performing those tasks.

Specifically, cash managers meet the cash management challenge by meeting the following goals:

- To understand when and how present cash funds are received and disbursed.
- To design and implement a simple system that estimates the amount and timing of future cash receipts and disbursements.
- To ensure that cash resources are available to meet the timely payment of obligations.

The County

St. Mary's County, on Maryland's western shore, has a population of 52,000. Five part-time elected commissioners oversee an annual budget of approximately $18,000,000 (FY 1978). In 1975 during a review of county bank deposits, Joseph P. O'Dell, Budget Officer, discovered that the county was losing large amounts of foregone interest income from uninvested cash. He initiated a process that convinced county officials to implement a new cash management program. It produced dramatic results for the taxpayers of the county.

The Results

Increased benefits:

- In the first year the county earned $360,000 from the short-term investment of idle cash even though interest rates fell in that period by 50%. That alone saved taxpayers 17 cents on the tax rate.
- The county continues to show improvement, earning $460,000 on interest income in FY 1979. It presently invests 98% to 99% of its available cash balances, a remarkable rate of efficiency.

Increased costs:

- To earn those benefits, the county expended little additional operating funds. Cash management operations were performed by re-assigning the duties of current staff. The county did pay its outside auditors an additional $1,000 for oversight and evaluation reports of the cash management program.

Factors for Success

Mr. O'Dell credits success to the county's four-step process of research, education, and implementation. It (1) identified cash management problems, (2) planned a course of action, (3) centralized cash management responsibility, and (4) designed a system to review cash management performance.

Local officials faced the most difficult hurdle first—how to convince their commissioners that the county had a cash management problem. Like most people, St. Mary's commissioners were not immediately familiar with the sizable benefits and low costs in excavating interest income.

To win the minds of the commissioners, O'Dell prepared a working paper that detailed cash management problems and offered specific courses of action in areas such as internal organization, accounting systems, and local banking arrangements. The paper convinced the commissioners that every day that they delayed action, the county lost money.

Since cash management changes also affected local banks, the county presented each with a copy of the working paper. County officials met separately with each bank president, seeking comments and recommendations. Since county cash management improvements offered attractive returns, the banks also supported the plan.

The commissioners authorized county officials to eliminate all excess bank account balances, make timely payments on accounts payable, invest idle funds in repurchase agreements and savings accounts, and eliminate advances to spending units until money was needed.

What was the reaction of the community? The new cash management program was well publicized, much discussed, and well received.

EXHIBIT 1.C / A Successful Cash Management Program: St. Mary's County, Maryland

- To minimize the costs of an efficient cash management program.
- To obtain and monitor high-quality, minimum-cost banking services.
- To evaluate short-term money markets and other opportunities for short-term investments.
- To ensure the safety of the funds invested.
- To preserve the value of local cash assets and increase nontax revenue by investing idle cash.

With these objectives in sight, cash managers operate within liquidity and risk constraints and statutory provisions. Although the local government wants to make the most money possible from an investment, it wants to ensure that no money is lost on investments and that enough money is available to meet its bills. Unfortunately, many state regulations unintentionally impede the functioning of good cash management programs. Nevertheless, cash managers must conduct their programs within state laws.

1.5 Roadblocks to Better Cash Management

Current high interest rates and taxpayer demands for better government performance have renewed interest in municipal management, but many municipalities have been slow to respond to the challenge. Some financial officers are only now becoming aware of cash management opportunities, but many more face a set of considerations that are in some respects unique to government.

This section lists some of the more common roadblocks to substantial cash management reform, as perceived by local officials. The discussion of these comments by practitioners should enable readers to better understand what circumstances may impede progress.

1. *Local officials do not want to run out of cash to meet disbursements while excess funds are committed in investments.* Local officials should be concerned about maintaining adequate cash balances to meet payment needs. The forecasting section of the manual (chapter 5) shows how to predict the amounts of cash needed for payments, and when they will be needed. It also shows how to build in a margin for error, or "reserve." Many investment opportunities keep invested funds available on a daily basis while still earning interest income (see chapter 6 on short-term investing).

2. *Better cash management might antagonize local banks.* Some local officials fear that the loss of idle balances might prompt local banks to be less supportive when the community needs financial assistance; for example, when it issues short-term notes. These fears are usually unfounded. Banks deal with their corporate clients

on a professional basis, and they expect customers to pay a fair price for their services, not an inflated price.

St. Mary's County, Maryland, in implementing its cash management program, developed a policy statement and proposed a set of goals. Then it invited discussion of the program from community leaders, including banks. Banks cooperated, and helped refine and improve the program.

Communities can assist banks in time of financial stress and still earn attractive interest. During the economic downturn of 1974–75, an Eastern county transferred many of its invested funds to local bank investments and earned a competitive yield. Many banks remembered that assistance when the county needed to borrow short-term funds months later.

One way to estimate the cost of inefficient cash management practices is to use an *Annual Loss Exposure Chart.* This is a device developed by Price Waterhouse & Co., the public accounting firm, to estimate the total annual cost of internal control weaknesses which allow repeated losses to occur. The chart can be applied readily to cash management practices. This example estimates foregone investment income.

Annual Loss Exposure Chart
(All figures rounded to nearest dollar.)

Estimated dollar value of each loss	Frequency of occurrence per working day: 1	10	50
$15.00	$3,750	$37,500	$187,500
10.00	2,500	25,000	125,000
5.00	1,250	12,500	62,500
2.50	625	6,250	31,250
1.00	250	2,500	12,500
0.50	125	1,250	6,250
0.25	62	620	3,100
0.10	25	250	1,250

Example: A municipal auditorium receives an average of one rental check per day, with an average dollar value of $600. The accounting staff holds these checks an average of three days prior to deposit. Prevailing short-term interest rates are 10%. The annual cost—foregone investment income—resulting from deposit delay is calculated as follows.

One day's interest income on $600 ($600 times 10% divided by 365 days):	$0.16
Foregone investment income per check ($0.16 times 3 days):	$0.48
Estimated annual cost of delaying deposits (intersection of $0.50 and once per day column):	$125

EXHIBIT 1.D / How Costly Are Inefficient Cash Management Practices?

3. *Withdrawal of idle balances from local banks will harm the local economy.* After an in-depth study in the state of Oregon, Deloitte Haskins & Sells concluded that better cash management programs had no measurable impact on the financial condition of local banks.

   Many community banks in different areas of the country do not have sufficient commercial demand to lend out much of the idle balances from government deposits. This is especially true since municipal demand deposits tend to show large fluctuations. Many community banks instead invest demand deposit balances in short-term loans to other banks.

4. *Cumbersome state laws do not permit local governments to use modern management techniques.* Many current state laws were written years ago to safeguard public funds, and in some cases, to ensure that funds remained in local depositories. For example, many states regulate the choice of depositories and investments, and some limit the amount that a community may deposit in each bank.

   Local governments have no choice but to follow mandated restrictions. However, many states are amending laws to allow communities to preserve their cash assets while still ensuring the safety of local funds. For example, eleven states now sponsor local government investment pools (see section 6.4) that encourage the short-term investment of idle cash balances.

   Many state laws are vague as to actual restrictions. Some communities react by interpreting these laws too strictly. Instead, local officials should meet the intent of the law while ensuring that their taxpayers have the maximum benefit of nontax revenues.

   Where laws specifically regulate cash management practices, local officials should consider legislative action through their financial officers' associations. Knowledgeable local officials may exert considerable influence in amending or repealing state laws that prevent their communities from preserving cash resources by means open to other segments of the economy.

5. *Local governments lack sufficient personnel to operate a cash management program.* Fortunately, most cash management techniques not only increase investment income but also save local officials time and effort. Some methods shift the costs of processing payrolls, debt service disbursements, and tax collections to banks, while other methods allow the transfer or investment of funds by telephone. Two investment media, money market funds and local government investment pools, also allow communities to make daily investments in and withdrawals from professionally managed short-term investments. Plus, a small investment of a local official's time often returns many times more investment income.

6. *The community might lose funds if forced to sell investments prematurely or if investments are bad.* First, good forecasting helps communities plan cash flows. By knowing when cash is needed, officials can plan investments to free cash at appropriate times to ensure that enough cash is available for disbursements.

Second, short-term investment options, in particular some money market instruments, are extremely safe. United States Treasury obligations are backed by the United States government, while others, such as overnight agreements with banks, offer collateral.

7. *Local officials lack the time to keep current with the array of new cash management services, and they lack the budgeted funds to attend expensive seminars.* This manual is designed to provide a relatively inexpensive, understandable explanation of better management techniques, and it is organized so that the reader may use any and all sections of interest. The manual also offers specific how-to instructions and provides the information that local officials need in order to bring more efficient cash management practices to their communities.

Disbursements 2

A local government's disbursement system is its set of mechanisms for paying employees, vendors, recipients, bond holders, and others. In effective cash management systems, disbursement mechanisms decelerate the outflow of funds from the local treasury so that more funds are available for investments. However, this control still ensures that a municipality can make timely payments on its obligations. Section 2.1 explores these objectives. Understanding the goals of efficient disbursing helps local officials build a sensible disbursement network of accounts.

The actual time that funds are released for payments depends on the procedures that banks and the federal government use to move money and settle payments. This national payment process delays the effective transfer of funds for several days after a check is released. This effect, called float, emerges from the banking system of check collection and creates natural opportunities for investing funds until they are called on by their recipients. Section 2.2 describes the timing of funds movement that results in float, and section 2.3 explains check collection from the point of view of those making payments. Knowing how payments are collected when checks are issued helps local officials anticipate extra investable funds in the community's bank accounts.

The prospect of gaining float can motivate communities to use more efficient disbursement techniques. Section 2.4 describes how local officials may calculate float for their own community's routine payments. With that information, officials can time funds movement so that cash is available for disbursements only as needed, and they can evaluate the benefits of management techniques introduced later in the chapter.

Section 2.5 discusses methods that allow communities to efficiently transfer funds between bank accounts or to disburse funds to recipients. Some money management techniques move funds quickly, while others place a premium on low cost; this section explains each method and discusses its advantages and disadvantages in local government operations.

Moving funds quickly and safely centralizes more cash for investment. New account services contribute to maintaining a larger central pool of cash by demanding municipal deposits only on the day that checks clear the bank. Other account services reduce internal processing costs by shifting payment mechanisms to banks. Section 2.6 discusses three types of cash management accounts at banks: zero-balance accounts, direct-deposit accounts, and paying agent agreements. Each account needs to be assessed in light of local conditions.

Following this description of cash management techniques, section 2.7 shows how to design a simple, efficient disbursement network. Essentially, disbursement systems use a central bank account to concentrate cash from municipal collections. Cash transfers from the central account are released only as funds are needed to cover checks drawn on disbursement accounts. This section gives an example of a simple disbursement network and explains its separate pieces.

Finally, section 2.8 offers suggestions that have helped reduce some of the more common errors in improving a disbursement system, including guidelines on when to take discounts that suppliers offer for accelerated payment of bills (trade discounts).

This chapter on disbursement management explains the concepts and techniques of municipal payments and shows how local governments might assess their value in their own communities' financial operations. With this information local governments may immediately start to improve their cash management operations.

2.1 Setting Disbursement Objectives

Disbursement systems should time cash outflow so that cash is removed from the treasury at the latest possible moment. Disbursement management, like the management of cash resources in general, is an art rather than a science. Although many cash management techniques are available, and more are appearing each day, the skill comes in applying those techniques to the particular circumstances of a municipality to maximize nontax revenue or minimize borrowing. If a town decelerates cash outflow and minimizes the time that cash lies idle, it will increase the amount of cash available for investment.

When a municipality pursues the following five disbursement objectives, it will increase its free cash.

1. Disburse money only when necessary. A cash manager needs to determine the payment due date of bills and the last mailing date to take advantage of trade discounts (section 2.8), and he should investigate zero balance accounts that allow communities to deposit funds only when payments are requested by recipients (section 2.6.1).

2. Centralize free cash in a master bank account so that a large pool of cash is available for investment (section 2.7).

3. Minimize the funds needed to operate a disbursement system by reducing the number of bank accounts (section 2.7) and implementing a zero-balance system (section 2.6.1).

4. Minimize the costs, such as clerical costs and service fees, of operating a disbursement system through a central disbursement network (section 2.7) and potentially through direct deposits (section 2.6.2) and paying agents (section 2.6.3).

5. Ensure that disbursements conform to state laws regulating money management, and further ensure the safety and reliability of disbursements. (Section 2.5.1 discusses the legal aspects of the principal instrument of payment, checks.)

Understanding Float 2.2

One of the main techniques for increasing the accumulation of investable cash comes from exploiting a community's payment *float*. Float is the amount of money that sits in a bank account from the time that funds are deposited until checks clear the bank. For illustration, if the town of Anyville pays ACME Construction $100,000 on Wednesday, but the check does not clear the town's bank until Friday, it has two days of float. In other words, the town has two days to invest the $100,000.

More specifically, this is an example of *disbursement* float, since it occurs when a town sends out checks. This float means towns have additional time to invest cash balances. The other float, deposit float, occurs when a town deposits collections in its bank account but waits one to two days for its receipts to be collected via the banking system.

Disbursement float has three aspects. First, there is the lag in mail time from the time that the town mails the check until the time that the vendor or payee receives the check. Second, the vendor or payee takes processing time to record the payment and deposit the check in its bank account. Third, it takes time for the vendor's bank to present the check to the town's bank to collect those funds. Only then are funds collected. Until that time, those funds are available for investment.

Disbursement float is the sum of the checks that have not been presented to the bank at any time. In other words, it is the difference between the collected balance in the bank and the amount recorded in the treasury's checkbook.

In astute municipal cash management, one pool of cash may serve three purposes at once. The town issues payment and receives credit from vendors on that pool of cash. It also invests those funds until the day checks are presented to its bank for payment, and it uses the remaining balances in the accounts to compensate the local bank for its services.

Tracing Check Clearing 2.3

To better understand disbursement float, let's follow a check through the collection and clearing process. For purposes of illustration, the example will follow a check that the town of Lincoln disburses to a contractor for building a new elementary school. See Exhibit 2.A.

When Lincoln receives and processes the construction company's invoice, it disburses a check to pay for a portion of its construction costs. If Lincoln sends the check by mail instead of presenting the check directly to the contractor, it gains one or more days float before the vendor receives the check. Mail float increases through a variety of circumstances. If Lincoln mails the check on a Friday, the town gains extra float because business and banking operations are closed on weekends. It also gains mail float if the mail is delayed or if the vendor is located far from the municipality. Some private consulting companies, such as the Phoenix-Hecht group in Chicago,

1. Check is generated. Local government (a) mails or (b) hand delivers check to recipient.
   - Delay clearance by mailing on Friday. May result in one to two day delay.
2. Vendor or employee receives check. Vendor records payment. Vendor or employee deposits check in bank.
   - Vendor may take many days to record receipt of check and deposit check.
   - Employees usually deposit check on same day.
3. Bank credits recipient's account and begins process of collecting funds. Based on bank location and local clearinghouse affiliations, bank selects fastest method of collection. May be same day or one day lag in initiating collection.

   Recipient's bank receives funds from local government's bank in one of three ways.
4. A. Federal Reserve. Guarantees that collecting bank will receive funds within two days. But, may take longer for check to clear local government's bank, creating *Fed float.*

   B. Clearinghouse. Check presented to local clearinghouse where checks are exchanged. Usually immediate or next day.

   C. Correspondent bank. Check sent to correspondent bank in the same district or clearinghouse group as local government's bank. Usually one to two day delay.
5. Local government's bank transfers funds to taxpayer's bank and charges local government's account. At end of month sends cancelled check to local government with bank statement.

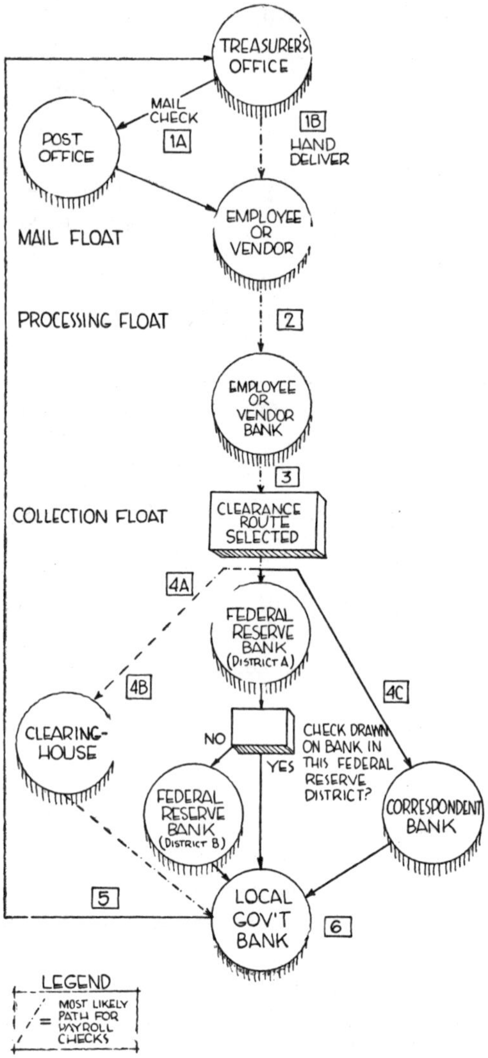

EXHIBIT 2.A / Check Clearance (Disbursements)

make a business of analyzing the mail float between locations around the country. This service would not indicate potential mail times for intracity mail, but it might be helpful for regional or national payments, such as a Colorado municipality's paying New York bondholders.

Once the contractor receives the check, it takes time for the company to record payment and deposit the check in the bank. Not all payees deposit checks immediately. Smaller companies use checks as a method of posting their credits to accounts receivable and therefore delay deposit until all bookkeeping records have been updated. On the other hand, companies with inherent cash flow problems, such as contractors who pay for salaries and materials before being paid, are likely to deposit their payments immediately.

After the contractor deposits the check, the bank begins the process of collecting those funds from Lincoln's bank. This time delay is the *bank collection float*. The contractor's bank may collect from Lincoln's bank in one of three ways.

1. If the two banks are in the same city, the contractor's bank may send Lincoln's check to a local clearinghouse, where local banks meet every day to trade checks. Funds from Lincoln's account are placed in the contractor's account in his bank. Then the funds are collected. Many such clearinghouses are automated and are thus called *Automated Clearing Houses* or *ACHs*.
2. If the contractor's bank and Lincoln's bank are located in different towns but in the same Federal Reserve District, the contractor's bank might send the check to a correspondent bank in the disburser's town. The correspondent bank presents the check to Lincoln's bank, receives the funds, and credits the account of the contractor's bank. The funds are then collected.
3. If Lincoln's bank and the contractor's bank are in different Federal Reserve districts, the contractor's bank sends the check to the local Federal Reserve bank, which then sends the check to the Federal Reserve bank in Lincoln's district. That Federal Reserve bank draws funds down in Lincoln's bank account, then transfers those funds backwards to the contractor's bank. The Federal Reserve System guarantees that checks within its system will clear in two days. If they do not, the Federal Reserve bank puts up the funds for the vendor even though it has not yet collected funds from Lincoln's account.

In all cases, when Lincoln's check is presented to its bank for payment, Lincoln's bank debits the town's account; at the end of each month, the bank returns the cancelled check to the town with an account statement. The elapsed time on the bank collection float should be no more than two days, because of the Federal Reserve guarantee. In many cases the float might be one day or none at all. However, when processing, mail, and bank collection floats are combined, total disbursement float can be significant.

Understanding the disbursement float will help a town determine how long it takes checks to clear its account and, therefore, how long it will have funds to invest. It will also enable a town to discover possibilities for extending its disbursement float and the time it has to invest those funds.

Some private corporations fully exploit delays in the check clearance system by releasing checks drawn on banks located in remote areas of the country, a practice known as *remote disbursing*. With remote disbursing, the paying entity draws its checks on a bank not readily accessible to the payee. For example, a Midwest company pays its California suppliers with checks drawn on a South Carolina bank. The result is that the company disbursing the check has many extra days of float while the payee's bank tries to collect the funds on that check. The big loser in this case is not the payee or his bank, but the Federal Reserve System. The Federal Reserve guarantees the payment of those funds to the payee's bank within two days after the check is presented to the Fed. If it takes more than two days for the Fed to collect those funds, in this case from the South Carolina bank, then it gives the payee's bank, in this case the California bank, credit for those funds anyway. Since the South Carolina bank still has those funds, the funds are in two places at once, compliments of the Federal Reserve System. This is called *Fed float*.

Remote disbursing is not directly relevant to municipalities. Almost all state laws require communities to conduct their regular banking in institutions within state borders. Remote disbursing, however, promotes the development of funds transfer systems, since the Federal Reserve reaction is likely to encourage practice that reduce this advantage to those making payments.

To counter remote disbursing, which is essentially a loan by the Federal government to those making payments, the Federal Reserve is introducing *truncation* to the check clearing process. This procedure automatically sorts out checks greater than a specified dollar value, then the Fed processes their collection by wire. This and other federal check clearing processes will make increasing use of the electronic transfer of funds to speed check collections.

2.4 Determining the Float

Even though the check collection process may be complicated, actual float times are easy to measure. Direct measurement takes little time, and it enables a cash manager to understand the float delay for each type of municipal disbursement.

A local official can use the results of a float analysis to assess the real benefits of different cash management techniques. Float information also helps a treasurer plan an investment strategy that frees funds from investment only as they are needed to meet collections.

To measure the float, a cash manager takes a sample of a particular kind of check, notes the day that the city releases the checks, and records the day the checks clear its bank account.

To illustrate, let's follow payroll checks for a municipal hospital. Disbursement information from checkbooks or check release logs shows the day that checks are

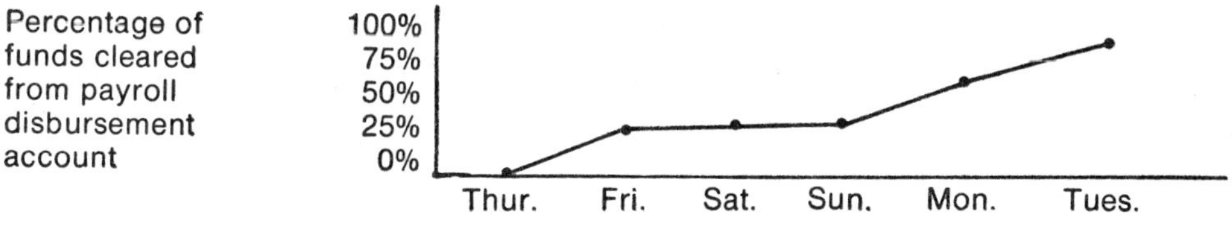

Checks are disbursed on Thursday.

EXHIBIT 2.B / Clearing History of Thursday Payroll Checks

released from the town's treasury. On the back of the cancelled check, the hospital's bank stamps the date that the funds were collected from the account.

The hospital develops a history of the check float of one type of payment, say payroll, by examining a sample of those checks. If the hospital looks at 5% of the payroll checks released in a recent pay period, it can graph the results as shown in Exhibit 2.B.

Payroll checks should have a relatively short float. Most will be collected within a week. Because payroll checks are distributed manually, there is no mail float, and because most employees cash or deposit their checks within one or two days, the processing float is minimal. Collection float is also short because most employees bank in the immediate vicinity of the hospital's bank. If checks are distributed on Friday, however, the hospital will at least gain a weekend's float.

The information in the preceding graph can be used to calculate the float on upcoming payroll disbursements. If the town will release $100,000 in payroll, then the float prediction based on the information would look like Exhibit 2.C.

Since 50% of the dollar amount of the checks clear on Monday, the town has on average four days of float of $100,000. In this payroll disbursement alone it could earn: 100,000 × 10% × 4/365, or $110. This is just the approximate income from

Dollars collected from bank accounts (cumulative)	
Thurs. (release day) (0%)	$0
Fri. (25%)	$25,000
Sat. (25%)	$25,000
Sun. (25%)	$25,000
Mon. (50%)	$50,000
Tues. (75%)	$75,000
Wed. (100%)	$100,000

EXHIBIT 2.C / Liquidation of Payroll Disbursement Float

this disbursement. In reality, the town treasurer would have to deposit $25,000 in the account on Friday and another $25,000 on Monday, Tuesday, and Wednesday to cover clearing checks. A town's collection history can, therefore, show when checks are likely to clear the town's account, and how much the town might expect from the investment of those funds.

A town treasurer should save each float sample. After several pay periods the operating history will reveal a regular pattern of check collections. There might be seasonal adjustments, a faster float around the December holidays or a slower float during summer vacations, but most floats for recurring disbursements are regular and predictable. After the initial sampling phase, the town financial officer need only return to sampling if the regular float predictions become inaccurate.

Effective use of float information requires the following:

1. The town's payments must abide by a firm, prearranged schedule.
2. Even though a department may collect bills, approve payment, and mail disbursements, the central financial officer must control all bank statements, execute all wire transfers and deposits, and conduct all banking business. (In most governments payment functions are centralized anyway.)
3. Transfers into the disbursement account must occur only when checks are presented for payment.

2.5 How To Move and Disburse Funds

In an entire cash management network, including collections as well as disbursements, there are a variety of ways to execute payments and transfers. The method chosen determines how quickly funds move, which in turn affects availability of funds for investment. If funds must be transferred between master and disbursement accounts, for instance, one technique may take an hour while another may take two to three days.

The four techniques described in this section differ in the cost of the service, the speed of delivery, and the planning necessary for execution. The decision rule for choosing among them, in most cases, depends on the amount of funds transferred. The larger the amount of funds, the greater the benefit of extra availability, the greater the need for predictable movement, and the greater the need for cash security. In these cases one does not mind paying a small premium for a significant amount of investment income and the certainty that the funds will be where the local officials want them when they want them.

Of the four techniques described, checks are the normal method of payment. Since their disbursement pathway was amply described in section 2.3, the discussion of checks in this section focuses on the security of check payments.

Payments are also made with payable-through-drafts, which moves funds in the same manner as checks, except that the maker of the draft reviews the payment one more time before releasing funds from the community's bank account. Although not created for this purpose, drafts may be used in some cases to decelerate cash disbursements.

Wire transfers move funds rapidly between accounts via electronic communications among banks and the Federal Reserve System. Wire transfers rapidly concentrate collected funds, and because they move funds almost immediately, local treasurers do not need to make deposits in the community's bank accounts until checks are presented for payment.

Like a wire transfer, a depository transfer check moves funds between the community's bank accounts; but it is a slower, yet less costly, method of making transfers.

Using Checks 2.5.1

Even though checks are the most common instruments for payment in the United States, most citizens know little about how checks are collected and processed through the country's banking system. And they know little about their legal rights and liabilities as agents for issuing or demanding payment on checks.

The law governing checks, as negotiable instruments, is the Uniform Commercial Code. The UCC is a body of law regulating commercial operations that has been adopted by forty-eight of the fifty states. This review does not claim to be a summary of that code, and any question of law should be directed to a lawyer. This highlights some of the more interesting features of the law that are relevant to municipal operations, and it also offers a brief description of the physical features of checks.

A check is an order to pay money on demand to the payee from the drawer's bank account. More specifically, the law says checks are: (1) unconditional orders, (2) written on paper, (3) addressed by one person or institution, (4) to a bank, (5) signed

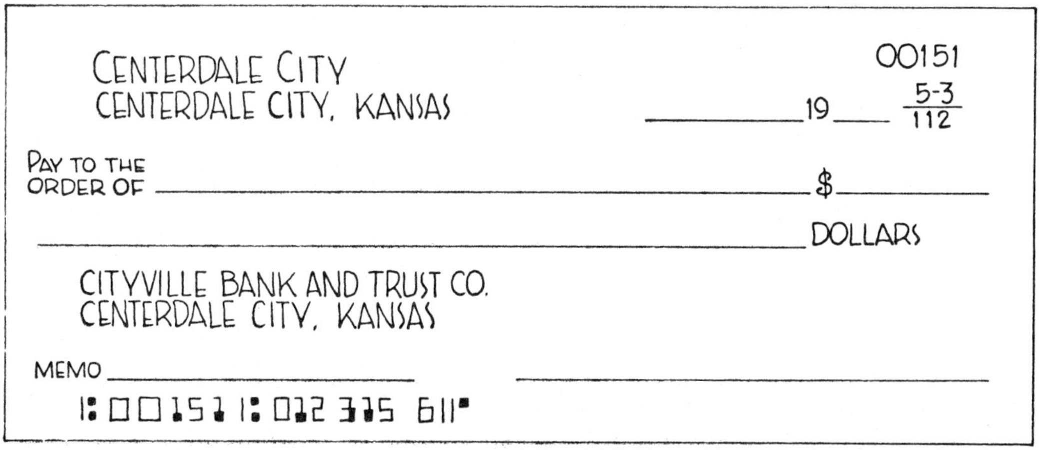

Check

by the person or agent making the check, (6) requiring the bank to whom it is addressed, (7) to pay on demand, (8) a sum of money, (9) to order or to the bearer. Checks are not cash; they are credit instruments that are presented by their holders for cash. Checks impose no obligation on the drawee (bank) until they are accepted by the drawee, and checks are revocable by the drawer (the person making the check) until the checks are presented and paid.

The following are some of the more interesting legal aspects of checks.

Signatures. Signatures are essential to the validity of checks, but there is no standard that says that checks must be written and signed in ink. In fact, signatures may be written, typewritten, stamped, or written in pencil, and if a town so desires, it may use any name or mark in lieu of a signature, so long as that is the signature or record at the bank. Once the customer and the bank agree on the form of the signature, the bank is under no obligation to honor checks that are not signed in that format. When a line is drawn through a signature, the bank does not have to honor that check unless the person requesting funds can prove that the line was not an attempt by the maker to cancel the check.

Facsimile Plates. In most cases banks are not liabile for accepting fraudulent payments that result from the illegal or unauthorized use of a city's facsimile plates. On the other hand, banks are responsible for their acceptance of false or forged signatures from phony signature plates.

Agents. Those who sign checks as an agent of an institution, such as the town treasurer for his municipality, are not personally liable for the payment of checks (1) if they have authority to sign, (2) if the government is clearly named on the check, and (3) if the check shows that the agent signed in a representative capacity. For example, the check should have printed somewhere on the face, "Town of Podunk," and it should be signed "Harvey Toast, Treasurer" or "Harvey Toast, Authorized Signature." If the treasurer merely signed a blank check, "Harvey Toast, Treasurer," he might be liable if the check was dishonored.

Check Dates. An undated, postdated, or antedated check is valid provided that the dating is not meant to defraud. When an undated check is issued, the holder has legal authority to fill in the date. Postdated checks are payable on or after the date on the check, and a bank that makes payment on a check before the check date may be liable for payment.

Check Blanks. If any information is left blank on a signed check, the holder of the check has a prima facie authority to fill in the banks, including the amount of the check.

Ambiguities. When there is confusion about the amount of the check, the following rules apply.

- Words control figures, except where the words are ambiguous.
- Handwritten terms control typewritten and printed terms.
- Typewritten terms control printed terms. For example, if the numbered amount of the check reads *$20.00* but the written amount reads *two thousand and 00/100 dollars,* then the check would be worth $2,000.00.

Cash-in Time. The Uniform Commercial Code says that a check should be presented for payment within a reasonable length of time. This usually means that the check should be presented no later than thirty days after the issue of the check or the date of the check (whichever is later). However, an unreasonable delay does not mean that the issuer is no longer liable for any debt, it means only that the check may not be valid.

Wording. A check made payable without the word *order* is not negotiable. A check written *Pay John Vendor* is invalid.

Forgery. Forged checks are invalid. Any bank making payment on forged endorsements does so at its own risk. However, when dealing with someone who uses a false name, that person may properly endorse the check with the phony name, if he's the person the community intended to pay.

Alterations. If checks are materially altered, they are invalid. Changes to the following items are material alterations if they are made without the consent of the person writing the check.

- Date
- Amount payable
- Place of payment
- Currency in which payment is to be made
- Any of the principals
- Any change that alters the effect of the instrument

Endorsements. The words *For Deposit, For Collection,* or *Pay any bank* restrict the collection and payment of funds to the payee's account only.

Payable-through-Drafts (Warrants) 2.5.2

Payable-through-drafts, also called drafts or warrants, look like checks, they are disbursed like checks, and they are paid like checks, except for one notable difference. When a warrant is presented to a municipality's bank for payment, the bank does not automatically release available funds to the party requesting payment, as it

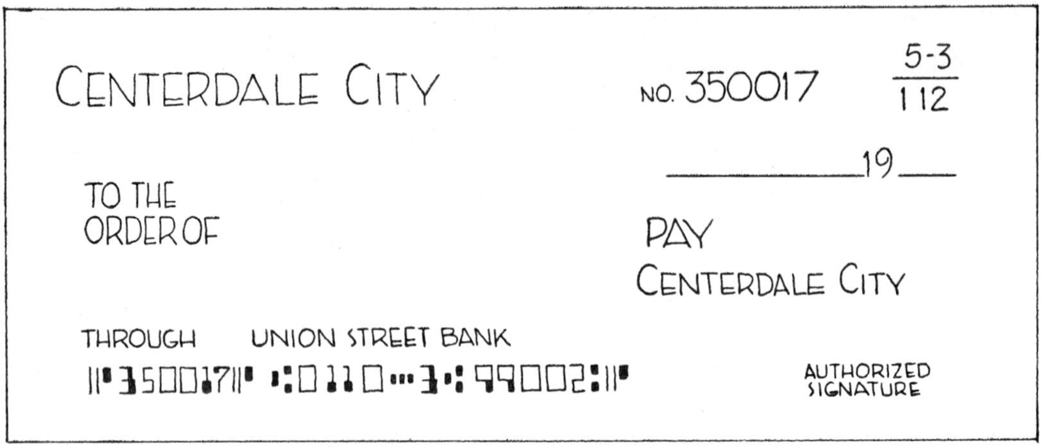
CENTERDALE CITY

NO. 350017 5-3/112

_______________19___

TO THE ORDER OF

PAY

CENTERDALE CITY

THROUGH UNION STREET BANK

AUTHORIZED SIGNATURE

Warrant

would if a check were presented. Instead, it passes the warrant back to the issuer for approval within twenty-four hours. A more exact definition of a draft would say that it is "an agreement to pay a sum of money when the warrant is presented to the issuer" (not the issuer's bank), assuming that the payee has met the terms of the payment.

To better understand drafts, let's look at the procedures for their issuance and payment. Assume a municipality generates a draft to pay Digitron Computer Systems for its new automated payroll system. Digitron deposits the draft in its bank account, and Digitron's bank presents the draft to the municipality's bank for payment. The municipality's bank then presents the draft to local officials for their approval and payment. If an official approves the draft, he signs the release and deposits funds in the bank to cover that amount.

Whereas the issuance of a check assumes that funds will be available in the bank to cover that check, a draft does not. Funds do not need to be available until the draft is approved. In a few communities where states strictly prohibit the issuance of checks against accounts with insufficient funds, local officials use drafts to keep idle funds invested until payment is requested.

Drafts were introduced in 1932 so that companies could avoid paying the federal check tax, then in effect. This tax lasted only two years, but drafts survived for two reasons. First, they freed cash until the drafts were presented for payment. Second, companies used drafts to keep control of payments made by people outside their normal, centralized operations. If claims adjustors for insurance companies are making payments in the field for emergency situations, then the home office has time to examine the documentation and the circumstances surrounding the draft before releasing the funds. Since governments issue checks from a central location on the basis of documentation, governments use drafts primarily for the former reason, to maximize the time they have to use free cash.

On the other hand, drafts have some significant disadvantages.

- Vendors prefer checks, if they notice the difference. With warrants they may have to wait an extra day for payment.
- A community using drafts may incur extra internal processing costs since a local official examines the draft before funds are released.
- Communities incur extra bank processing charges, since drafts need extra attention outside the normal check clearing process. They usually require manual processing.

For most government operations, warrants are uneconomical and inefficient. They should be used only in special circumstances where the municipality is prevented by legal or other reasons from delaying cash disbursements until the last possible moment and where the investment gain from the use of the extra cash exceeds the costs of issuing the warrant. In most cases a centralized, controlled disbursement network with zero balance accounts accomplishes the same purpose at lower cost and with greater efficiency.

Wire Transfers 2.5.3

Wire transfers move funds electronically, and therefore almost immediately, between bank accounts, from revenue sources to larger payees and to and from investment sources. They increase the predictability of payments, and in some cases allow communities to release large amounts of funds only on the day requested.

Wire transfers move money between bank accounts by telephone (by "wire"). The transfer is relatively fast, and it permits the same day use of the funds transferred into the account. For example, if a town treasurer wanted to transfer funds from the town's central account to its disbursement account, he might initiate a wire transfer, and the disbursement account would be replenished that day. Exhibit 2.D describes the processing of a wire transfer order.

The great advantage of wire transfers in disbursement systems is the extra time that cash remains in the central account for investment. Wire transfers also simplify the control over cash flow between bank accounts. Many corporations use wire transfers for many major payments because it makes the timing of their disbursements predictable. If a local treasurer moves funds between accounts by check and it takes two days for this check to clear then he has to estimate the amount that will be presented for collection two days later. Wire transfers may be implemented immediately based on current information.

Wire transfers are used mostly for transferring large amounts of cash, as the profitability formula shown later in this section demonstrates, and they are used only to transfer funds between banks. Exhibit 2.E shows some minor difficulties encountered by businesses using wire transfers. These concerns might be expressed when this service is being arranged with banks, to ensure smooth transactions.

Several wire services are available. The Federal Reserve Wire Service, or Fed Wire, moves funds between banks that maintain balances with their local Federal Reserve district banks. If a local treasurer calls the bank with the central cash account and requests that funds be transferred to the bank with the disbursement account, then the central bank has the Federal Reserve transfer balances from its account with the Fed into the disbursement bank's account with the Fed. The central bank then notifies the disbursement bank that the municipality's account should be credited. If the central account does not have sufficient collected funds, then the transfer will not be executed.

Another wire service is the Bank Wire System. The Bank Wire System is composed of cooperating banks that maintain balances with each other. For example, a treasurer calls the bank with the central account and requests that funds be transferred to the bank with the disbursement account. The central bank reduces the town's balance and increases the disbursement bank's balance. The central bank then notifies the disbursement bank that the town's account should be given credit for the increase. Overdrafts are possible with Bank Wire System, so local treasurers must make sure that their central accounts have adequate collected funds before the transfer takes place or else their community will incur unnecessary charges. Bank Wire is privately operated by 200 cooperating banks in 60 cities across the country.

The drawback to wire transfers is the cost. Since they are more expensive than other methods of moving funds, local officials may have to determine the minimum

Wire transfers occur through a sealed set of telephone lines among banks. Banks and other financial institutions that do not have direct access to the system generally maintain an account with a bank that does, thus wire transfers can be made between virtually any two banks or institutions.

When making a wire transfer, a cash manager should call the bank or institution from which the funds will be removed and provide the following information:

- Account number of the account to be debited.
- Amount of the transfer.
- Recipient bank's name and the account number of the account to be credited.
- Name of a person at the recipient bank to whose attention the funds should be wired.

Most banks have an early afternoon cutoff time past which they will not guarantee transfer of funds on the same day. Cash managers should also call the recipient bank prior to the transfer in order to inform it that funds will be wired. The recipient bank should provide a confirmation of receipt when the transfer arrives.

EXHIBIT 2.D / Using the Wire Transfer System

> Coopers & Lybrand, the public accounting firm, conducted a survey in 1978 on the use of wire transfers by private corporations (*Coopers & Lybrand Special Report*, Jan.–Feb. 1979). The survey identified several problems which government cash managers should be aware of.
>
> - Incorrect or incomplete addresses result in wire transfers being sent to the wrong bank or account.
> - Delays in sending the wire transfer wipe out the benefits intended in using the system.
> - Delays in advising the key officer in the recipient organization also wipe out the intended benefits.
> - Arranging and following up on wire transfers can consume an excessive amount of personnel time.

EXHIBIT 2.E / Problems with Wire Transfers

transfer to justify the cost of the wire. The following formula can be used to determine that amount.

$$\text{Minimum amount transferred to be profitable} = \frac{(\text{Cost of wire transfer}) \times (365 \text{ days})}{(\text{Current short-term interest rate}) \times (\text{Additional float gained from wire transfer})}$$

For example, if the community is currently receiving 7% on its short-term investments, if a wire transfer costs \$6, and if the wire will save two days float, then the town will only want to wire transfer funds that exceed \$15,650:

$$M = \frac{(\$6) \times (365)}{(.07) \times (2)} = \$15{,}640$$

Notice that the decision changes with the interest rate of investments. If interest rates fall to 6%, then transfer amounts less than \$18,000 are uneconomical. Still, these amounts are relatively small. If a treasurer wants to replenish a disbursement payroll account, then he will more likely be transferring hundreds of thousands of dollars rather than tens of thousands. The formula indicates, however, that local officials should consider the cost of wire transfers and not become wire happy over small amounts.

Depository Transfer Checks 2.5.4

Depository transfer checks are inexpensive instruments that are used to move funds between municipal accounts in different banks. A depository transfer check (or DTC) moves funds through the regular check clearance process, and it looks like a regular demand deposit check except that it is unsigned. It is nonnegotiable, meaning that the check cannot be used except to move funds between the municipality's accounts; it is preprinted and payable only to the municipal account.

The general procedure for using DTCs to disburse funds is as follows. First, the local community arranges with its banks to use DTCs by signing a resolution statement for the bank. That statement gives the bank authority to process DTCs.

Then suppose that a local treasurer wants to move funds from the town's central account to its disbursement account to meet vendor payments. Assume that he mails $100,000 worth of checks today and knows from past experience that in two days 25%, or $25,000, will be presented at the town's bank for payment. He also knows that it takes one day for the local banks to process the DTC transfer between the two accounts so tomorrow he will generate a DTC for $25,000—perhaps a little more just to be safe.

DTCs in disbursements require some planning to time the transfer process. Local officials should be certain that sufficient funds are available in the central account to cover the transfer. In the case of collections, a municipality may leave standing instructions for the bank to process a DTC whenever collected funds reach a certain balance, so collected funds are automatically transferred to the central account.

The foremost advantage of depository transfer checks is their cost. Most DTCs cost about 30 cents per check, so they efficiently move even the smallest amounts of money.

The disadvantage to DTCs is that they may take one to two days to move the funds between accounts. Unless the town manager wants to transfer the funds into the disbursement account when checks are mailed, and thus lose the float, he has to estimate when checks will clear the account. This may be accomplished by using the method described in section 2.4.

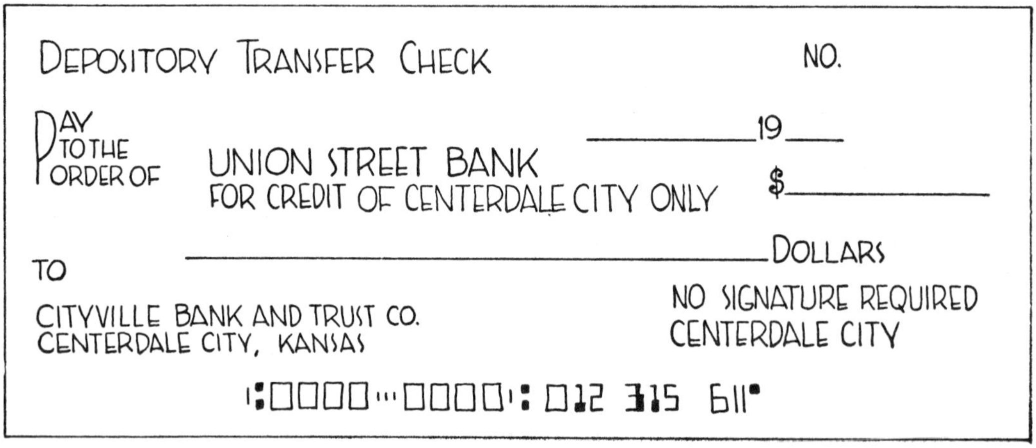
DEPOSITORY TRANSFER CHECK NO.

PAY TO THE ORDER OF UNION STREET BANK
FOR CREDIT OF CENTERDALE CITY ONLY ______19___ $______

TO ______DOLLARS

CITYVILLE BANK AND TRUST CO.
CENTERDALE CITY, KANSAS

NO SIGNATURE REQUIRED
CENTERDALE CITY

:0000···0000: 012 315 611

Depository Transfer Check

A community might also want to consider maintaining the disbursement account in the same bank as the central account, if there are no losses of float time. Then transfers may be processed immediately with a telephone call.

Wire transfers move funds almost immediately. Thus the amounts needed for transfer are more predictable; in the case of collections, funds are moved quickly to the central account for disbursement. However, when it is not economical to use wire transfers for smaller amounts of funds, then DTCs are affordable alternatives.

Managing Disbursement Accounts 2.6

An efficient disbursement system creates a central bank account from which funds are moved to separate accounts when needed for disbursement. These disbursement accounts may free funds for investment, increase the safety and predictability of payments, and even reduce processing costs.

Three types of payment accounts are zero-balance accounts, direct deposits, and paying agent accounts. Zero-balance accounts (ZBAs) maintain no available cash balances; they only retain balances sufficient to compensate the bank for its services. As checks are presented to a ZBA for payment, the municipality reimburses the account. Thus funds are free for investment until they are actually needed for payment.

Communities use direct deposits to transfer funds directly to employee accounts, thus reducing payroll payment costs, increasing cash flow predictability, and increasing the payroll disbursement convenience to municipal employees.

Paying agent accounts, now widely used, have banks make payments from community funds for principal and interest payments on municipal debt. With paying agent agreements, the time and effort of processing debt service payments falls on the banks. All three accounts help local officials efficiently control disbursements and economize resources.

Zero-Balance Accounts 2.6.1

Zero-balance accounts allow communities to disburse payments on schedule, yet relinquish funds only as those payments are presented to the municipality's bank for collection. Although zero-balance accounts may maintain minimum, reserved balances to pay for bank services, these accounts maintain no idle balances available for payments. (For compensation amounts, see chapter 4.)

Zero-balance accounts (ZBAs) literally maintain no balance. As checks are presented for payment, funds are automatically transferred from the central account to the ZBA for the amount of those checks. Actually, the community's account is overdrawn daily since funds are not transferred into the zero-balance account until the end of the day, when the bank knows how many checks have cleared the account. Communities compensate the bank for this service in one of two ways. They may pay the bank on a fee basis, say 15 cents for every check processed, or they may leave a

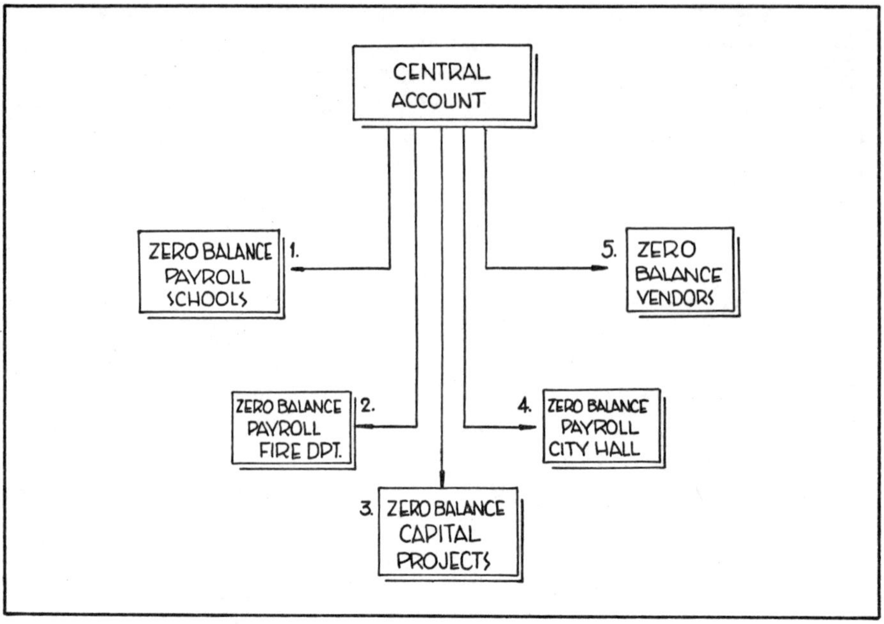

minimum, or "compensating," balance in the account that is available to the bank to invest. The computation of compensating balances is discussed in section 4.7. Either way, funds do not have to be deposited to a zero-balance bank account to cover checks until the day they are presented. Meanwhile, the community has use of those funds in its central account for short-term investment.

The great advantage of zero-balance accounts, of course, is that they allow communities to invest funds until the funds are needed. Zero-balance accounts also allow a town to maintain a central account with local disbursement centers. It allows a simple system that permits disbursement of funds, say a payroll, at a location that is convenient for municipal employees.

Zero-balance accounts do not, however, tell how much money will clear the account the next day. Local officials still have to rely on cash forecasting for short-term cash flows. Forecasting estimates the funds to be collected tomorrow and the checks to be presented for payment. That estimate enables the town to minimize the funds that are not invested in securities.

The operation of zero-balance accounts requires attention from cash management officials. Care should be taken to keep the account at a zero balance rather than allowing it to be overdrawn any longer than necessary. Smaller municipalities can avoid overdraft problems by having the bank automatically transfer enough funds to cover the checks that have cleared. Some banks take one day to collect funds from the concentration accounts. Thus larger municipalities can avoid overdrafts and unnecessary charges by maintaining an equivalent day's charges in the account, wire transferring the funds to the disbursement accounts for immediate transfer, or maintaining the zero-balance account and the central account in the same bank.

When a municipality implements a zero-balance account, it should remind its bank to "flag" the accounts for tellers. If zero-balance accounts are not identified, an employee cashing his paycheck, for example, may be told that the account is overdrawn and that the bank cannot honor the paycheck.

Zero-balance accounts require a few extra considerations, but they are simple to operate. They simplify control and reporting, increase the amount of free cash, and clarify information on float.

Direct Deposits 2.6.2

Direct-deposit accounts allow communities to increase the predictability of cash flows for regular municipal payments, such as weekly or biweekly payrolls, and reduce processing costs.

A direct-deposit system deposits the employees' or recipients' checks in their bank accounts. It reduces the time and cost of generating checks, since the deposit information is automated, and it is much more convenient for the payee. An employee does not need to rush down to the bank on Friday to deposit his paycheck; the funds are automatically transferred to his account Friday morning.

There are several advantages of direct-deposit systems besides convenience to the employee. If local officials have reasonable controls over their payroll tape, there is better security with direct deposit. Checks do not get lost or stolen, an advantage that has proven to be an important feature of the new federal direct-deposit system for Social Security payments. Direct-deposit also reduces distribution costs: the postage cost if checks are mailed or the labor costs if they are hand delivered. Transaction costs may also be lowered, since all those checks are not processed through the bank account, and of course the community saves the costs of labor and materials for printing, generating, and signing checks.

The significant disadvantage to direct-deposit systems is the loss of float. If checks are drawn against a regular checking account, then a town that distributes checks on Friday has the extra cash to invest until Monday or Tuesday. With a direct-deposit system, the funds are credited to the employees' accounts on Friday. Also, direct-deposit systems are not free. Local officials should ensure that the direct-deposit service is worth the effective price. The effective price is the difference between the new banking charges for a direct-deposit system plus the income loss from reduced disbursement float and the savings from reduced distribution, transaction, and material and labor costs.

Direct-deposit systems work well with government organizations that use computerized payroll systems. The payroll department generates a payroll tape (a computer storage disk, tape, or punch cards) that contains all payroll information (payee, payee's bank account, etc.), and it delivers the tape to the bank with the payroll disbursement account information. The bank then presents the tape to the automated clearinghouse (ACH), which credits the employees' accounts and reduces the funds in the municipality's account.

Many municipalities find that the advantages of increased predictability and decreased processing costs outweigh the loss of payroll float and make direct-deposit arrangements attractive disbursement mechanisms.

2.6.3 Paying Agents

Paying agents, banks under contract to local governments, relieve communities of the burdensome processing of debt service payments to bondholders. The use of paying agents reduces internal processing costs, increases the predictability of cash flows, and, just as important, increases control over a large volume of cancelled bonds and coupons.

As paying agent, banks collect and redeem municipal bonds and coupons, which represent the principal and interest payments on capital borrowing. The municipality is freed from processing thousands of coupons. Instead, it merely makes a lump sum payment on the due date to cover scheduled redemptions.

Arrangements for paying agent services with a bank are contracted when the bonds are issued. At that time, the bank creates a separate account for the municipality's debt service disbursements and generates a schedule of funds transfers based on bond and coupon due dates. Using that schedule, the local government transfers sufficient funds into the municipal account in time to meet upcoming debt service payments. (Bond and coupon payments are typically processed every six months.)

When their coupons and bonds come due, bondholders remit them to the paying agent. The paying agent verifies the redeemed coupons and bonds, pays the bondholder, and returns the cancelled instruments to the municipality along with a statement of items processed.

The most significant advantage of paying agents is that they save municipalities cost and time in processing redeemed bonds and coupons. Since banks service many municipal customers, economies of scale permit them to hire a full-time staff to process these instruments. A municipality would otherwise have to hire a specialized staff every six months to carry out the same service. Some very large banks have automated processing, increasing their efficiency and lowering costs even further.

Another advantage of paying agents is that they assess only a front-end fee. When the community signs a processing agreement, it pays a one-time fee for services over the life of the issue. This limited charge means that the service cost may be included in the initial cost of issuing the bond and does not need to be an annual budget item. Such an arrangement insulates the community from rising labor costs involved in manual processing. However, a community can choose to be billed annually for paying agent services, as corporations are.

Bank paying agent fees vary widely. Some banks charge from ten to seventeen cents per coupon and one to two dollars per bond, while others provide the service free. Banks estimate that it costs approximately thirty cents to process each coupon, so most paying agent fees do not reimburse the bank's direct costs. Banks profit from the float in processing bond and coupon redemptions.

In exchange for low processing fees, municipalities lose the debt service float that banks gain. Since municipalities draw investors from national markets, the collection lag between disbursement of redemption checks and payment from the community's bank account may be significant. A town in Wisconsin, for example, may make payments to investors living in Arizona or Florida.

If local officials think that it is possible to save funds by eliminating paying agent services, they may perform a rough cost-benefit calculation. The benefits from investing idle funds should exceed the costs of internal processing. These types of calculations may become exceedingly difficult, since the payment life of bond issues usually spans twenty years and since towns experience uneven patterns of borrowing.

To simplify matters, a local official should calculate the annual investment income from debt service disbursement float by examining the checks for interest and principal payments from the last few years; this calculation assumes that capital payments will remain relatively constant for several years. By examining these checks to find the date that they were presented to the bank, as described in section 2.4, the local official estimates the average float on each payment date. This average float is then translated into annual investment income.

An example clarifies this calculation. Suppose that a community makes four debt service payments a year, two for interest and principal payments of \$200,000, and two for \$100,000 each. Further assume that each payment, on average, takes five days to clear the community's bank, and the community earns at least 6% on invested balances. The calculation would be as follows:

$$\text{Annual interest income} = \frac{(\text{Investable balances}) \times (\text{Average float}) \times (\text{Interest rate})}{(365)}$$

or

$$\$500 = \frac{(\$600{,}000) \times (5) \times (.06)}{(365)}$$

An annual interest income of \$500 on debt service float is minuscule if it costs the community \$3,000 to hire a part-time employee to process bonds and coupons and mail out checks. If there are four payment dates and if 4,000 coupons and 100 bonds are redeemed, a bank might charge the following:

$$\begin{array}{r} (\text{Number of coupons}) \times (\text{Charge per coupon}) \\ +\ (\text{Number of bonds}) \times (\text{Charge per bond}) \end{array} = \text{Bank charges for debt service}$$

$$(4{,}000) \times (\$.35) + (100) \times (\$1.00) = \$1{,}500$$

This $1,500 the bank charges compares with the $2,500 ($3,000 processing costs less $500 investment income) that it costs the community to process payments itself. If one further considers the costs of managing and auditing the debt payments process, the attractiveness of bank paying agents is apparent.

Usually, the services of a paying agent benefit all but the largest and smallest communities. Large cities find some economies in maintaining a full-time processing staff. A small town, on the other hand, rarely needs to raise funds on its own and may sell its bonds to a single bank, thereby simplifying debt service processing.

2.7 Building the Disbursement System

Payment instruments, methods of moving funds, and disbursement accounts may be used in the design of a simple system to disburse funds.

A concentrated disbursement system collects all the free cash in one central location for short-term investment. It consists of a network of bank accounts and the appropriate instruments for transferring cash between accounts, matched to the requirements of each type of disbursement.

The central feature of a centralized cash management network is a *concentration bank account*. This account, which is just a regular checking account in a local bank, receives all cash that is not used to compensate banks for their services. Any collected funds from property taxes and other revenues are immediately transferred to this account, and the funds that are used for disbursement leave the account only when needed for payments. Thus, a large investable cash balance is left in a central location. Since this account is the repository for all idle cash, all investment purchases are paid from this account, and all investment sales are returned to it. Concentration accounts are also called *lead banks, master accounts, central depository accounts, parent accounts, mother accounts,* or *central accounts.*

The second feature of the system is the *disbursement account*. Disbursement accounts are special accounts usually used for one type of municipal payment. When checks are released, funds are moved from the central account to the disbursement account as late as possible to cover the amount of the checks issued. For example, a disbursement account may be maintained for payroll, for debt service, or for accounts payable payments. To show how a municipality takes advantage of controlled disbursements, assume that a town makes payroll disbursements from a single payroll bank account. If the municipality issues its payroll on Friday, but the checks do not clear the account until Tuesday, the town leaves the funds in its central account until Tuesday. Then it wire transfers the correct amount to the disbursement account to cover the checks being presented for payment.

Exhibit 2.F shows how these accounts form a disbursement network. The town in this example classified major disbursements into four categories: payments to vendors, investors, employees, and all others.

To pay vendors, the town consolidated four or five separate departmental accounts into one zero-balance account. By prearranged agreement, the local treasurer phones

Funds enter central account from collections and the sale of investments.

1. A. Treasurer draws vendor checks on zero-balance account and mails checks.
   B. Vendors deposit checks. Their banks collect funds from local government's bank.
   C. Zero-balance account bank notifies treasurer daily of amount needed to cover checks presented for payment.
   D. Treasurer wire transfers funds into zero-balance account.
2. A. Payroll tape sent to local government's bank on the day before each payroll date.
   B. Bank credits employee accounts at the bank, then sends tape to Automated Clearinghouse (ACH).
   C. ACH credits employee accounts in other local banks.
3. A. Paying agent notifies treasurer of amount of coupons and bonds coming due.
   B. On date coupons and bonds mature, treasurer transfers funds to paying agent account.
   C. Paying agent redeems bonds and coupons.
4. Miscellaneous expenses paid by checks drawn on central account (or miscellaneous disbursement account).

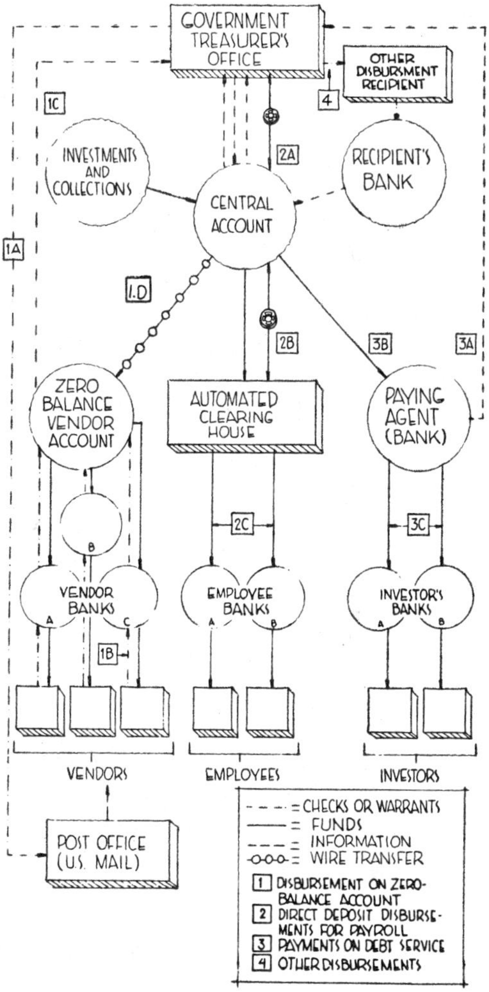

EXHIBIT 2.F / The Disbursement Network

the bank each day at 3 p.m. to learn the dollar amount of checks presented for payment. The bank then automatically transfers sufficient funds to the zero-balance account to bring its balance up to the minimum necessary to compensate the bank.

The town also found that greater predictability of payment, reduced processing costs, and increased employee goodwill made direct deposit of employee salaries an attractive service. One to two days before the biweekly payroll disbursement, the town presents its bank with a computer tape of employee and payroll data. On payday, funds are immediately transferred from the central account into employee accounts throughout the town.

Local officials knew that with their relatively low volume of semiannual bond and coupon redemptions, hiring a bank as paying agent would cost less than processing those payments themselves. Two days before the due date for debt payments, the treasurer sends a depository transfer check to the paying agent, so funds are available in the paying agent account on the due date. If the community maintained its central account with its paying agent bank, funds could be transferred from the central account to the debt service account by telephone.

Finally, the town processes a small volume of irregular payments, such as reimbursements for travel expenses and insurance payments. Those payments are disbursed with checks drawn directly on the central account.

The town maintains a highly efficient, yet simple, disbursement system. Because it controls disbursement times, it retains a significant amount of idle cash in its central account and earns nontax revenue for the town. The treasurer knows when cash is needed, and investment decisions are simplified because two of the town's three major cash disbursements, payroll and debt service, are highly predictable. The town also lowered its processing costs. Since it shifted debt service and payroll payment processes to banks, the town operates its check generation process only for payments to vendors.

2.8 Factors for Successful Disbursement

In building and maintaining an efficient disbursement network, experience shows that communities achieve better results if local officials follow a few simple guidelines. These tips, suggested by local financial managers, have helped many communities make good cash management systems better.

Maintain one central bank account; at most, two accounts. The great advantage to a concentrated disbursement system is that all the free cash is located in one account. This simplifies cash control and maximizes the amounts available for investment. It is much harder to control two or more accounts and still invest those idle funds, and it is almost impossible to control and invest cash from more than five. In addition, maintaining more than two central accounts increases service costs.

Keep the number of disbursement accounts to a minimum. Again, it is much easier to control cash and minimize costs with fewer accounts. Most concentration systems maintain four to six disbursement accounts, primarily for major disbursements such as payroll and debt service payments; at least one is a multipurpose account for the many smaller, infrequent disbursements. If there are legal reasons for maintaining a separate account for a department or a specific purpose, local officials should carefully review the legal aspects of that requirement. For instance, a state grant might require a separate grant funds bank account for better cash control and reporting. Still, a municipality should minimize the number of accounts within any such external constraints.

Maintain separate bank accounts for the few major disbursement items. For major disbursement items this separation helps control the accounting; just as important, it allows local officials to identify separate float patterns for similar types of items. Except for an all-purpose account, communities generally should not maintain a separate disbursement account for disbursements that make up less than 10% of the annual budget.

Use A/B disbursement accounts for major items. For some major disbursement items, the float is sufficiently long that what is being paid and when will become confusing. With an A/B disbursement account system, two bank accounts for the same purpose are rotated each payment cycle. For example, a town that is not using a direct-deposit might maintain two payroll accounts. If it has a biweekly payroll, it uses account A to pay the first two weeks' payroll, then uses account B to pay the second two weeks' payroll. By the end of four weeks, payroll account A has essentially cleared all the first two weeks' payroll checks and is ready to be used for the next biweekly payroll. The additional time allowed for clearing checks makes it much easier to estimate the float on each account. These A/B accounts should be used only if the costs of maintaining the extra account justify the increased control over cash and the additional float information necessary to make markedly better investment decisions.

Locate the disbursement accounts and the central account in the same bank. If the fees for these accounts are competitive with accounts in other banks, maintaining disbursement and central accounts in the same bank facilitates the transfer of funds between accounts and may lower transfer costs. It also ensures the timely transfer of funds.

Delay the transfer of funds from the central account to the disbursement accounts to the latest possible moment. Delaying the transfer of funds to the last possible moment increases the amount of idle cash available for investment. The use of wire transfers, depository transfer checks, and zero-balance accounts facilitates the transfer of funds and maximizes the amount of free cash. They allow communities to move funds from the central account to disbursement accounts only as funds are needed to meet checks presented for payment. Transferring funds too early decreases the amount available for investment.

D = Discount offered by vendor

D	D/10 net 30	D/10 net 45	D/10 net 60
½%	9.0%	5.1%	3.6%
1%	18.0%	10.3%	7.2%
2%	36.0%	20.6%	14.4%

Example: Paying a bill in 30 days rather than paying in 10 days with a 2% discount is financially rewarding if funds may be invested at an annual rate of 36% or better for the subsequent twenty day period.

Source: William Donoghue, *The Cash Manager*.

EXHIBIT 2.G / Effective Interest Rates of Trade Terms

Take timely trade discounts. Trade discounts, reductions in bills that vendors offer municipalities for quick payment, are a significant yet overlooked source of savings. Whether a municipality should take the discount depends on the terms of the discount and the interest rate that the community can earn from investments. If the terms are *2/10, net/30,* the municipality may deduct 2% from the amount of the bill if it pays within ten days. If not, the entire amount, or net amount, of the bill is due in thirty days. A discount of 2/10, net/30 has the equivalent interest rate of 36% (see Exhibit 2.6). Thus if a community has funds invested in securities that yield 8%, then it is more profitable to take the trade discount. Communities should file their payables by the date that checks should be sent out to take advantage of discounts (*aging* the payables). The due date is usually counted from the date of the invoice, but some vendors allow the discount based on the postmark date while others use the day of receipt. Aging payables also helps with very short-term cash forecasting. The town treasurer may examine the aging profile to estimate the amount and timing of vendor payments for the next ten to thirty days.

Develop written procedures. When local officials determine the policies for the disbursement system, they should write a clear statement on what payment procedures they will follow. This will define for others in the payments operation the working guidelines for cash management, and it will help outside parties, such as auditors and larger vendors, understand the disbursement program. The statement might include the following guildelines:

- Disburse checks on a regular schedule. This includes vendor payments, perhaps scheduled for weekly or biweekly release of checks. There is little reason for issuing checks on a daily basis, except to meet trade discount dates. Issuing checks daily may increase processing costs and reduce the amount of cash on hand.

- Pay bills at the latest possible date to take advantage of trade discounts. The savings from trade discounts may be significant. A cash discount of 2% for payment within 10 days with the net payment due in 30 days is the equivalent of 36% annual interest savings. On the other hand, the treasury should not pay bills sooner than the due date when taking discounts. Those funds could otherwise be invested.
- Ensure that all department heads receive a copy of the written disbursement policies, so that they are aware of the bill-paying schedule and may submit invoices on a timely basis.

Collections 3

Collection systems have the same general purpose as disbursement systems. They centralize as much free cash as possible for investment, but they use different means. Collection systems speed receipts to a central account so that more funds are available sooner for investment, thus enabling local officials to protect the value of their community's cash assets as well as increase its nontax revenues.

The first section in this chapter highlights the purposes of a collection system. It sets general standards that explain the intent of accelerated collections and sets targets that local officials may use to formulate and assess changes in their community's systems.

As with disbursements, the process of accelerating collections depends in part on the check collections process. Section 3.2 describes check clearing from the point of view of those collecting funds, since a community wants to collect funds from revenue sources as quickly as possible. This section also reviews other methods used to move and collect funds, including depository transfer checks and wire transfers, and demonstrates how they accelerate collections. It shows when it is economical to use the techniques that move funds most quickly and how to move them relatively quickly using cheaper means.

Some of the opportunities in accelerating receipts come from reducing processing time. Any system that reduces the time that checks and other payments sit undeposited increases collected funds for investment. Section 3.3 introduces collection accounts and procedures that ensure the speedy deposit of receipts and the possible reduction of processing costs. It shows when special processing arrangements speed the collection of funds and save money.

Methods for moving funds quickly and the use of collection accounts for concentrating cash are most effective when tools and techniques are meshed in a centralized system. Such a system generally uses satellite bank accounts to collect different types of major revenue receipts, then it speeds those funds to a central account, most likely the same central account that pools free cash in the disbursement system. The central account makes funds available for investment or as needed for disbursement. Section 3.4 describes an example that shows how different accounts, techniques, and procedures form a central system. The chapter ends by exploring some of the information needs of collection systems and some of the most recent techniques (really techniques of the future) which may someday help local governments run more efficient cash systems with less effort.

Setting Collection Goals 3.1

The first goal of collection systems is to increase investable cash by speeding collections to a central account. The impact of sluggish receipts is illustrated by a situation in an Eastern community with a population of 75,000. An annual state aid payment of $5 million takes seven days from the day of release to the day of collection in the recipient community's bank account as a result of mail float, processing time in the local treasury, and collection time between the community's bank and the state's bank. If local officials had those funds wire transferred to the local account on the day of release, the community would be able to invest those funds for an additional seven days. At a 9% investment return, those funds in that period of time could earn an additional $8,600:

$$\frac{\$5 \text{ million} \times 9\% \times 7}{365} = \$8{,}630$$

When a community collects most of its receipts this quickly and invests them, it can earn additional revenues for its citizens merely from improved collection management.

As this shows, increased investable cash balances result from some money management techniques that reduce mail time between those making payments and the municipality. Other management techniques reduce the processing time in the treasury department for receiving and depositing revenue collections. Still others, such as the wire transfer in this example, accelerate the collection process.

Part of the goal of centralizing free cash is to reduce the number of collection bank accounts. With fewer collection accounts, fewer funds are sitting idle in bank accounts or kept there to compensate banks for their services. Having fewer accounts enhances cash control, since it is easier to manage two or three collection accounts than ten or twenty.

Although the acceleration of receipts is the primary goal of collection systems, communities should also aim to reduce processing costs or ensure that gradual increases in service costs mean an even greater increase in investment income. Some collection accounts, such as lock boxes, have banks process and deposit tax payments, with the bank passing on the paperwork for municipal posting to collection records. The community saves the time and energy of processing deposits, including the intangible costs of management oversight of the process. But the benefits of the service should exceed its costs.

As a community analyzes its current collection methods and assesses cash management techniques intended to increase the efficiency of its collection system, it should keep in mind the goals of its programs. Its goals direct it toward successfully achieving its bottom line: improved collection of funds, greater accountability, and increased nontax revenues.

3.2 Methods of Moving Funds

As in disbursement management, an efficient collection system accumulates idle cash in a central bank account. In this case, collection systems move funds quickly so more is available sooner for investment. The methods of moving funds are discussed in this section to enable those managing cash to spot opportunities in their systems for speeding up the receipt and processing of funds. These mobilization services help local officials invest those funds more quickly.

Chapter 2 introduced different techniques for moving funds. This chapter discusses those techniques from the perspective of those collecting, rather than making, payments. Section 3.2.1 follows the collection process for checks and highlights in each step possible options for improvement. Section 3.2.2 describes how funds can be moved quickly and suggests times when wire transfers are most economical. When a less expensive method makes more sense, section 3.2.3 uses an example to show how smaller amounts of funds can be moved efficiently with depository transfer checks.

Check Collection 3.2.1

Almost all municipal revenues are paid by check from taxpayers, grantors, state and federal governments, and other users of municipal services. The check collection process through the nation's banking system determines when funds will be available for municipal use.

Section 2.3 described the check collection process from the point of view of those making payments. For those collecting funds, the process is the same but reversed, with the exception of certain federal guarantees on collection times.

The check payment and collection process diagrammed in Exhibit 3.A begins when someone who owes the community money, say a taxpayer, submits payment. If the payment is sent through the mail, it may take one to seven days to reach the local treasurer's office. Municipalities can have only a limited impact on mail float in collections, unless they are able to place the receiving address for the payment, perhaps through the use of a lock box, close to the payment source. Many private corporations use lock boxes to reduce collection mail float. For example, assume that corporation A does a good deal of business with customer B in a city across the country. To reduce the mail time for payments from B and other customers in that area, corporation A places a post office box in B's town. B mails its payments to that post office box rather than to A's home office three thousand miles away. Mail float is greatly reduced, and once that payment is collected, the local bank wire transfers it to corporation A. Point-to-point mail time is local, and collection is local, saving company A valuable time on available funds. Most municipal collections are nearby, so lock boxes can do little to reduce already short mail times.

Municipalities may affect mail times, however, by avoiding the mails altogether. Some communities arrange for their taxpayers or water and sewer users to pay tax or utility bills at local banks. The bank immediately deposits those checks in the town's account and sends the paperwork to the treasurer's office. If the service is equally or more convenient for local citizens, the municipality should eliminate the mail float.

Collections can also be delayed by inefficient payments processing in local treasuries. When the treasury receives tax payments, it usually credits the taxpayer for the

1. Local government mails tax bills. Collections accelerated by early mailing.

2. Taxpayer remits tax payment (a) by mail or in person at city hall, or (b) by mail to lock box. Tax payments accelerated by penalties for late payment or installment payment system.

3. A. Collections department records payment and deposits checks in bank account. Collections accelerated by same day deposit.

   B. Local government's bank opens mail from lock box and deposits checks immediately. Sends tax payment forms and other collection information to collector's office.

4. Local government's bank begins collection process. Based on bank location and local clearinghouse affiliations, local government's bank chooses fastest method of collection.

   A. Federal Reserve. Guarantees that local government's bank will receive funds within two days.

   B. Clearinghouse. Check presented to local clearinghouse where checks are exchanged and accounts settled. Usually immediate or next day.*

   C. Correspondent Bank. Check sent to correspondent bank in the same district or clearinghouse as taxpayer's bank. Usually one to two day delay.

5. Taxpayer's bank transfers funds to local government's bank and charges taxpayer's account. At end of month, sends cancelled check to taxpayer.

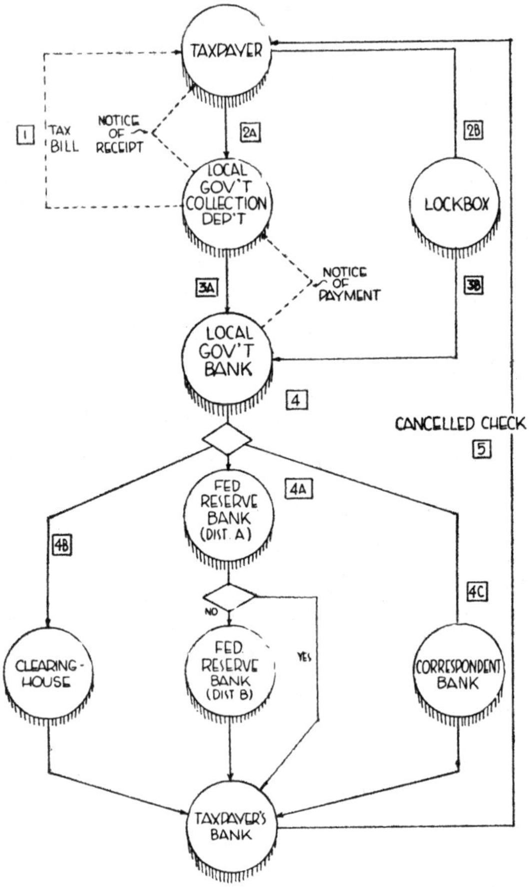

*Automated clearinghouses. Since 1979, a network of regional automated clearinghouses have been linked together in a national exchange to batch process electronic payments. The federal government uses ACHs to distribute its national payroll and revenue sharing disbursements. Municipalities can designate local banks as depositories for the latter payments and thus receive direct and immediate credit for large sums of money. Otherwise, revenue sharing funds are distributed by check.

EXHIBIT 3.A / Check Clearing (Collections)

payment and prepares the check for deposit. The time that the check remains in the treasury, the internal processing time, is significant in some localities. The community loses interest from those funds not being deposited when received. Two procedures may help local governments reduce this delay.

First, local officials should have treasury clerks prepare and deposit funds on the day they are received. For some, this is a significant departure from current practices if checks are used to post collections directly to tax receivable accounts. Accounting records should be posted after checks are deposited, from tax payment remittance slips returned with payments. Same-day or next-day deposit is a realistic goal.

Second, special processing procedures can be used for larger checks. In one community the clerks open the mail as it arrives each morning. For all payments over $50,000, payment remittance forms are stamped "paid," checks are prepared for deposit and deposited that same morning. This ensures that the largest dollar volume of checks, a much smaller percentage of the number of checks, is deposited immediately.

After checks have been deposited, the community's bank begins the process of collecting those funds from the taxpayers' banks. This lag, *deposit float* (section 2.3), may take one of three routes. First, the bank may collect those funds through a local clearinghouse (automated clearinghouses, ACHs) if the taxpayer's bank belongs to that group. Second, the bank might send the check to a correspondent bank who collects those funds and in effect, sends them back to the community's bank. Third, the bank may process the check through the Federal Reserve System. Since the Fed guarantees that the collecting bank will be given credit for those funds within two days, the community's bank will collect its funds within two days after the checks have been deposited.

Even with the Federal Reserve guarantee, banks may want to delay the availability of funds to their customers while they wait to see whether deposited checks will bounce. Although funds are collected in two days, it takes up to ten days for a check to return if there are not enough funds in the taxpayer's account. If a taxpayer's bank finds insufficient balances after it has made payment to the community's bank, the check is returned to that bank in exchange for the funds. The process may take up to ten days. Local officials may, however, arrange with the community's bank to make funds available as they are collected, with immediate reimbursement on bad checks.

When funds are finally returned to the community's bank, those funds are considered to be collected, and they are then available for investment or disbursement.

Examination of current collection and deposit practices may reveal opportunities for accelerating investable funds by reducing mail, processing, and deposit float. One such technique is the wire transfer.

Wire Transfers 3.2.2

Wire transfers move funds rapidly from bank to bank, or to and from investment media. Because they make funds available almost immediately, they can accelerate collections and therefore increase investment income. The example in the introduction to this section demonstrated that using wire transfers to collect state aid could increase the nontax revenue to that town by $8,600 per transfer!

Section 2.5.3 described wire transfers in detail and explained how to use them. Wire transfers have two major uses in collections. First, they collect funds from large payment sources such as the state government or perhaps a grantee. If for some reason the source of the payment, in the opening example the state treasurer, declined to wire funds, a municipality might open a bank account in the same bank as the source. If the check can be deposited immediately, the collection involves merely a transfer of funds between two accounts in the same bank. This type of "on us" payment would be made the same or the following day. Then the local treasurer could wire transfer those funds to the municipality's central account. This additional account and transfer involves extra costs, and local officials should assure themselves that these additional costs are exceeded by the extra income from reduced float.

Wire transfers are also used to move funds quickly from outlying collection accounts to a central account. Of course, if the collection account and the central account are in the same bank, then a local treasurer merely processes a transfer that moves funds immediately and saves the cost of the wire transfer. If the accounts are not in the same bank, the treasurer may move collected funds between accounts in different banks by telephone. Wire transfers not only move funds quickly between banks; they also allow the treasurer to move funds on the basis of current information. He knows at the time of transfer how much is collected in each account.

A simple calculation can be used to determine the minimum transfer needed to cover the cost of the wire transfer order. The following formula was described in section 2.5.3 and may be used here.

$$\text{Minimum amount transferred to be profitable} = \frac{(\text{Cost of wire transfer}) \times (365 \text{ days})}{(\text{Current short-term interest rate}) \times (\text{Additional float gained from wire transfer})}$$

For example, suppose that a town receives a 6% annual return on its investments, it gains an extra two days if it uses a wire transfer rather than a depository transfer check or some other method, and a wire transfer costs $6.00. Then the calculation would look something like this:

$$\text{Minimum amount} = \frac{(\$6.00) \times (365)}{(.06) \times (2)} = \$18{,}250$$

The town would not want to wire transfer funds in amounts less than $18,000, solely on the basis of cost.

There are other reasons than economics for using wire transfers, and these are part of the consideration. If, for example, the community is moving funds to cover a potential overdraft in another account, then the cost of the wire transfer is secondary.

Depository Transfer Checks 3.2.3

When wire transfers are not economical, depository transfer checks (DTCs) can be used. DTCs transfer smaller amounts of funds almost as effectively yet cost much less than wire transfers. Section 2.5.4 described DTCs and explained how municipalities use them.

DTCs pass through the normal check-clearing process, so they may take several days to move funds. Even so, this may not be excessively inefficient. The following example describes how a local treasurer uses DTCs to transfer funds between a collection and a central bank.

When a local treasurer generates a DTC, he moves funds on the basis of the expected amount in the collection account one to two days hence, when the DTC effectively transfers funds. This may not mean, however, that the community loses one to two days in collection float. It takes one to two days for the checks that have been deposited in the collection account to clear the taxpayer's bank, so a DTC may clear a collection account at the same time that the collection account is collecting funds from the taxpayer's bank. Funds could not have been transferred any sooner by wire transfer since only collected funds may be moved. DTCs are less accurate than wire transfers, since one must estimate how much funds will be collected when the DTC clears. However, local officials correct for that uncertainty by leaving a cushion to prevent the account from being overdrawn.

When local officials prepare DTCs, the amount transferred from collection accounts to a central account depends on several factors. It depends first on the amount of collected funds on hand in the collection account when the DTC is expected to clear. Local officials estimate the collected funds that will be on hand at the time the DTC reaches the collection account. The amount transferred should leave sufficient funds in the account to compensate for banking services. (Chapter 4 describes how to calculate compensating balances for banking services.) Finally, some communities leave a little extra from time to time to maintain a smooth working relationship with their bank. This reserve balance sometimes includes a buffer for uncollected or returned funds. Over time, local officials get a good idea of the percentage of checks that will bounce, making this buffer more predictable.

Many local officials do not have the time to monitor and estimate smaller account balances. They instead have their bank prepare the DTC based on standing instructions. In this case DTCs are not generated until collected balances are known, but some efficiencies are gained because banks are in a much better situation to know and meet bank cutoff times for depositing funds. For example, if a bank cutoff time is 10 a.m. for same day availability of local checks, then the DTC should arrive at the bank by 10 a.m. to ensure that the collection of funds is not delayed a day. Banks should guarantee that DTCs meet cutoff times and eliminate DTC transport time to the bank, which is otherwise a worry to the muncipality. Banks may, therefore, write a DTC on the basis of more up-to-date information, such as the number and amount of checks deposited and collected that morning.

The easiest way to manage the DTC transfer process is to agree with the bank on the proper compensating balance, then instruct the bank to automatically transfer out any excess. This works well if communities transfer amounts via DTC that are smaller than necessary to justify the use of wire transfers. With banks automatically transferring excess funds, funds move relatively quickly to a central account, providing greater opportunities for investment.

3.3 Managing Collection Accounts

Collection bank accounts help local officials manage the collection process, accelerate the concentration of funds, and contain processing costs.

Although most collection accounts are simply regular checking accounts, sometimes earmarked for special revenues and separately managed, one type of account has special bank processing arrangements: lock boxes. In addition, letters-of-credit can be used to collect funds from federal agencies. For municipalities that receive federal grant monies, the proper management and collection of grant funds at least ensures that cash is available when needed to pay for federally funded project disbursements. Otherwise, communities find that they are delaying these disbursements or continually disbursing cash that has not yet been reimbursed by the United States Treasury. Lock box arrangements and letter-of-credit procedures are not the only means of managing collection accounts, but if used effectively, they may considerably accelerate the collection of municipal revenues.

3.3.1 Lock Boxes

Lock boxes accelerate the deposit and therefore the collection of municipal receipts. Thus, even though banks charge for the service, lock boxes may reduce internal processing costs. If located properly, they also reduce mail float.

A lock box is a post office box to which a community's citizens send revenue payments, such as tax collections. The community's bank empties the box daily, immediately deposits all funds, and sends the local treasurer the payment information to adjust receivable accounts. The community has its collected checks almost immediately deposited.

A more detailed description of how a town manages a lock box should clarify its procedures and purpose. The town rents a post office box and shows this address on its tax bills. The town's bank then sends a courier to the post office two to three times a day, around the time that the post office receives large mail shipments. The bank opens the envelopes, processes the checks for deposit (including making out the deposit slip), arranges the return documentation for processing (including the computer cards or tapes that record payment information), deposits the checks, and sends to the town the detail of the deposits and the documentation (deposit slips, return tax forms, computer cards, and the like). If there is a delay of one or more days in having the deposit documentation reach the town, the town may ask the bank to notify a local official by phone each day of the amount deposited.

Used correctly, local boxes have strong advantages. They reduce the time that it takes to process tax returns and deposit the funds. Since tax payments cause peak processing periods that stretch the capabilities of the collection department's staff to get funds into the bank, the reduced deposit time is significant. Lock boxes also shift some internal processing costs to the bank since the town collector's staff performs fewer functions, such as opening envelopes and depositing checks. If the bank produces the collection information on machine-readable cards or tapes, then other processing costs are essentially reduced to running the tape or cards through the town's receivable system. Banks specialize in high-volume lock box processing, so they often offer a lower per item processing cost than the municipality itself could achieve. Besides, processing costs at peak times are sometimes expensive for communities, since staff may have to work overtime or communities might have to hire and train temporary help.

Locating a lock box near the source of payment may also reduce the mail float. If, for example, a town receives regular payments from its state capital located 200 miles and two or three days of mail time away, it might locate a lock box near the source, in this case in the state capital. Presumably the two to three day mail time would be cut down to at most one day. Since most collections for state and local government are nearby, mail float alone is not a major manageable factor in government cash collections. However, when collection times are extended as a result of mail float from distant sources, local officials should consider lock boxes to accelerate cash mobilization.

Lock boxes also provide greater security for collected checks. Since checks are sent directly to the bank through a post office box, the municipality need not worry about the security of transporting checks to the bank for deposit. If it hires an armored car service to collect and deposit checks, it may further save money by eliminating this service.

Lock boxes also reduce errors. The bank ensures that all checks are properly signed, dated, and endorsed to the proper payee and thus reduces the error from that oversight by treasury personnel.

As with any service, lock boxes have several disadvantages. Lock boxes may delay the arrival of cash management information at the collector's office. Tax payment information reaches the bank first, and there may therefore be a one-day to one-week lag in the time that the information reaches City Hall, thus delaying the updating of receivable accounts. However, communities often reduce information lags to tolerable levels by some suitable arrangement with their banks.

Lock boxes may increase the department's expense for making corrections and following-up on incorrect payments. Since the collector's office does not inspect and determine the accuracy of the remittance before funds are deposited, an error in a payment may require that another check be generated to refund money to the taxpayer.

Net earnings from a lock box that processes 10,000 checks per year.

Annual check volume: 10,000
Investment yield on available cash: 9%
Processing charge: $0.40 per item
Annual net earnings rounded to nearest 250

Number of days saved	Average dollar value of checks		
	$10,000	**$1,000**	**$500**
1	$21,000	(1,500)	(2,750)
2	46,000	1,000	(1,500)
3	71,000	3,500	(250)
4	96,000	6,000	1,000
5	121,000	8,500	2,250

EXHIBIT 3.B / Evaluating Lock Box Arrangements

The most important consideration, however, is the economics of the lock box. Generally, communities do not want to use a lock box unless they can demonstrate that its benefits exceed the costs of the service.

The following calculation can be used to determine the minimum size check that makes a lock box economical.

$$\text{Minimum size check} = \frac{(\text{Marginal cost of lock box}) \times (365\text{ days})}{(\text{Interest rate of short-term investments}) \times (\text{Additional float gained from lock box})}$$

The marginal cost of a lock box is the additional cost incurred to process a lock box check over the cost of processing a check through the regular collection and deposit process. If, for instance, it costs 10 cents to deposit a check received directly from the taxpayer, and the bank charges 40 cents to process a lock box check, then the marginal cost of a lock box item is 30 cents:

Cost of lock box (per check)	$ .40
Cost of regular deposit (per check)	.10
Marginal cost of lock box	$. 30

Let's look at an example. Suppose that interest rates are at 7%, the marginal cost of a check deposited with a lock box is 30 cents, and the community gains one day of mail float and one day of processing float with a lock box. Then the minimum economical size of a check routed to a lock box would be as follows:

Dear City Collector:

According to our mutual understanding, the arrangement for the Centerdale City lock box service is to be as follows:

1. A post office box will be rented in the name of Centerdale City. Post office box rental fees will be charged to your account semiannually.
2. Contents of the post office box will be removed according to our hourly schedule each day and processed by the Lock Box Department. Mutually agreeable "cutoff" times may be arranged to achieve optimum processing and/or delivery of posting media.
3. The total of all checks processed will be credited to your account each day, it being understood that the credit and collection of such checks will be subject to the same terms and conditions as would apply to deposits received directly from you.
4. The following municipal name, or a reasonable derivation thereof, would be acceptable as payee: City Collector, Centerdale City.
5. Each check processed will be endorsed: "Credited to the account of the within named payee, absence of the endorsement guaranteed, Cityvale Bank."
6. One photocopy will be produced for each processed remittance check. Photocopies and invoices (proof documents) will be tape listed in total.
7. Miscellaneous documents received without a remittance check will be reinserted in the proper envelopes and segregated.
8. All miscellaneous documents enclosed with the check, one check listing, one proof document listing, all photocopies and advices will be mailed to you.
9. Postdated checks will be forwarded to you unprocessed, unless the date is current enough for the check to be paid in the normal course of banking practice.
10. Checks not containing special or restrictive endorsements, and such other items as the bank designates as irregular, will not be included in the daily work process, but will be forwarded to your office for disposition.
11. A microfilm record of each remittance check processed will be maintained by us for research or reference purposes.
12. Checks which are returned for reason of "insufficient funds" or "uncollected funds" will be automatically redeposited on the first occasion of dishonor. On the second occasion of return, we will charge you with our usual advice and return the item to you.
13. In addition, all checks bearing typed or handwritten notations reading "payment in full" will not be included in the daily work process, but will be forwarded to the City Collector for review. Any check bearing a similar printed legend will be processed in the usual manner.
14. Based on your estimated volume of 1,000 items per month, and the specifications outlined in this agreement letter, we would charge $.30 per item. Our minimum charge for the service is $100 per month.
15. Charges for the lock box service can be factored in the analysis charges of your account each month.
16. Lock box service charges are subject to periodic review and adjustment.
17. In addition, you would need to maintain collected balances in support of deposit, maintenance, and account activity charges on the checking account.
18. Our earnings allowance for collected balances is presently 8%, before deducting for our 15% reserve requirement. This allowance is based on a three-month rolling average of 91-day Treasury bill rates and changes monthly.
19. This agreement is subject to termination by either party with a minimum of thirty (30) days written notice.
20. The offer to provide the lock box service at the price indicated herein shall remain in effect for ninety (90) days subsequent to the dating of this proposal.

If you find this agreement satisfactory, please sign one copy and return it to my attention.

Sincerely,	**Accepted & Confirmed**
Calvin Boscombe, Vice President Cityvale Bank	By: Title: Date:

EXHIBIT 3.C / Sample Lock Box Agreement

$$M = \frac{(.30) \times (365)}{(.07) \times (2)}$$

$$M = \$782.$$

The minimum size check of $780 shows that for most payments a lock box will pay off. Remember, too, that this calculation does not consider the savings from reducing internal processing costs, assuming that a municipality may have to hire more people or have people work overtime to process tax payments.

One way of using this information is to segregate tax payments. A community could, for example, have all tax bills over $800 show the lock box post office number, and all the bills less than $800 returned to City Hall for manual processing. These arrangements are called *bullet* or *wild card* lock boxes.

The calculation for the minimum amount changes with changes in the short-term interest rate, the additional gain on float, and the marginal service charge. If any of these variables changes (the short-term interest rate will most certainly change significantly every quarter) local officials should recalculate the minimum feasible amount. As interest rates rise, a municipality will want to have more checks processed through its lock box; the reverse is true when interest rates fall. Also, the longer it takes municipal personnel to process and deposit checks, the more attractive the lock box becomes.

For corporations the profitability of a lock box depends on the bank's location and the services provided by the lock box bank. For local governments services are much more important than location, since most tax collections are from local sources. A corporation, for example, would locate its lock box near the source of its collections to reduce mail float. More important for local governments, however, is to choose lock box banks that have the facilities to process lock box checks on the same day and to wire funds, automatically or otherwise, immediately to a central account.

3.3.2 Letters of Credit

Improved management of one collection process in particular, the federal letter of credit payments system, helps communities guarantee the availability of federal funds when needed to make disbursements for federally funded projects. This process generally does not enable municipalities to accelerate federal collections for local investment, but it should ensure that payments are supported by federal money rather than by what is essentially a loan from the local government until federal funds are received.

The federal government disburses grant monies to state and local governments largely with letter of credit agreements. Instead of issuing lump sum checks to state and local governments, the federal government authorizes municipalities to draw down federal bank accounts only as the local government needs cash to meet grant disbursements.

1. Agency awards federal grant to local government. Sends letter of credit to the Bureau of Government Financial Operations (BGFO) and a copy to the local government.
2. BGFO sends letter of credit to Federal Reserve Bank (FRB).
3. When cash is needed, local government deposits a payment voucher in its bank account.
4. Bank credits local government account and collects funds by submitting voucher to FRB.
5. FRB charges U.S. Treasury account and credits local government's bank. Sends copy of voucher to BGFO.
6. BGFO sends copy of voucher to Federal agency that awarded grant.
7. Federal agency charges local government's grant account.
8. At specified intervals, local government sends periodic cost reports to Federal agency.

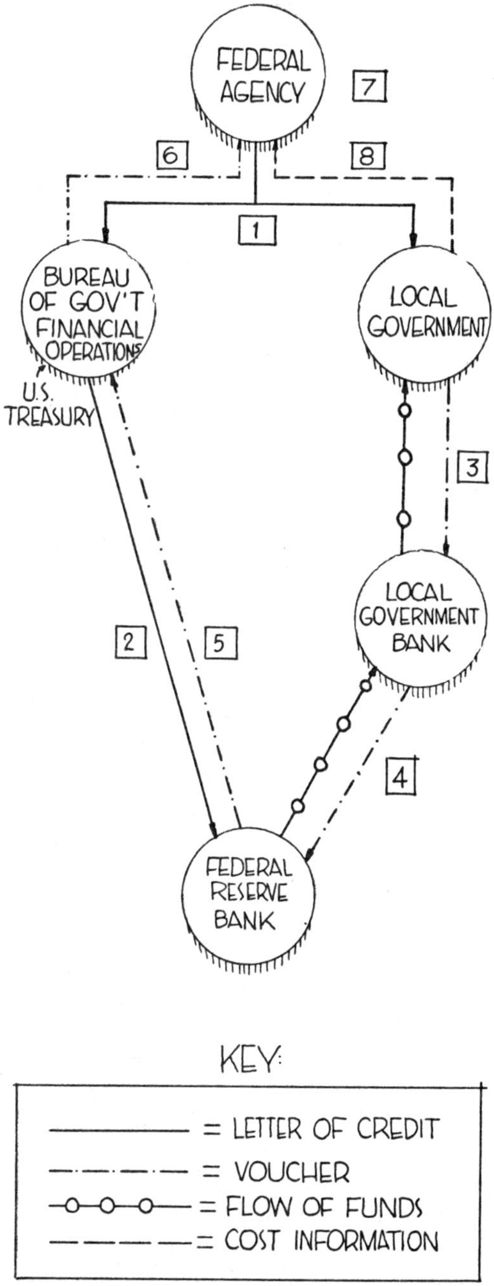

EXHIBIT 3.D / Letter of Credit Process—Federal Reserve Bank (FRB) System

The federal government instituted letters of credit for a variety of federal agencies in the late 1960s to improve the U.S. government's cash flows. Before that time, a recipient of a federal grant collected a check for the entire amount of the grant when it was awarded. As a result, the federal government was disbursing funds that might not have been needed until much later and it lost some of its control of funds because it could not examine the propriety of payments until after the funds had been released. To reduce the interest costs of advancing cash and to improve authorization control, the federal government began a letter of credit system.

To qualify for the letter of credit system a grantee must meet the following criteria. First, the grantee must have a relationship with the federal government that extends at least one year, and the annual advances must be expected to exceed $120,000. Second, the grantee must draw funds only as they are needed, and it must report periodically its cash disbursements and grant balances to the federal agency that has awarded the grant. Third, the federal agency can review the financial practices of the grantee and initiate remedial measures if the grantee does not comply with the terms of the grant or with the letter of credit agreement.

In addition to these criteria, local restrictions may prevent some state and local governments from participating in the letter of credit program. Some state laws, for example, require that funds be available in local treasuries before obligations are incurred, and some require that funds be on hand before bills can be processed for payment. These restrictions necessarily impede the application of the letter of credit system.

To better understand letters of credit, let's examine the procedure for their use and processing. When a grant is awarded, the federal government opens a letter of credit in favor of the grantee (local government) against the Treasury's account with the Federal Reserve bank nearest to the community. If a payment is approved, the Fed is permitted to draw down the U.S. Treasury's account to pay for grant payments. When the community needs funds to pay for grant expenses, it submits a payment voucher by depositing the vouchers in its bank account. The community's bank then presents the voucher to the Federal Reserve bank. The Fed inspects the voucher for authenticity and makes sure that the amount of the voucher falls within the letter of credit ceiling. Once it approves the voucher, the Fed charges the Treasury Department's account and credits the commercial bank's account.

Specifically, there are two primary letter of credit processing paths. In the first and older process, the Federal Reserve Bank (FRB) system (see Exhibit 3.D), the recipient processes payments as just described. In a second and newer process, the Treasury Regional Disbursing Office (RDO) system (see Exhibit 3.E) has the recipient submit payment vouchers to a regional disbursing office of the U.S. Treasury. The RDO examines and approves the voucher, then sends the local government or its bank a check for the amount. To collect those funds, the municipality deposits the Treasury check in its bank, which collects funds through the regular check clearing system. Depending on the location of the RDO, the letter of credit process may be very long since submission of vouchers and return checks depend on the U.S. mail.

The local government's management of letters of credit is relatively straight-

1. Agency awards federal grant to local government. Sends letter of credit to U.S Treasury Regional Disbursement Office (RDO) and a copy to local government.

2. Local government sends advance copy of payment request to agency.

3. Agency reviews advance copy of payment request and can ask RDO to withhold payment.

4. When cash is needed, local government submits payment request to RDO.

5. RDO sends check to (a) local government's bank or (b) local government. Sends copy of payment request to agency (5C).

6. Local government deposits RDO check.

7. Local government's bank credits local government's account and presents check to Federal Reserve Bank for payment. Federal Reserve charges U.S. Treasury account and credits local government's bank.

8. A. Monthly, RDO reports total agency charges to Bureau of Government Financial Operations (U.S. Treasury).

   B. Monthly, agency reports total agency charges to Bureau of Government Financial Operations.

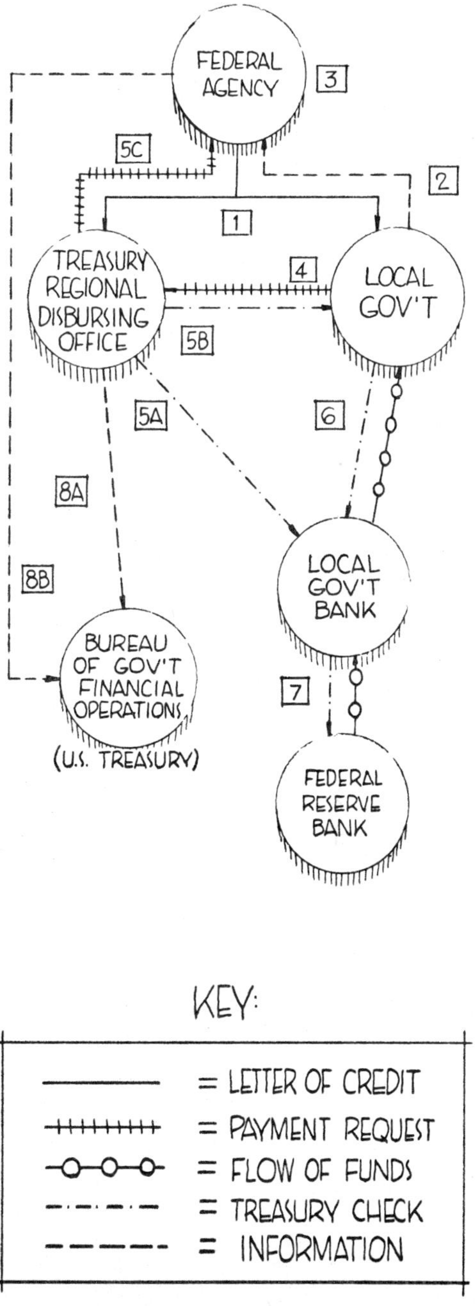

EXHIBIT 3.E / Letter of Credit Process—Treasury Regional Disbursing Office (RDO) System

forward. The local government should ensure that payment vouchers are submitted as soon as possible, in order to maintain adequate cash reserves to meet incoming bills. The federal government is trying to simplify the payment process for itself and the grantee by consolidating all letters of credit from each federal agency into one for each municipality. This consolidation reduces the administration costs for federal, state, and local governments. Information describing federal regulations, forms, and procedures for letters of credit may be found in Transmittal Letter No. 236 and Circular No. 1075, published by the Department of the Treasury, Fiscal Service, Bureau of Government Financial Operations, Washington, D.C. 20226.

If a community finds that mail delays significantly slow grant collections in an RDO letter of credit system, and the community collects a significant amount of

Some frequently asked questions regarding federal grant cash management are answered below.

1. Does the grantee have to set up a separate bank account to deposit grant funds?

No. Federal Management Circular 74-7, Attachment A *(Cash Depositories)* states that "no grant program shall require physical segregation of cash depositories for Federal grant funds." That is, grant funds can be pooled with other funds if accounting controls can identify all deposits and withdrawals. Some federal grant officials ask, but cannot legally require, grantees to set up separate accounts.

2. Does the federal government impose any restrictions on the selection of banks?

Generally, no. FMC Circular 74-4 prohibits any grant program from "imposing eligibility requirements for cash depositories" of grant funds. However, monies advanced which are determined to be "public monies" owned by the federal government must be deposited in a bank with FDIC coverage, and balances exceeding the FDIC coverage must be secured by collateral. Also, FMC Circular 74-7 encourages but does not require the use of "minority banks."

3. When can local governments request federal grant payments?

Grant regulations specify the timing of federal advances. The letter of credit system is designed to advance funds only for *immediate* disbursement needs. *Immediate* is not precisely defined but auditors of grant funds are advised to disclose if drawdowns materially exceed three days' cash requirement.

4. Can the grantee retain interest earned on unspent grant funds?

According to law, no; but the law is poorly enforced. FMC Circular 74-7, Attachment E, requires local governments to return all interest earned on advances of grant funds. This is in accordance with a decision of the Comptroller General of the United States (42 Compt. Gen. 289). (The Intergovernmental Cooperation Act of 1968 excludes state agencies from this requirement.) The decision has had minimal impact because of poor agency enforcement. Also, the letter of credit system has reduced federal advances to a point at which investment income, in the eyes of many auditors, is immaterial. In any event, the law does not prohibit a grantee from using federal advances as compensating balances, thus freeing up local revenues for investment.

General revenue sharing funds may be invested so long as the investment income is added back to the unspent revenue sharing balance.

EXHIBIT 3.F / Federal Regulations Regarding Grantee Cash Management

funds from that office, local officials should consider methods of accelerating at least the collection process, perhaps by using a lock box with the same bank as the RDO and wiring funds to the community's central account.

Building the Collection System 3.4

Knowing the nature and processing characteristics of major types of revenues, the local treasurer's objective is to build a simple system for collecting and centralizing funds expeditiously.

As in the disbursement network, the key feature of the collection network is the central account, the account in which funds are pooled for short-term investment. Although a municipality usually uses separate collection accounts for significant funds or special payments, most deposits are made directly to the central account.

The collection network is composed of a central demand deposit bank account, often the same central account used in the disbursement network, and several collection accounts that feed collected funds to the central account.

Exhibit 3.G shows how one town might process collections to mobilize idle cash. Payments for tax bills over $500 are sent directly to a lock box. Since checks are deposited on the same day they are received, and since most taxpayers keep checking accounts with local banks, lock box funds are collected and transferred to the central account for investment within days. Other receipts, such as currency from the parking meters, are deposited in a bank account near the headquarters of the department that receives the money. An officer of the bureau then generates a depository transfer check for the amount of each deposit, to move those funds to the town's central account. The town in this example also receives significant revenues from the state and federal governments. Arrangements were made with the state treasurer to wire transfer funds directly to the town's central account on the day that the state releases local aid payments, and the town collects federal grant funds by depositing vouchers which are processed through the FRB letter of credit system. Infrequent or miscellaneous revenues are deposited directly to the central account. This small, simple collection system efficiently collects and concentrates cash for short-term investment.

The key to this and other controlled cash management systems is that they reduce the number of bank accounts to minimize the time that cash lies idle. They also reduce banking costs and simplify cash control. Communities maintain separate bank accounts to segregate certain receipts for preferred processing or to increase the security of currency collections or reduce mail or collection float. Some of the considerations in creating collection accounts to meet special control and processing needs are outlined here.

Processing considerations. A community may want to maintain a collection account to shift the costs of processing a large number of payments during peak periods. Banks may sell lock box services whereby the bank receives collection payments from taxpayers, opens and sorts the mail, deposits funds as soon as

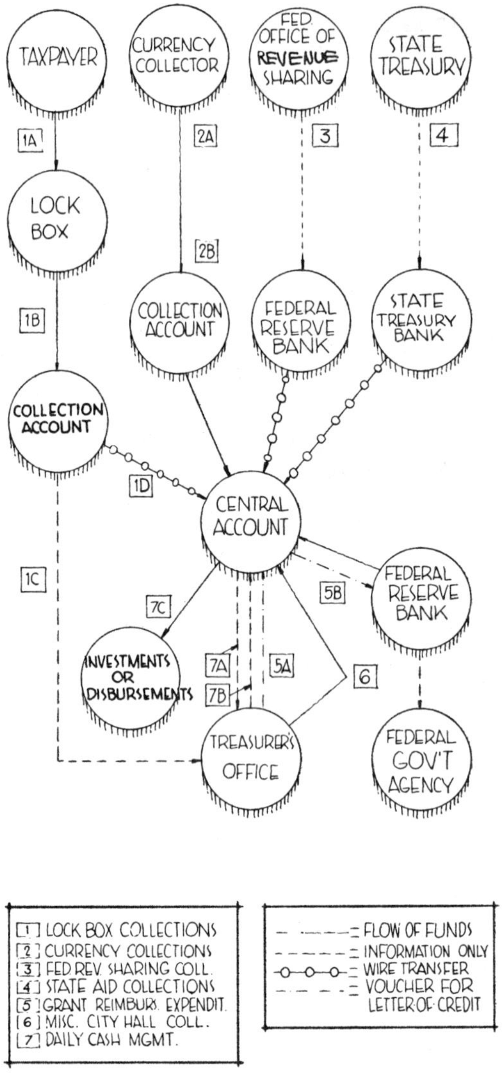

1. A. Taxpayers mail tax payments to designated lock box (lock box address may be assigned to only those with payments in excess of a minimum amount).

   B. Bank empties lock box and deposits checks in local government's collection account on the same day.

   C. Bank notifies treasurer daily of lock box receipts and available balances.

   D. Funds in excess of compensating balances wire transferred to central account on day of availability.

2. A. Collection agent deposits cash receipts from parking meters, golf course fees, etc., daily.

   B. Upon deposit of currency, collection agent generates depository transfer check which is deposited in the central account.

3. When revenue sharing funds are disbursed, the Office of Revenue Sharing deposits funds directly into local government's central account.

4. On payment date, state treasurer wires state aid funds to municipality's central account.

5. A. Local government deposits federal grant voucher in central account.

   B. Central bank collects funds from Federal Reserve Bank.

6. Local government deposits cash collections into central accounts.

7. A. Central bank notifies treasurer daily of available balance.

   B. Treasurer issues orders to central bank to buy or sell investments or transfer funds.

   C. Funds leave central account for disbursements or purchase of investments.

EXHIBIT 3.G / The Collection Network

possible, and sends the local collector records of the check, often a photocopy, with the taxpayer's payment form. The municipality then updates tax collection records. The use of lock boxes reduces processing float and reduces the community's internal management costs.

Security considerations. Some municipalities, usually larger cities or counties, maintain a collection bank account near the site of cash collections, if there is a security risk of moving the cash across town to the central account office. It also allows more frequent cash deposits during the day. Local officials should determine, however, that the cost of maintaining the bank account is "worth" the insurance for those funds.

Large collection float. In a few cases, local governments might establish collection accounts to accelerate collections from remote locations. The most efficient method is wire transfer directly from the source to the community's bank. But if wire transfer is not possible, a community might maintain a bank account near the source of the payment to reduce mail and collection times.

These reasons for keeping separate bank accounts, the last two of which are somewhat unusual, mean that most communities need only a few collection accounts. Accounting controls and legal requirements also influence the number of bank accounts. Where special revenues require separate cash accounts, there is little a local treasurer can do. For accounting purposes, however, control may be maintained over cash receipts by separate cash ledgers (or cash subaccounts on the general ledger) with periodic reconcilement to accounts receivable records and aggregate bank balances. Bank accounts used merely for control purposes should be consolidated to centralize free cash.

Generally, collection accounts should be created only if the location or operation of the account significantly increases the availability of funds for investment. This criterion is the best guide to designing an efficient system.

The Information Network

An effective, centralized collection system requires an efficient and accurate information network that keeps local officials up-to-date on the cash balances in local bank accounts. A community must know how much money is collected in its accounts and how much it expects to collect in the next days and weeks so it knows how much to transfer and invest. If funds are transferred automatically, then local officials need advisements from collection accounts on how much is being collected to plan investments.

Most local governments have only a few local depositories; thus information gathering is simplified. The most efficient way to get account information is to call the bank at the end of the day or in the morning, depending on bank clearing schedules, to find out how much cash has been collected in municipal accounts. Local officials should also know the amount of the checks recently deposited and still awaiting clearance to estimate incoming cash flows. A centralized system of cash control should eliminate departmental deposits and resulting delays in collection information. Generally, it is better to call banks than to wait for them to call. On occasion, hectic bank days may delay bank notification of cash balances.

Large municipalities with a network of distant bank accounts may use national services that collect balance information on all municipal accounts and relay that to the city collector. Such services are provided by the National Data Corporation in Atlanta, General Electric, the Automated Data Processing Corporation, Interactive Data Corporation, and Rapidata Corporation.

Ideas for More Effective Cash Management

This section discusses ways that other local governments have improved cash flows, either by controlling disbursements or accelerating collections, thus making more cash available for short-term investment. These means will not be useful for every community, but most of the practices should contribute to better cash management in many communities.

To control disbursements, managers should:

- Create two vendor paydays a month rather than having continuous payments.
- Make timely payments to take advantage of trade discounts.
- Release checks after banks have stopped processing deposits for the day. This does not mean that employees will not be able to cash their checks, but their accounts will be credited on the next day.
- Release checks immediately before a weekend.
- Write checks on slow clearing banks.
- Reduce prepaid vacation payments.
- Keep petty cash funds to a legal minimum.

Accelerating collections:

- Mail tax bills promptly, and consider moving forward the mailing date.
- Consider collecting sales and hotel taxes monthly rather than quarterly or semi-annually.
- Increase the penalties and interest charges on late tax payments.
- Review the list of delinquent taxpayers and take follow-up action.
- Establish procedures for the prompt filing of federal and state grant claims.
- Consider installment billing for property taxes on a voluntary basis.
- Send out utility bills promptly.
- Deposit each day's receipts on the same day, or ensure that large checks are deposited promptly.

Part 2

Banks and Banking Services

Banking Relations 4

Efficient cash management systems—those that consolidate idle cash, accelerate collections, control disbursements and invest available funds—depend greatly on the quality of banking services. This part introduces local government managers to a straightforward process of reviewing and acquiring cash management services.

Until recently, communities often took banking relations and services for granted because cash management meant merely that local officials kept sufficient balances in checking accounts to meet payments. Banking services consisted of a series of checking accounts to keep accounting information on different types of municipal disbursements.

Part 1 on disbursements and collections shows that cash management opportunities have changed greatly from the time when bank service consisted of moving funds through the check collection system, a sizable task, but now only part of the services offered by banks. Greatly expanded investment opportunities mean greater returns from investing idle cash, and added investment income simultaneously protects cash assets from the ravages of inflation. In response to active financial cash management, banks have developed services to help local officials manage their cash resource.

More active cash management and expanding local government cash flows make the hiring and use of banks a more important and more complex decision. The first sections of this module describe the steps involved in the hiring decision: assessing needed services (section 4.2), inviting banks to bid for local accounts (section 4.4), analyzing banks and their bids (section 4.5), and awarding bank services, including the subsequent working contract (section 4.6).

This assessment and award process helps officials choose the most effective services from the ever-expanding bank menu. Officials accustomed to traditional financial management or those new to their positions may find the array of bank services and their value to the community bewildering. Section 4.3 describes the range of banking services (the application of many to local systems was discussed in Part 1).

Local officials need a method to determine the true costs of services, called an *account analysis*. Banking services were formerly thought of as free if banks levied no special charges, but in fact they are not free, since idle balances can instead be invested in income-producing securities. Section 4.7 shows how to determine the costs for banking services measured against effective compensation in the form of idle deposit balances. One aspect of bank compensation, the separate pricing of services, is further discussed in section 4.8, which explains much of the variance in the prices that banks charge. Bank account analysis is necessary, not only to assess bids for accounts, but also to review bank costs on a regular basis. Account analysis is an ongoing process requiring regular review.

4.1 Managing Banking Relations

Banking relations improve when each side recognizes its benefit to the other. Government-banking relationships are best when the bank provides services at lower cost and greater efficiency than the government could provide itself and is compensated fairly for its efforts, that is, when local governments and banks see opportunities for mutual gain. The final sections of this part, *The ABC's of Banks and Bank Regulation,* explain how banks operate. These sections should enable the reader to develop a general understanding of banking management and appreciate the value of local government accounts to those institutions.

A good banking relationship emerges when local officials pursue a constructive, professional approach. The following observations help communities develop that approach.

Banks are in business to make a profit. Banks provide services to a municipality at a reasonable profit, because they have an obligation to their depositors and stockholders to maintain an ongoing, profitable concern. A municipality that demands unreasonably low bank prices will develop a reputation as an unattractive account.

Banks are in competition. The best insurance that banks do not make unreasonable gains from municipal accounts is competition. Competition is the basis for new, improved services, lower costs, and greater efficiency. Except in extreme situations, local officials should not threaten banks with loss of business, but they should give notice that accounts will be awarded to those that provide the best services at the lowest cost. This encourages banks to continually make their best efforts.

Bankers are professionals. Bankers should not be treated as political cronies, or a source for a free lunch, nor should they be treated as all-powerful masters. These types of relationships occur in many areas of the country. The symptoms of these relationships are bloated bank balances, poor service, misinformation about the availability and legality of certain bank services, and administrative chaos. The municipality should not tolerate inadequate services at unreasonable prices. Local officials should not expect banks to accept unreasonable terms, but neither should they apologize for creating an efficient cash management system. Bankers can understand that local officials wish to save money for their jurisdiction, since it is the goal of every client they serve.

How will a new cash management system affect the community's relationship with its bank? Much depends on the approach taken by municipal officials. If they deal with bankers professionally and if bankers know the town expects to pay a fair price, then most banks are delighted to help create a well-designed cash program. If banks have been making unreasonable profits from very high deposit balances, then they are likely to be disappointed, but it is difficult to argue with fair and open arrangements.

Communities also enhance their relationships with banks by developing an understanding of the banks' business. Local officials should understand how and why banks make profits, and they should understand how and when banks deal with financial difficulty. In the latter case, without sacrificing cash management performance, municipalities can find areas that enhance their own effectiveness and are profitable to the bank as well.

Professional banking relationships depend on good will. Older urban areas in particular need a steady relationship with banks. In times of credit shortages, such as the economic downturn of 1974–75, older cities relied on banks for short-term funds when banks might have otherwise chosen less risky loans. These cities compensated banks for that good will either by buying bank investments when banks needed funds or by maintaining slightly higher deposit balances when funds became available. One Eastern county helped local banks survive the tight money crunch of the early 1970s by increasing the size of its certificates of deposit with its main banks. The county maintained a competitive yield on its investments, and banks were grateful for the source of funds in a difficult financial environment. That gesture of financial good will had positive effects when the county later sought additional services.

Many states limit the placement and activity of local government deposits. Naturally, communities must conduct their activities within legal statutes, but within the law there is much room to acquire economical and efficient services. This part takes a nonlegalistic view of banking management, since it is impossible to recommend a set of practices based on the combined regulations of fifty states. However, the reader will quickly see areas limited by law as well as many new opportunities for acquiring economical service.

How to Hire Your Banker 4.2

Some localities are required by law to spread their accounts among several banks, while others are required to rotate their banks every few years so that each bank eventually has part of the business. Except when prohibited by statute, many local governments find compelling advantages to opening accounts for bid to eligible banks in the community. A competitive atmosphere encourages banks to offer services at the lowest reasonable cost and to provide quality, timely service. Competition means that communities have access to a variety of bank services, choosing those that each bank provides best.

Selecting banks through competitive bid involves a multi-stage process: specifying desired services, preparing a request for proposal, receiving and analyzing bids, and awarding a contract.

Communities must first identify and define the services they need. The chief financial officer should develop a clear design of the municipality's disbursement and collection bank network, including its central account, and then should specify each service needed, whether it be lock boxes, wire transfers, armored car services, zero-balance accounts, or regular demand-deposit accounts. (Section 4.3 describes the range of bank services.) To assess the benefits of each service and provide descriptions for bank bids, a local official should estimate the anticipated volume of each service (say 3,000 items per month for a lock box), the average amount of each item (the lock box items may average $10,000 each), the frequency of the service (lock box payments may be received on the 20th of each month), and any special circumstances. Special circumstances might include the location of the service or unusual security requirements.

When the municipality has defined the needed services, it should determine which banks are most likely to be able to provide those services. Size, reputation, service capabilities, costs, convenience, and processing efficiency would qualify banks for further attention. The most important account is the central account maintained in the *lead bank*. Officials should see that each bank competing for lead bank status is large enough to keep secure the sizable amount of funds that will pass through the account, and that each can efficiently transfer large amounts of cash. The lead bank should have adequate wire transfer facilities or the capability to generate and process depository transfer checks, and it should have an adequate deposit base and capital structure to diminish the effect of deposit fluctuations.

In this first step of the selection it is not necessary to perform a detailed analysis of a bank's qualifications. If a bank might qualify for a local account, then the community should invite it to bid for town accounts and send the bank a request for proposal (see section 4.4).

4.3 Surveying Banking Services

As a town financial officer becomes more familiar with banking services, he should ask local banks about the types and prices of their services. As with anything else, it pays to shop around. Can the bank provide any services at a lower price than the town now pays? The larger metropolitan banks generally offer more cash management services and sometimes devote an entire department to attracting local government business. Prices for banking services vary widely, so it makes sense to compare.

Exhibit 4.A lists many common banking services now available to local governments, although not all banks provide all of these services. Services in this exhibit are divided into management areas.

Depository Services

Bank depository services help towns process and protect their currency and check receipts.

Towns might use *night depository services* if they collect cash after the close of the banking day. If the town recreation center takes gate fees during the evening, the town may not want that money unsecured overnight. A city employee could drop those funds into a night depository box after the town program closes. This service is useful when funds are sufficiently large and their safety is sufficiently exposed to justify the cost of the service.

Depository Services

- Night depository services
- Special deposit messengers
- Armored car services
- Branch deposits

Custody Accounting—Safeguarding Services

- Storage of stocks and bonds
- Storage of cancelled checks
- Safe deposit boxes

Cash Mobilization Services

- Checking accounts and check processing
- Concentration accounts
- Zero-balance accounts
- Lock box systems

Cash Control Services

- Wire transfers
- Depository transfer checks
- Payable-through-drafts
- In-bank transfers
- Balance monitoring and control services
- Direct deposit systems
- Federal tax payment services
- Preauthorized payment systems
- Account reconcilement

Investment Services

- Investment advice and strategy
- Savings accounts
- Time deposits
- Investment instruments:
    - Certificates of deposit
    - Repurchase agreements
    - Other money market instruments
- Paying agent services
- Trustee services for pension and retirement plans

Credit Services

- Lines of credit
- Note purchases
- Bond underwriting

Special Services

- Food stamp transactions
- Tax and utility collections
- Account profitability analyses
- Economic seminars and advice
- Optional cash management models

EXHIBIT 4.A / Financial Services of Banks

Specialized courier service is available to move check deposits from local government collection points to the bank. Since the Comptroller of the Currency prohibits banks from sending messengers to pick up deposits (it amounts to mobile branch banking), banks will contact couriers who then serve as agents of the municipality. These messengers are usually bonded and are particularly useful for carrying small numbers of large-dollar checks that should be deposited as soon as possible to meet check collection deadlines for out-of-town checks. Bonding certificates should be reviewed periodically for dollar coverage and other details to ensure that funds transferred by courier are sufficiently insured. For coin and currency collections, armored car services offer specially equipped vehicles with armed guards for regular cash pickups.

Branch deposits are convenient for collections that are received far from the main office of the bank but close to a branch office. However, deposits should be credited to the town's account on the same day. Usually, banks stipulate a cutoff time, such as noon or later (typically 2:30 p.m.), for branch deposits to qualify for same day deposit credit. Local officials should know and meet those deadlines.

Custody Accounting—Safeguarding Services

Banks will also store valuable items for municipalities. A standard service is *storage of stocks and bonds*. With a major New York bank's "misplacement" of over $400 million of securities owned by a New York City employee pension fund, a town manager might want to inspect bank storage facilities or periodically receive confirmation of securities held. Banks are also experimenting with the storage of cancelled checks, known as *check retention*. Rather than return checks with monthly statements, banks merely return a reconciled statement with a list of checks processed. It saves the bank the effort of sorting and returning checks, reduces paper flow, and saves the municipality the trouble and cost of storage. Few cancelled checks are actually needed, so the city is not inconvenienced if it has to send to the bank for one it might need. The bank retains the checks for the time required by state law, then it supervises check destruction.

Specifically, banks believe that paid-check retention is attractive to its customers because it is convenient, safe, voluntary, and less costly. Some banks are considering offering reduced charges to customers who adopt bank check retention services.

Finally, banks offer *safe deposit boxes* for unusual storage needs, for valuable items such as insurance policies, bonds, or items of historical significance. Some communities keep cameras for making licenses or check signature plates in safe deposit boxes.

Cash Mobilization Services

Banks service a variety of bank accounts, but most are merely a variation of a *regular checking account*. Prices for account services vary widely from town to town and bank to bank; some checking accounts do not directly charge for account activity while others assess a fee for every item processed. In reality, no account is free; it is unrealistic to expect banks to work for nothing. Later, this chapter describes how town officials may assess the true cost of account services.

A bank also provides *concentration accounts,* the checking accounts in which towns pool their free cash. As with regular accounts, the town should have a clear understanding of the necessary compensating balance or per item charges that it will pay for bank account services. Because some state and local laws either restrict the gross amount that a town may deposit in any one bank or require collateral for amounts above certain levels, the town should arrange to monitor even the momentary balances in concentration accounts so that deposited amounts conform to local law. With deposit concentration accounts, depository transfer checks may be made payable to the concentration bank to move funds into the account. Transfer checks can be prepared by the concentration bank based on telephone or electronic information.

Zero-balance disbursing accounts (see section 2.6.1), sometimes called *imprest accounts,* are a mainstay of efficient cash disbursement systems since they allow towns to disburse funds at the latest reasonable moment. These accounts are indvidual disbursement accounts. When checks or drafts are presented for payment, the master account is debited for an amount equal to the total of checks presented and the zero balance account is credited to cover the disbursements. Banks are compensated by per item charges or by a level compensating balance maintained in the master account or the disbursement account (see section 4.7 on bank compensation). To maintain smooth operations, town managers should ensure at the end of every day that account balances do not fall below prescribed minimum compensating balances, and they should see that the master account has enough funds to reimburse daily cash demands from the disbursement accounts. Drawing down agreed upon minimum balances strains bank relations, yet maintaining excessive balances costs the town money.

Banks also operate *lock boxes*. The local government rents a post office box in its name and designates the bank as its agent in accessing the incoming mail. The bank deposits the funds sent to that box in the town's account, and sends deposit information to the town on the following day. Section 3.3.1 describes the uses of lock boxes.

Cash Control Services

Cash control services at banks help financial managers monitor cash balances and move funds efficiently between bank accounts.

Banks can arrange for *wire transfers* of funds between banks. A town financial officer carries out the action by calling the town's banker who initiates the transfer. Funds are moved within hours, and the banker returns written confirmation, usually within one to two days (see sections 2.5.3 and 3.2.2).

Depository transfer checks (DTCs) also move funds efficiently through the check clearance system. Because DTCs are preauthorized, they may avoid detailed check disbursement and warrant mechanisms in city government. They also offer security, since DTCs move funds only between city accounts. As section 3.5.4 describes, DTCs cost less than wire transfers, but they require more coordination if timing is crucial. Depository transfer checks usually cost, per check, the same amount as bank charges for regular checks.

As discussed in section 2.5.2, towns should carefully consider the value of *drafts* (or payable-through-drafts). They are useful for two limited types of payments: payments of insurance claims and reimbursement of expenses. Traveletter Corp. of Minneapolis, Minnesota, offers a draft package that allows employees to reimburse themselves for expenses within a certain limit while away from town. Drafts must be reviewed, then approved or rejected, by local officials prior to payment. Since banks guarantee one-day deferred availability, rejected drafts must be returned to the bank before the deadline on the day after presentment.

In-bank transfers allow regular checking account depositors to transfer funds immediately between accounts within the same bank. To move these funds, a town manager completes a transfer form and presents it to the bank, or he may simply call the bank to make the transfer.

An essential part of banks' customer service is information that keeps customers current on account balances and activity. The extent and timing of notification depends on when customers want that information.

Balance monitoring and control services inform a town treasurer of the account activity and the amount of available funds in each bank account on a daily basis. A town treasurer may learn the previous day's ledger balance, debit and credit activity, lock box and concentration service deposits, zero-balance disbursement activity, drafts presented for payment, and wire transfers. The treasurer may then transfer funds to bring account balances to targeted levels or invest funds to make use of excess balances. Banks may charge up to two dollars for each notification, and local officials may receive notification by either telephone, Telex, TWX, or data transmission via facsimile, magnetic tape, or time-sharing terminals.

With a *direct-deposit system* a town may deposit employee paychecks directly into the employees' bank accounts. It is an efficient and cost effective way of processing what often constitutes the bulk of regular municipal payments, and employees appreciate the convenience of having funds available in their account on payday. Other bank payroll services will perform a payroll calculation and maintain an employee data base, then disburse paychecks by check or direct deposit.

In addition to payroll disbursements, banks offer *Federal tax payment services* which efficiently process, disburse, and account for tax payments. Banks perform this service simultaneously with other tasks, then send customers proof of payment and a recordkeeping system to supplement municipal records.

Towns may arrange for *preauthorized payment systems* for regular payments such as utility bills. With these agreements, the bank transfers prearranged amounts each month from taxpayer accounts for tax payments to the municipal account. This saves taxpayers the headache of paying monthly bills, and it assures the town of regular payments of its accounts receivable. Preauthorized credit arrangements with banks and customers, however, require an initial planning phase and a minimum level of technical processing capability at the bank and in the town. The timely collection of preauthorized amounts must earn enough investment income to compensate for the costs of the system.

If a town sends its bank a list of checks on magnetic tape written during the month, the bank can perform an *account reconcilement,* by computer, that confirms a ledger balance at the bank and includes a list of outstanding checks. In a simple case, the bank ledger balance less the total of outstanding checks should equal the *book balance* in the treasury at the end of the reporting period. On the town's statement, the bank also lists account activity for that month.

Banks offer three types of account reconcilement plans. The first, a sort-and-list plan, sorts cancelled checks by serial check number and lists those checks on the bank statement. Second, a paid-check plan performs the sort-and-list function and produces a list of serial numbers of outstanding checks. Third, a complete plan offers the services of the second plan and in addition reconciles the bank statement balance to the community's checkbook or ledger balance. The first two plans are offered by most banks; the third is not. However, the third service may be offered by any bank that has a correspondent relationship with a bank with complete reconcilement capability.

Investment Services

Banks are usually excellent sources for *short-term investment advice,* since bank money desks buy and sell short-term instruments on a daily basis. They invest funds that exceed reserve requirements or borrow funds, through repurchase agreements, to meet reserve requirements. For long-term investments, such as pension fund and retirement plan investments, the trust departments of banks offer advisory services.

In addition, banks offer a variety of *investment instruments*. Better-known options, such as savings accounts, allow for investment of small amounts of funds for short periods of time. Rates are kept artificially low by law, however, and savings accounts at thrift institutions offer ½% to ¼% higher interest rates. Time deposits pay slightly higher rates than savings accounts in return for a longer commitment of funds. Some time deposits require 30 to 90 days' notice to withdraw funds without penalty. Usually, certificates of deposit (CDs) offer highest yields. For amounts larger than $100,000 customers may negotiate the interest rate with the bank, so CDs offer competitive rates. CD maturities begin at 30 days. For investments of very short duration, as short as overnight, banks will sell repurchase agreements (*repos;* see section 6.1). Repos are short-term loans that towns make to banks in return for competitive interest rates. Repos are collateralized with high-quality securities.

At the request of the towns, some banks will arrange to have idle balances invested overnight, usually by buying repos for the town's account. This can be done automatically by the bank or simply on the basis of a telephone call from the town treasurer. However, this investment service should compare favorably with the return from other investments. Do bank investments or pooled money funds offer a higher yield? Which charges the least for comparable services? Which is most convenient and tailored to the frequency and size of the town's investments?

Paying agent services are used by most municipalities to process principal and interest payments on local debt. Banks receive and process maturing bonds and coupons from municipal offerings, thus saving communities the job of processing large numbers of coupons. Communities in turn pay banks the gross amount of debt due, plus a fee for service, on the due date of the bonds or coupons. These fees may be set when the bond is issued. It pays to shop before buying this service, because paying agent charges for processing bonds ranges from $0.50 to $10.00.

Credit Services

Although the borrowing side of financial management is not explored in this chapter, it is nonetheless an essential aspect of banking relations.

Banks offer businesses lines of credit which allow the customer to make and repay periodic short-term loans as the customer needs funds. Banks usually lend short-term funds to municipalities by buying town or city notes. Notes have a maturity of less than one year, and their repayment is pledged against the receipt of some type of city revenue, taxes, or the proceeds of bond sales. Lines of credit have also been arranged on certain municipal accounts, and if these are convenient and within local law, they are worth exploring.

Special Services

The kind and range of special services vary from bank to bank. Some banks, for instance, distribute food stamps while others collect tax or utility payments. Banks are convenient locations for citizens to pay tax or utility bills, and having a bank collect these payments saves the town the cost of processing collections and ensures that funds are deposited immediately in the town's account.

Municipalities can request banks to provide an *account profitability analysis* for each local account; banks provide this analysis to their business customers. It shows whether deposit balances overcompensate, undercompensate, or properly reimburse the bank for its services. It is an important tool that local officials use to keep noninvested cash to a minimum. (See section 4.7 for a detailed discussion of an account analysis.)

Some banks also help local officials keep abreast of financial and economic developments by holding local seminars or subscribing to financial newsletters published by larger banks or other sources. Financial newsletters are good, relatively short summaries of the latest financial events, and town officials need merely skim these periodically.

Larger banks offer large clients, such as major cities, *optimal cash management models,* which are computer models that recommend the types and location of city collection and disbursement accounts that maximize cash flow and minimize cost. Since these models are costly, they are useful only when the best structure of a cash management system is not obvious.

4.4 RFPs: Bidding for Services

Requests for proposal (RFPs) are the detailed descriptions that communities send to banks asking them to bid for local accounts. An RFP lists and describes desired banking services, describes the format banks should use to submit bids, and notifies

Proposal submitted by:
Bank:
Address:
Bank office to be contacted:

Telephone number:
Signature:
Title:
Date:

I. General Provisions

A. Bids must be presented in duplicate to the following address at the stated bid closing time.
Time: 2 p.m.
Date: Friday, November 16, 1980
Address: Director of Finance, City Hall, One City Hall Plaza, Cityville, Kansas

B. Bids should be signed and sealed in an envelope marked, "Bid—Not to be Opened Until 2 p.m., November 16, 1980."

C. Each bidder should also submit its most recent audited financial statements and annual report. This information should reach the Director of Finance no later than November 16, 1980.

D. Bids will be opened and read at the above time and date. Interested parties are welcome to attend the bid reading.

E. Bank selection should be announced by November 30, 1980. The city reserves the right to reject any and all bids.

F. The bid price for services may be in the form of a fixed minimum daily balance and/or a fixed fee. The bidder may also submit a formula used to set these balances or fees based upon the changes in volume, earnings credits, float, or any other factors banks normally use in pricing services. Bidders are encouraged to price each service separately, as well as collectively, where feasible.

G. The successful bidder(s) shall act as the depository of city funds beginning January 2, 1981, and must agree to a three-year contract incorporating the provisions of this proposal.

H. For further information contact Alfred Inglethorpe, Assistant to the Director of Finance, City Hall, (403) JU5-1140.

II. Required Banking Services

A. Depository for Funds

1. Checking accounts.
   a. Central operating account. Per month deposits average $10,000,000 in aggregate with 45 deposits, 1,000 checks, and 22 wire transfers.
   b. Payroll account. Per month, deposits average $6,000,000 in aggregate with 20 deposits and 7,000 checks. It is expected that no balances be maintained in this account for transaction purposes.
2. Checking account services.
   a. Bank statement. Service will include the provision of a bank statement within five (5) working days of the closing date of the statement. Statements are to begin with the first day of the month and end with the last day of the month.
   b. Cancelled checks. Checks should be returned with the bank statement in numerical order.
   c. Account reconcilement. On the first day of each month the city shall deliver to the bank a computer tape (technical description of the tape) containing a description of each check generated in the prior month. The description shall include the check number, the amount of the check, the date the check was generated (and presumably mailed), and the payee. The bank should then produce a report that includes an account reconcilement, a list of outstanding checks and deposits-in-transit, a list of missing check numbers, and a float analysis by payment type (central operating and payroll accounts).
   d. *Stop payment orders. There shall be no service charge for stop payment checks.*

(continued on next page)

EXHIBIT 4.B / A Request for Proposal (RFP) for Banking Services

e. Account information. There shall be same day notice of all available balances through telephone communication with the Office of the Director of Finance.

B. Property Tax Payments Processing

1. Mail payments. The city will provide a post office box and the bank will be provided with access to the box. Processing consists of the bank picking up mail at the post office daily, matching of checks with the property tax forms, forwarding the checks and forms of any discrepancies immediately to city hall, running tape totals, depositing checks on a same day basis, and returning all paperwork to city hall on the next working day. Approximately 10,000 property tax bills of amounts over $1,000 are mailed semi-annually, on the first of November and the first of May, and are due on the last day of those months. Each semi-annual mailing of bills greater than $1,000 totals approximately $25,000,000.

2. Over-the-counter payments. All city property tax payments may be accepted at the bank's main office and all of its branches. This should account for approximately 600 payments.

C. Depository Services

1. Provide for daily armored car pickup of deposits from city hall.

2. Provide for weekly armored car pickup of parking meter receipts from Police Headquarters.

3. Provide night depository services for the city recreation program. Approximately 80% of the volume will occur during the summer months. The bank will provide 20 night depository bags free of charge.

D. Other Services

1. Continuous-form accounts payable checks, payroll checks, and deposit forms to city specifications. Approxmately 9,000 checks and 300 deposit forms are used monthly.

2. Local messenger service to City Hall for pickup of special deposits, tax payment discrepancies, and returned checks.

III. Compensation for Providing Required Bank Services

$ ______________________________

Bid may be stated as either an average daily compensating balance or as a direct charge. Average daily balances should be computed from the monthly bank statements based on a full-year average.

Comments:

Alternative method of compensation proposed:

IV. Compensation for Alternative Services

List any other bank services that the city should consider and include the charge for each service.

the banks of bid requirements and deadlines. RFPs should be sent to any bank that can meet performance and price expectations. If possible, RFPs should be sent to at least three banks to ensure adequate competition.

Exhibit 4.B is a sample of an RFP. The preparers of the RFP define each requested service. The types of accounts, the volume, dollar average, frequency of service, and special conditions are carefully described.

The RFP also includes a form for the bidder to complete with the price of his services, including the per item cost and the total cost based on volume. The form may also leave room for the bank's composite bid for providing all the required services, which may be stated as a direct fee or an average daily compensating balance (see section 4.7 on bank compensation). Such a package deal might offer a reduced price in exchange for winning all services. In either case, it is important that the form supply the municipality with adequate information to evaluate the price of each service that the bank offers: the community wants to evaluate each service separately, or *unbundled,* as well as collectively (see section 4.8 on unbundling bank services). Unbundling encourages banks to charge only for services that the community will use, and it offers the community the option of awarding an account to the bank that charges the lowest price for that service.

RFPs usually leave room for the bidder to list the nature and price of any additional or alternative services that the bank thinks the community may need or wish to substitute for requested services. In this section the bank might call to the attention of local officials a service that had not been previously considered.

The RFP also describes the terms under which bids are submitted. It should say when the bid is due (the time as well as the date), where it is due, and when the bid will be awarded. It should mention that only bids in the required bid format will be accepted and that the municipality has the option of rejecting any and all bids for whatever reasons it deems necessary. It should also note the length of service covered by the bid (one, two, or three years, etc.), extenuating circumstances that might cause the cancellation of the contract, and any other general provisions relating to the length and service of the agreement.

An RFP is only a circular that invites banks to bid for accounts. It does not bind the community to contract for listed services or to the volume estimates for each item, although local officials should provide their best estimates. Nor does it require that the community award all services to one bank.

Interview and Analysis of Banks 4.5

After bids have been received, the community should analyze the bids with respect to (1) the quality and price of services to be offered, (2) the managerial resources of the bidding banks, and (3) the financial condition of the bidding banks. Exhibit 4.C lists several key questions to ask a bidding bank.

All else being equal, the community should choose the bank that offers the *lowest composite price* for services to be provided. (Sections 4.6, 4.7, and 4.8 explain

1. **Are the bank's prices reasonable?**
   Generally, communities choose banks that meet service requirements and offer the lowest prices. When a bank's bid is substantially lower than those of other banks, local officials should find out why. A bank that lowers prices below its costs may be in financial difficulty. A town should be confident that its bank can provide services at bid prices for the length of the agreement.

2. **What is the financial size and stability of the bank?**
   If a community inadvertently places funds in a bank in poor financial condition, it runs the risk of accounting confusion, immobilization of deposits, loss of funds, and damage to the community's reputation. Local governments should not overextend any bank with large deposits (Exhibits 4.D and 4.E show how to assess a bank's financial condition). One eastern state found that it could not withdraw large amounts of funds from several depositories during the banking squeeze of 1974 and 1975 for fear of causing those institutions serious harm.

3. **Are bank officers available for consultation and discussion?**
   Choose a bank that has a reputation for consistent, courteous customer contact. The bid process should include an interview with the account officer who the bank will assign to the community's account. When difficult situations arise, local officials want to contact a bank officer who is prompt and effective.

4. **Is the bank capable of providing modern services and developing new techniques to meet the emerging needs of the community?**
   As a cash management system develops, communities should ensure that its lead bank can meet new technical and operating requirements.

5. **Is the bank known for its municipal expertise? What other government entities does it serve?**
   Ask the bank for the names of other local governments that use the bank's services. Did the bank serve the local governments well? These clients provide candid and valuable information not found in financial statements or service descriptions. Does the bank respond well to emergencies? Does it provide information correctly and promptly? Does it offer professional service?

6. **What are the bank's facilities for moving funds efficiently?**
   A lead bank should have facilities for wire transfers, such as a membership with the Bank Wire System, as well as clearinghouse affiliations that move and collect funds quickly.

7. **Is the location of the bank convenient?**
   When a bank is used for disbursement accounts, such as payroll accounts, it should be accessible for employees to cash checks. If the bank is used as a depository for currency collections, then it should have an office near the collection source.

8. **Can the bank satisfy the community's credit requirements now and in the future? What is the bank's maximum lending capacity?**
   At some time, the community may need to borrow funds by selling notes or bonds. A major, mutually-agreeable bank-government relationship fosters understanding, which in turn makes it easier for local governments to borrow money. In choosing a lead bank, local officials should see that the bank can meet the community's borrowing requirements for as long as the next two to three years.

9. **What are the bank's current affiliations?**
   Is the bank a member of a holding company? If so, local officials should evaluate that relationship. For example, a strong bank with a financially insecure holding company weakens the bank. Is the bank a Federal Reserve member or a state chartered bank? Does the bank have Federal Deposit Insurance or other state deposit coverage? If the bank is a member of the American Bankers Association or the Independent Bankers Association, contact those national offices for references.

EXHIBIT 4.C / Questions to Ask Prospective Banks

pricing.) Contracts for very simple banking services may be awarded purely on the basis of price. But there are other important considerations. These must be addressed if the community is going out to bid for the first time, if the services asked for are complex, or if the total package of services requires substantial banking resources and expertise.

The *quality of the services* offered may vary between bidding banks. Make sure to distinguish differences that are inconsequential to the performance of the community's cash management system from differences that materially influence mobilization of funds and overall control. Bid analysts may find it difficult to compare competing systems, for example, an "apple" check reconcilement system with an "orange" reconcilement system. Moreover, a bidding bank may propose an attractive service feature that will not be available until sometime in the future.

To compare the quality of services offered, local officials should make the maximum use of site visits to bank offices and, more important, phone or on-site interviews with some of the banks' customers. Systematic interviewing and inspections will clarify the practical implications of alternative service features.

The *managerial resources* of the bidding banks should also be considered, particularly if the package of services desired is complex and modifications to the package are expected in the future. Local officials should interview the executive to be assigned to the community's account. They should also examine the qualifications of the account executive's backup.

Large-sized banks often appear to have a strong managerial advantage over small banks. Large-sized banks often manage all data processing in-house. They may have entire departments devoted exclusively to cash management, government services, lock boxes, and other operations. On the other hand, small banks can afford to give a community's account more top-level, day-to-day supervision and may be more attentive and flexible than large banks because the account is more important to them.

If there is some question that a bank may not be large enough to offer adequate security deposits, officials can perform an *analysis of the financial condition* of bidding banks by completing the form in Exhibit 4.D. Even with a bank in good financial condition, it is unwise to allow the average demand deposit level to exceed 5% of the total demand deposits of the bank, since both the community and the bank become too dependent on each other's financial performance.

The treasurer of Grand Rapids, Michigan, Earl R. Hoenes, has developed several systems for evaluating the financial condition of banks. He was first introduced to the need for financial condition analysis in 1969 when Ann Arbor, where he was employed at the time, placed $2 million in a bank that failed shortly thereafter. (The city eventually recovered all its money.)

Upon his appointment as treasurer of Grand Rapids, Mr. Hoenes began to ask banks doing business with the city to submit financial reports that banks prepare for various federal agencies. In 1978 Sheshunoff & Co., an Austin, Texas, publisher, began providing Grand Rapids with computer analyses of twelve key financial ratios listed in Exhibit 4.E. Grand Rapids excludes from consideration any bank that does not meet or exceed the minimum standard for most of these ratios.

Name of bank	Approximate min. or max.	Bank A	%	Bank B	%	Bank C	%
Assets			%		%		%
1. Cash and due from banks							
2. U.S. Treasury securities							
3. Obligations of other U.S. govt. agencies							
4. Obligations of states & political subdivisions							
5. Total cash & govts.							
6. Other bonds & securities							
7. Net loans & discounts							
8. Fed. funds sold & repos. purchased							
9. Total current assets							
10. Real estate							
11. Other assets							
12. Total assets			100		100		100
Liabilities & Equity Capital							
13. Total deposits							
14. Fed. funds purchased & repos. sold							
15. Bills payable							
16. Other liabilities							
17. Total liabilities							
18. Capital -- common stock							
19. Capital -- preferred stock							
20. Surplus							
21. Undivided profits							
22. Reserve for contingencies & other cap. reserves							
23. Total equity capital							
24. Total liabilities & equity capital			100		100		100
Financial ratios*	**Approximate min. or max.**	**Points**	**%**	**Points**	**%**	**Points**	**%**
(1) Liquidity: #5/#12	15% min.						
(2) Liquidity: (#2 + #3)/(#4 + #8)	45% min.						
(3) Loans: Net charge-offs**/#7	75% max.						
(4) Capital: #23/#12	7% min.						
(5) Capital: #23/#13	5% min.						
(6) Capital: #23/#7	10% min.						
(7) Other: Income before security trans./#12	.5% min.						
(8) Other ratios*:							

* See Exhibit 4.E for description of ratios and point system (if used)

** Supplied by bank

EXHIBIT 4.D / Analysis of Bank Statement of Condition

The city of Grand Rapids, Michigan, requires that banks and savings and loan associations doing business with the city meet or exceed specific standards of financial condition. These standards are balance sheet ratios. Ten ratios are applied to bidding bank balance sheets and an overall "point" profile is derived to quantify the financial condition of each bank. To hold city demand accounts, a bank must achieve 165 "points" by reporting ratios equal to or better than the ratios listed below. It may underperform in some ratios only if it exceeds the standards set for other ratios. A slightly lower point total is permitted for banks that only sell certificates of deposit to the city.

Ratio #1 through #7 and #10 measure financial condition; the remaining ratios encourage favorable bank practices. Ratios #8 and #9 encourage banks to conduct business with the public sector. And, a local bank is awarded bonus points for more conventional 1–4 family unit residential mortgages (ratio #11).

	Standard percentage by asset size of bank (in millions)					
Ratio	**$25-39**	**$40-99**	**$100-299**	**$300-899**	**$900-5 b.**	**over 5 b.**
1.	10%	10%	10%	10%	10%	10%
2.	50%	45%	45%	35%	50%	40%
3.	31%	26%	26%	31%	41%	41%
4.	6%	6%	6%	6%	6%	4%
5.	7%	7%	7%	7%	7%	5%
6.	12%	12%	10%	10%	10%	8%
7.	10%	11%	9%	9%	9%	7%
8.	15%	15%	15%	15%	15%	15%
9.	35%	40%	40%	30%	40%	40%
10.	0.5%	0.5%	0.5%	0.5%	0.5%	0.3%
11.	20%	16%	20%	12%	10%	5%

Definitions of Ratios

1. Cash and securities maturing in one year as a percentage of total assets
2. Total Treasury securities and U.S. Government agencies as a percentage of total securities
3. Net charge-offs as a percentage of average loans. Note: this is the only criterion where a lower percentage earns more points
4. Total capital as a percentage of total assets
5. Capital as a percentage of total deposits
6. Capital as a percentage of net loans
7. Capital as a percentage of risk assets
8. Public time deposits as a percentage of total time deposits
9. Total municipal securities as a percentage of total securities
10. Return on average assets
11. Conventional mortagages for 1-4 family residential units as a percentage of total loans

EXHIBIT 4.E / Evaluating the Financial Condition of Banks

Economic and Social Factors in Bank Selection

Many local officials understandably wish to select banks that are favorably disposed to their community, *all other factors being equal*. They single out the banks that provide a large share of local mortgages, student loans and commercial loans, and those that regularly offer to buy the community's debt issues (short-term notes in particular). Some officials grant bonus points to bidding banks on the basis of their geographical proximity and economic and social performance. And many officials have tradtionally awarded bank business on a sole source basis as an explicit reward for community services rendered.

Using economic and social factors in bank selection is legitimate managerial policy, but the limitations of this policy should be kept clearly in mind. First, it is difficult if not impossible to identify and measure the value of services rendered by a particular bank that would not be provided by another bank in the absence of competition. The community should reward *exceptional* service, not normal service that other banks would gladly provide. Second, the data collection and analysis required to compare economic and social performance can be burdensome.

Third, the costs to the community in the form of foregone investment income can be substantial though not apparent to the untrained observer. Assume, for example, that a community awards banking services (at a competitive rate) to a prime purchaser of short-term notes and, to reward the bank's steadfast support, agrees to place the proceeds in a demand deposit at the bank, working the balance down over the lifetime of the loan. The net effect of this policy is to approximately double the costs of borrowing, as the foregone investment income would about equal the interest cost of the note.

Chapter 8 addresses the concept of social investing in detail.

4.6 Selection, Pricing, and Formal Agreement of Banking Services

Written bids detailing the offered price of each service, interviews, references, and bank analyses provide local officials with the necessary information to choose the bank or banks best suited to meet community cash management needs. If a financial condition test is made, only the banks that pass are candidates for final selection.

The following weighting scheme rates different qualities of bids for a typical package of cash management banking activities in a medium-sized local government.

Price of services	50%
Quality of services	25%
Managerial resources	25%

If the package of services is complex and subject to future modification, more weight can be given to service quality and managerial resources. If the package is simple and the services are easy to perform and involve little managerial supervision, price deserves great weight.

This is an example of a contractual agreement for banking services. An actual agreement between a local government and its bank would reflect their particular circumstances.

Parties: Centerville City ("the City)
City Hall
Centerville, Kansas

Cityville Bank ("the Bank")
Centerville, Kansas

Agreements:

A Bank proposal to provide certain banking services, as revised by the Director of Finance and approved by the City Council on May 1, 1980, is made part of this agreement (Attachment A).

1. **Term.** The agreement will become effective July 1, 1980, and will terminate June 30, 1983.

2. **Depository for Funds.** The Bank shall act as the demand depository for the City as follows:

   A. Central Operating Account. The Bank shall accept deposits and process withdrawals on the account.

   The Bank shall also accept, and receipt for, at each of its offices, over-the-counter property tax bill payments. Forthwith upon receipt by it, the Bank shall endorse and photograph all checks received, prepare appropriate deposit slips, and deposit the funds received to the central operating account of the City. On the next working day following the deposit, the Bank shall deliver to the City written confirmation of the deposit and the appropriate portion of the property tax bill.

   B. Direct Deposit Payroll Account. The Bank shall honor authorized transfers of funds to the account. On Thursday of each week, the City shall furnish the Bank with the details of the weekly payroll disbursements by means of magnetic tape. The tape shall include the name of each payee, the payee's bank, the payee's bank account number, and the gross amount of the payment less payroll deductions. On Friday, the Bank shall credit payee accounts and charge the City payroll account, then deliver the tape to the Automated Clearinghouse for credit to payee accounts in other local banks. No balance shall be maintained in the payroll account for transaction purposes. At the end of each working day, the Bank shall transfer from the central operating account to the payroll account funds sufficient to cover the daily drawdown in the payroll account.

   C. Lockbox Service. The Bank shall accept, and receipt for, property tax bill payments payable to the City per the attached *Agreement for Lockbox Services* (see Exhibit 3.C in the text).

3. **Demand Deposit Account Services.** For the demand deposit accounts listed in Section 1, the Bank shall perform the following functions.

   A. Checks and Supplies. The Bank shall furnish to the City, preprinted to City specifications, all continuous-form accounts payable checks, deposit slips, and other instruments pertaining to transactions for the accounts.

   B. Bank Statement. For each account, the Bank will provide a bank statement within five (5) working days of the closing date of the statement. Statements are to begin with the first day of the month and end with the last day of the month.

   C. Cancelled Checks. Checks shall be returned with the bank statement in numerical order.

   D. Account Reconcilement. For the central operating account only, the City shall deliver to the Bank a magnetic tape (include technical description of tape) on the first day of each month. The description shall include the check number, the amount of the check, the date the check was generated, and the payee. The Bank shall then produce a report that includes an account reconcilement, a list of outstanding checks and deposits-in-transit, a list of missing check numbers, and a float analysis.

(continued on next page)

EXHIBIT 4.F / Sample Agreement for Banking Services

E. Account Information. The Bank shall provide the same day notice of available balances in all accounts through telephone communications with the Office of the Director of Finance.

4. **Night Depository.** The Bank shall supply the City with such night depository bags, keys, and services as may be required by the City from time to time.

5. **Armored Car Service.** The Bank shall supply armored car service as may be required by the City from time to time, including, but not limited to, the following:

   A. City Hall. Pick up daily check, coin, and other deposits from City Hall. Delivery to City Hall each morning all night depository bags deposited the previous night and day.

   B. Police Headquarters. Pick up weekly coin deposits from police headquarters.

6. **Compensation.** The City shall compensate the Bank for services provided by maintaining a minimum balance in the central operating account. The Bank shall compute the compensating balance by projecting the total of monthly service charges to a minimum collected balance that, at the earnings rate, compensates the Bank for all charges. The Bank shall adjust the compensating balance to include balances that the Bank is required by the Federal Reserve System to keep in reserve. The earnings rate shall be a three-month moving average of the 91-day Treasury bill rate, and the Bank shall charge the City for services at the rate specified in the bid proposal as amended. The Bank shall provide the City with an account analysis, within ten (10) working days of the closing date of the analysis. Account analyses are to begin with the first day of the month and end with the last day of the month.

Approval of Form: **Signatures:**

	Centerville City
By ______________________	By ______________________
Mr.	Mr.
City Counsel	Director of Finance
	Cityville Bank & Trust Co.
	By ______________________
	Mr.
	Senior Vice President
	By ______________________
	Mr.
	Vice President & Manager

Upon award of the community's accounts, local officials should prepare a formal, written banking agreement that will be signed by both parties. There are several advantages to a formal banking arrangement. First, it strengthens the professional image of the municipality's money management operations since it openly defines the requirements for its cash system and negates any suspicions of improper dealing. For the same reason, it also provides excellent public disclosure. All banking information is clearly spelled out, and the prices for services are attached to each service. With competitive bids and other award information, the choice of the winning banks is justifiable to all outside parties. Formal agreements also improve performance evaluation. A clear description of the nature and price of banking services serves as a standard for bank performance. If banking costs rise, or if service falters, this written document allows local officials to determine the variance from the standard and assess the responsibility for the change.

A written agreement (an example is shown in Exhibit 4.F) should include a citation the parties involved (the municipality and the bank), a copy of the accepted bid, and the approval, if needed, of any legislative body or municipal officials. The agreement then spells out the specifics of the arrangement, including the length of the contract and the terms of each service. The agreement should briefly outline the procedures for performing each service and account and the responsibilities of each party. The awarded price should be either included in the description of the service or account or attached in the accepted bid; it should be stated as either a direct fee or a compensating balance.

Collateralization (Pledging) Requirements

Almost all states authorize or require that public deposits in banks be collateralized by federal, state, or municipal securities. A 1976 survey of pledging practices (performed by the Advisory Commission on Intergovernmental Relations) found that pledged assets were 116% of public deposits in commercial banks. In Minnesota, Missouri, and Pennsylvania, pledged assets exceeded 200% of public deposits.

It is not clear whether collateral programs are beneficial to state and local governments. The original rationale for collateral—security in the event of bank failure—has become increasingly irrelevant. Collateral requirements were first introduced in the 19th and early 20th centuries, when bank failures occurred with relative frequency and federal deposit insurance was not available. Today, bank failures are rare. The Federal Deposit Insurance Corporation, created in 1933, insures depositors up to $100,000, effectively providing complete coverage for all but the very large public depositors.

Collateral programs today serve a purpose other than providing security. They are believed to increase the demand for municipal securities by banks, who use these securities as collateral. This increase in demand is believed to reduce the interest rates on municipal debt. The ACIR found that net interest costs of municipal debt are somewhat less in states with high pledge requirements than in states with low pledge requirements. On the other hand, collateral requirements may also result in higher bank service charges and in the lessening of competition for public deposits. If all factors are accounted for, the net financial impact of collateral programs on public agencies may be nil.

4.7 How to Determine Bank Compensation (Account Analysis)

A bank account analysis is a standard format for comparing the price of services among competing banks. Indirectly, the analysis encourages banks to charge the community only for the services used, since the form separates the price of each item processed.

Once bank accounts are awarded, an account analysis also shows whether a community maintains sufficient balances to compensate the bank for its efforts. To determine what a community now pays for bank services and what the compensation should be, local officials can perform a regular cost analysis for all bank accounts.

Banks usually supply the following account analysis to their commercial customers. The bank's computer generates the monthly analysis, which is sent to the customer in addition to a bank statement. The procedure for producing an account analysis is explained here in detail so that local managers will understand what the analysis means and which areas of the analysis are open to different construction or negotiation with the bank. If a bank does not supply account analyses, local officials, with information from the municipality's bank statment and a few reasonable assumptions, may perform the analysis themselves.

Bank Compensation

Governments compensate banks for services in one of two ways. Either they pay a unit price for each item, such as 10 cents for every check paid, or they leave idle funds in their account that the bank uses for its own investment.

The first method, known as a *fee basis,* is a simpler, more direct method of pricing and paying for services. By accepting bids for each type of service, a municipality can easily determine, based on expected volume, which accounts will cost the least. For example, Exhibit 4.G shows that Bank B offers the least costly services. However, with a fee basis, the local government may have to appropriate funds for banking expenses. Not only does this require legislative review, but the less informed

Banking Service	Volume per Month	Bank A Unit Price	Bank A Total	Bank B Unit Price	Bank B Total
Deposits	1,200	25 cents	$300	25 cents	$300
Checks Paid	500	10 cents	50	15 cents	75
Lock Boxes	1,500	40 cents	600	35 cents	525
Total Monthly Cost			$950		$900

EXHIBIT 4.G / Banking Services Charged on a Fee Basis

members of the community are likely to ask, "We never paid for banking services before. Why should we pay for them now?" Of course, the community paid for its banking services by maintaining checking account balances that were at the bank's disposal; the costs were hidden. With account analysis, communities may discover the true cost of their banking agreements.

The second method, *compensating balances,* is an indirect method of paying for bank services. Essentially, the community pays the bank by leaving in its checking account a minimum balance which the bank is free to use as it wants.

Compensating balances have advantages over fees as a method of bank compensation. First, banks prefer compensating balances because the bank then shows larger deposits on its financial statements, and deposits are one important factor used by analysts to measure bank growth. Many governments also prefer compensating balances, since these indirect charges might not be a budgetary expense, as fees are, and therefore are less subject to inquiry and review.

The disadvantage to compensating balances is that they are more complicated to calculate and thus open to some disagreement between the bank and its customer. For example, necessary compensating balances change with the rise or fall of interest rates and the volume of items processed. Suppose that a bank should be compensated for $10,000 worth of services for the year. If the net earnings rate for the bank is 10%, then a compensating balance of $100,000 pays for the $10,00 worth of services. However, if interest rates fall to 5%, then $200,000 is necessary to meet a $10,000 service cost. Also, any earnings on account balances that exceed the bank service charges are absorbed by the bank and are in effect "excess profits."

The choice of the method of bank compensation depends on the community and its bank. Traditionally, banks have used idle balances to charge for financial services such as the depositing or cashing of checks and other account services. On the other hand, banks charged for data processing, investment, and trust services on a fee basis. The current trend is toward a greater use of fees, largely because corporate customers want to pay only for the services they use. Companies also prefer fees because they are dax deductible, and banks are prohibited by the Federal Reserve from investing a certain portion of customer deposits. As a result, a corporation must leave more money in its account to earn the required service cost than it could if it invested the money itself and paid the bank directly for the services. In spite of this corporate trend, local governments often pay banks with compensating balances.

Account Analysis

Exhibit 4.H illustrates a monthly account analysis. The upper portion of the form calculates the average investable balance, the true deposit balance available for bank investment (only the net amount may produce bank income). The middle section calculates the total service charges incurred by the municipality, then projects that amount into average annual balances necessary to return one month's income to cover those charges. The balance required to cover service charges is subtracted from the available balances to the bank, and the difference, the amount below the bottom line,

MASSACHUSETTS COMMERCIAL BANK
200 FEDERAL STREET
BOSTON, MASSACHUSETTS 02222

CITYVILLE, MASSACHUSETTS
TREASURER

STATEMENT OF ACCOUNT ANALYSIS
FOR THE MONTH
OCTOBER, 1980

BANK OFFICER:

ACCOUNTS INCLUDED IN THIS ANALYSIS ARE: 123-456-7

AVERAGE LEDGER BALANCE	81,909	
LESS: AVERAGE UNAVAILABLE BALANCE	4,559	
AVERAGE AVAILABLE BALANCE		77,350
LESS: LINE COMPENSATING BALANCE REQUIREMENT		10,000
OTHER COMPENSATING BALANCES		
NET AVERAGE AVAILABLE BALANCE		67,350
LESS: RESERVE REQUIREMENT AT 15.00%	10,102	
AVERAGE INVESTABLE BALANCE AVAILABLE FOR ACCOUNT SERVICES		57,248

BALANCES REQUIRED FOR SERVICE CHARGES BASED ON AN EARNINGS ALLOWANCE OF 6.%

ACCOUNT ACTIVITY	ACTIVITY	UNIT PRICE	TOTAL	BALANCE REQUIREMENT
MONTHLY ACCOUNT MAINTENANCE	1	3.00	3.00	600
DEPOSITS MADE	17	.35	5.95	1,190
CHECKS DEPOSITED	111	.04	4.44	888
TOTAL BALANCE REQUIRED FOR ACCOUNT ACTIVITY			13.39	2,678
OTHER SERVICES				
ZERO BALANCE ACCOUNTING	10	5.00	50.00	10,000
LOCKBOX SERVICE	600	.25	150.00	30,000
WIRE TRANSFER	10	2.50	25.00	5,000
TOTAL BALANCE REQUIRED FOR OTHER SERVICES			225.00	45,000
TOTAL BALANCE REQUIRED TO COVER SERVICE CHARGES				47,678
BALANCE AVAILABLE FOR OTHER SERVICES THIS MONTH				9,570

EXHIBIT 4.H / Account Analysis

is an excess (or deficient) compensating balance. In this case, a balance of $9,570 may be withdrawn for investment.

The average investable balance is the amount that the bank has on hand for investment. This amount is less than the average ledger balance (or the checkbook balance) for several reasons. First, the bank may not invest funds not yet available (or *floating*). The ledger balance reflects, among other items, checks recently deposited. Since it may take several days for the bank to collect the funds from those checks, those funds (the float) are not available for investment. The ledger balance less the float is the available balance, or the amount of funds that are actually on hand in the account. An illustration shows how the amount is calculated. If $100 is in the account and the municipality deposits a check for $50, the ledger shows a balance of $150. However, the bank cannot invest any of that $50 until the funds are available. Assuming that it takes two days for the bank to collect those funds, then for three days the ledger shows an average balance of $150 [(150 + 150 + 150) / 3], but the average available balance at the bank is $117 [(100 + 100 + 150) / 3]. Banks include the average available balance for the month on the account analysis. Without the analysis, the community will have to approximate that calculation by projecting an average float for those checks deposited and disbursed at the end of the month.

In practice, it is too cumbersome for banks to trace the exact float on each deposit or disbursement. Instead, they apply a formula based on the average destination and the average dollar value of those checks. To be sure that the formula is close to the community's deposit pattern, local officials should know on what banks the largest dollar volume of checks is drawn. If tax payments are drawn on local banks, then there should be no- or at most one-day collection float. If the bank is applying a two-day float, then that is a point for discussion. The delay should never exceed two days since the Federal Reserve guarantees collection within that time.

Similarly, the bank may not invest the portion of funds set aside to meet the Federal Reserve System's *reserve requirement*. The reserve requirement is the amount of funds that the bank must set aside for every deposit dollar received. The requirement changes, ranging between 15% and 17%. To illustrate the effect of the reserve requirement, assume that a bank receives a $100 checking account and that the Fed has imposed a 17% reserve requirement. The bank can not lend out that $100; it must reserve $17 and can lend $83 if it wishes. Because of the reserve requirement, which is designed to ensure stability in the banking markets, account analyses deduct the reserve requirement from the available balance. The bank cannot invest reserved funds, in the exhibit calculated at $10,102.

A few corporations do not deduct the reserve requirement from their average daily available balances because the corporation would otherwise be able to invest all of the $100. The reserve requirement, they argue, is an expense indigenous to the bank, and the corporation should not be charged for it. This is especially so because banks receive financial and operational services from the Fed in return for their reserve balances. The position that any community takes depends on its perspective. From the local government's point of view, that $100 could be fully invested if the funds were not on deposit with its bank. From the bank's point of view, it is prohibited by law from investing the reserve requirement, so it is providing services for which it is not being fully reimbursed. Because the community will have to pay for its banking services one way or another, and because banking relationships are crucial to the quality of service, most communities deduct the reserve requirement from the average available balance.

Certificates of deposit (CDs) with a 0% interest rate have an overwhelming advantage when used in place of demand deposit balances to compensate banks. Because CDs have lower reserve requirements than demand deposits, fewer funds are needed to compensate banks, and thus more cash is freed for investment. The following example illustrates this point (see Exhibit 4.I).

Using a Demand Deposit Balance

Collected balance	$100,000
Reserve @ 16.25%*	(16,250)
Investable balance**	83,750

Using a Certificate of Deposit (or Other Time Deposits) of 30-179 days

Collected balance	$89,095
Reserve @ 6%*	(5,345)
Investable balance**	83,750

Using a Certificate of Deposit (or Other Time Deposits) of 180 or more days

Collected balance	$85,897
Reserve @ 2.5%*	(2.5% = 2,147)
Investable balance**	83,752

Source: William Donoghue, *The Cash Management Manual*

* Reserve requirements of the Federal Reserve System and state reserve requirements for nonmember banks change from time to time. The Federal Reserve Bulletin or the community's bank can keep local officials abreast of current requirements.

** This is the balance that the bank credits to the community, at the earnings rate, against charges for bank services.

This example shows that a community, using a 0% CD of 179 days or less, needs to commit only $89,095 rather than $100,000 when using demand deposits. Or, it may use a 180+ day CD which requires only $85,897. This frees approximately $14,000 of each $100,000 for community investment.

EXHIBIT 4.I / Bank Compensation with a 0% CD Rather Than Demand Deposit Balances

CDs are short-term agreements (or money market instruments) that banks sell to investors who lend them a certain amount of money for 30 to 270 days. Since investors must keep those funds at the bank (in CD form) for at least 30 days, the law allows banks to reserve a much smaller portion of that balance. If a community maintained a compensating balance of $100,000 in a checking account at a national bank, the bank could invest only $83,000 since it is required to reserve approximately 17% of all demand deposits. However, the reserve requirement for CDs is only 5%, so if the community chose to keep a 0% CD with the bank instead, it would have to maintain only an $87,400 CD to give the bank $83,000 worth of investable funds. The community would have an extra $12,600 to invest.

The other side of the account analysis equation, the middle section of the exhibit, is the price of the bank's services translated into an equivalent deposit balance. Exhibit 4.J shows the *costs* that banks across the country charge for various services.

Average Unit of Service Costs of Banks:	
Clearing a depositor's check:	$0.05
Processing a check deposit:	$0.10
Cashing a check:	$0.17

These standard costs are approximate. Banks recoup these costs, and make a profit besides, by setting unit service charges sufficiently high. The service charges are then transformed into desired compensating balances by answering the question, "What annual balances will produce a monthly income, at the earnings rate, equivalent to the service charges?" The calculation then becomes:

$$\text{Balance required} = \frac{\text{Service charges} \times (12)}{\text{Earnings allowance}}$$

In the account analysis, Exhibit 4.H, the account activity charges translate into a required balance of $2,678.

$$\frac{(13.39) \times (12)}{(.06)} = \$2,678$$

The earnings allowance, at the top of the middle section in the exhibit, is the interest rate that banks offer communities for the use of municipal deposits. Most analysts use a 30- or 90-day Treasury bill rate as an indicator of a fair earnings rate. These T-bills are highly liquid (they can be bought and sold before maturity quite easily), and they have very low risk. Local officials and bankers, in their discussions of the price of bank services, should agree on a consistent market instrument as a basis for an earnings allowance during times of changing interest rates. Then, banking relations will not erode through technical misunderstandings.

The following 1979 prices for banking services were compiled in a national survey by Sheshunoff and Company, an Austin, Texas, firm monitoring bank activity.

PER ITEM CHARGES FOR:

BANK ASSETS	Federal reserve bank transfers (outgoing)	Bank wire transfer	Outgoing draft collections	Incoming draft collections	Payroll check
0-10 Million Range	1.00-10.00	1.00-10.00	.25-7.50	.25-7.50	.25-.45
Median	3.00	4.00	1.00	1.00	.35
10-25 Million Range	1.50-10.00	1.00-10.00	.25-10.00	.25-7.50	.10-.80
Median	4.00	5.00	1.50	2.00	.40
25-50 Million Range	1.50-10.00	1.00-10.00	.25-10.00	.25-9.00	.10-.75
Median	3.50	5.00	2.00	2.00	.40
50-100 Million Range	1.00-10.00	1.00-10.00	.25-10.00	.25-9.00	.05-.80
Median	5.00	5.00	2.00	.40	.06
100-250 Million Range	1.50-10.00	1.50-10.00	.25-10.00	.25-8.00	.09-.80
Median	5.00	5.00	2.00	2.00	.40
250-500 Million Range	1.50-10.00	1.50-10.00	.25-10.00	.25-9.00	.25-.60
Median	4.00	5.00	2.50	2.00	.45
500 Million - 1 Billion Range	1.50-8.00	2.00-8.00	.50-7.50	.50-8.00	.09-.80
Median	3.00	3.00	3.00	3.00	.40
Over 1 Billion Range	1.50-7.50	1.50-5.00	.50-5.00	.75-5.00	.10-.56
Median	3.00	3.00	2.50	3.00	.40

Prices in Dollars
NC = No charge
Source: Sheshunoff and Company, Inc.

EXHIBIT 4.J / Prices of Banking Services

Checks paid on commercial DDa account	Checks deposited (non encoded)	Deposits to commercial account	Returned items	Stop payment orders	Commercial account reconcilement	Monthly maintenance fee
NC-.15 .05	.025-.05 .03	NC-.50 NC	NC-5.00 NC	NC-10.00 2.00	NC-.04 NC	.50-5.00 1.00
NC .15 .05	.015-.05 .03	NC-.50 NC	NC-8.00 NC	NC-10.00 2.00	NC-.06 NC	.50-5.00 1.00
NC-.15 .05	.015-.08 .03	NC-.50 NC	NC-6.00 NC	NC-12.00 3.00	NC-.08 NC	.50-7.50 1.00
NC-.20 .03	.015-.08 NC	NC-.50 NC	NC-12.50 5.00	NC-.12 NC	.50-7.50 1.00	NA
NC-.20 .07	.015-.08 .03	NC-.50 .03	NC-7.00 NC	NC-12.50 4.00	NC-.12 NC	.50-5.00 1.00
NC-.15 .08	.025-.06 .03	NC-.30 .03	NC-8.00 NC	NC-10.00 3.00	NC-.07 .015	.50-5.00 2.00
.04-.12 .08	.025-.08 .04	NC-.60 .05	NC-5.00 .40	NC-8.00 4.00	NC-.05 .01	.75-5.00 2.50
NC-.15 .09	.025-.07 .03	NC-.50 .10	NC-4.00 .50	NC-7.50 4.00	.005-.06 .03	.75-7.50 2.50

The Bottom Line

The average investable balance available for account services should equal the balance required to cover service charges. In other words, the price paid for services (in the form of investable balances) should equal the value of the services received (in the form of the balance requirement). Whenever the investable balance exceeds the required balance, the community has overpaid and may remove excess funds for investment. Whenever the reverse is true and the required balance is not covered by the investable balance, the community has underpaid and needs to replenish its account.

An account analysis should be performed periodically, and ideally every month, to ensure that bank compensation is fair for the services provided. A shortfall or excess in compensating balances in one period can be made up in the subsequent period by raising or lowering the level of the compensating balance.

4.8 Pricing Practices of Banks

Perhaps the most lasting legacy of the 1970s in banking is a greater sensitivity on the part of bankers to the need for accurate pricing. The rise in operating costs, the expansion of services being rendered, and greater customer sophistication have pressured banks to come up with realistic and up-to-date prices for their services. There is ample evidence that many banks still are not using good cost accounting procedures. Communities may occasionally receive a set of bids for banking services in which a few bids state extremely high or extremely low prices. Inquiries would reveal that these banks may have chosen their prices at random rather than from a reliable cost accounting system. Local officials do not need to be experts in bank cost accounting, but it is useful to understand the way in which prices are arrived at by bidding banks, and how prices might change significantly over the space of several years.

Banks price their services with effort, partly because it is not clear which operating costs should be included in the price of a particular service. For example, if a bank is offering a new service, such as an automated payroll system, should it include just the extra cost of providing the new service, or should it also include a portion of all the indirect costs of running a bank, such as a portion of the president's salary? The first method, called *incremental* pricing, would only include the extra time and labor costs of running the payroll tape on the computer. The second method, called *full absorption* pricing, would also include a portion of the cost of buying and operating the computer.

The details of either method of pricing bank services are not important to local officials, but they can see how the choice affects current and future prices. If a bank uses incremental pricing and the community plans to gradually increase its use of a particular service, then at some point the price of the service might leap upwards. This effect is illustrated in the following example. Perhaps a bank has had unused capacity on its computer, and therefore has charged a very low price for services requiring additional computer utilization. As unused capacity dries up, the bank decides to acquire a new computer and increases charges to reflect the full cost of acquiring and maintaining the new computer. A large customer of the bank, such as a city, may find to its dismay that pricing for services rendered has switched from an incremental to a full cost basis.

Introduction of new bank productivity can also cause prices to change significantly. Over time, bank productivity is very sensitive to changes in wage rates and to technological innovations. Bank wages have increased steadily in the post-World War II era. But check processing costs declined sharply in the early 1960s due to the introduction of automated bookeeping machines that did away with manual posting of customer debits and credits. In the late 1960s, computers began to process magnetically encoded checks. This innovation, like other computer innovations in the 1970s (such as computer preparation of account analyses) added to the capacity of banks to handle large volumes and to offer sophisticated services but probably at increased costs.

Traditionally, banks have priced only a few standard services, offering the rest without charge. For instance, deposits, wire transfers, and ledger entries have been charged on a per item price, but other activities such as trust administration and data processing services have been offered either without charge or at a customized price. According to Federal Reserve System studies, banks appear to have undercharged for these services, perhaps because they did not collect accurate cost data themselves, or perhaps because bank marketing officers viewed these special services as loss leaders to attract and hold customers.

One approach banks have used toward a more accurate pricing of services is called *unbundling,* or separate pricing of each discrete type of service. The unbundling approach has become very popular with large banking customers. Separate pricing of each banking service is becoming more and more prevalent as money managers strive to keep banking costs low. Whether they choose to pay for banking services on a fee basis or with compensating balances, many cash managers insist that banks price services separately. It allows the community to compare the prices of services among local banks, and it encourages banks to charge only for services used.

The Federal Reserve System has assisted banks in cost accounting by compiling periodic surveys of cost trends. Each Federal Reserve bank has a *functional cost analysis* department that collects detailed operating data from a sample of community banks within its district. District-compiled data are subsequently merged to provide annual, nationwide profiles of bank operations. The profiles are crude—they do not, for example, separate out the costs of servicing large customers—but they are widely read by bankers, many of whom set prices according to the data contained in the profiles. Exhibit 4.J shows data for 1979, the most recent year reported on as of early 1980.

The ABCs of Banks and Banking 4.9

To acquire and maintain effective banking services, local officials need to understand how banks do business and earn profits, and thus how their accounts are of value to banks. This section presents an overview and description of banks, how they make money, and how the government regulates their activities. Only with a general understanding of the banking business can local officials establish mutually beneficial banking relationships. Local governments should pay a fair price for services they could not provide with comparable efficiency, and banks should earn a fair return for providing those services.

In managing community cash, local treasurers may do business with any of three kinds of banking institutions: savings banks, savings and loan institutions, and commercial banks. Local governments use savings banks and savings and loan institutions primarily as depositories for investable funds, while commercial banks play the central role in providing cash management accounts and services. In the following discussion of their operation, commercial banks are referred to as *banks* or *trust companies*.

Commercial Banks

Commercial banks function as businesses. They receive funds from capital supplied by bank shareholders, retained earnings, and demand and other deposits. They make money by loaning those funds, investing those funds in securities or other forms of investment, and selling their services to their customers. Interest from loans constitutes the major part of bank income, approximately 66% in 1972. Interest from securities amounted to 19%, and fees from trust department operations and account services, the remaining 15%.

Banks also get funds from bank shareholders and retained earnings. To invest in the bank, shareholders buy stock. The bank uses the money from those sales to develop capital facilities and support operations. Retained earnings are profits, less the amounts paid to shareholders in the form of dividends, that the bank reinvests in its operations.

The bank's largest source of funds is deposits, but commercial banks do not merely collect and reinvest depositor funds; they lend out more than the original deposit. The original deposit, the *primary* deposit, generates other, or *derivative,* deposits. To show how a bank generates derivative deposits (called the *multiplier effect*), the following simple case describes a one-bank national economy.

With any demand deposit, the Fed requires member banks to reserve a portion of the balance and allows the bank to lend the remaining amount. For example, if the reserve requirement is 20% and a bank receives a $100,000 deposit from Morristown, the bank reserves $20,000 and can lend the remaining $80,000. If it lends that money to Acme Construction, it credits Acme's checking account for $80,000. In addition to the primary deposit of $100,000 held by Morristown, the bank now has a derivative deposit of $80,000 held by Acme. The multiplier effect continues since the bank may then lend up to 80% of the Acme Construction deposit. Exhibit 4.K summarizes the cumulative effect.

The banking system has generated $400,000 worth of loans from a $100,000 deposit. At 10% interest for the loans, the bank effectively earns 40% on the original deposit.

$$\text{(Annual income interest rate)} \times \text{(Investment principal)}$$
$$\$400{,}000 \times .10 = \$40{,}000$$

Cycle	Deposit	Reserve Requirement (20%)	Excess Reserve (Loanable)
1.	$100,000	20,000	80,000
2.	80,000	16,000	64,000
3.	65,000	12,800	51,200
4.	51,200	10,240	40,960
•	•	•	•
•	•	•	•
Total	$500,000	100,000	400,000

EXHIBIT 4.K / The Multiplier Effect

In a multi-bank economy, a 40% interest rate for a single bank is possible only if all loans are redeposited in the same bank and no customer draws down deposits.

This is an extreme example of deposit growth for any single bank in a multi-bank system. There are many reasons why the deposit will never reach this amount of loanable funds. Depositors will make withdrawals, or Acme's account may be with another bank. The point is that one deposit may generate many more funds for the bank to invest. The bank does not merely deposit and reinvest depositor funds.

Banks earn money, not only from interest on loan investments and the sale of services, but from excess balances. When reserve account balances exceed the reserve requirement, a bank can lend those funds, called *Federal funds,* to other banks on a short-term basis (as short as overnight). Such loans help other banks reach their reserve requirements. The interest rate charged, called the *Federal funds rate,* is one indication of the availability of short-term funds. If reserve balances represent a longer-term increase in the bank's deposit base, then the bank might draw down the funds and invest them in longer-term securities, or it may make customer loans.

Because banks keep accounts at the Federal Reserve Bank, the Fed has sometimes been described as the member banks' bank. The amount that the Fed requires members to reserve in their accounts affects the growth of the money supply in the national economy. It also affects the actual amount of funds that a particular bank may lend.

Banks naturally manage their assets to return the highest yield, or profit, that is possible. However, they must meet profit objectives within the constraints of safety and liquidity. They must ensure that any investment, in loans or securities, is safe enough to preserve capital and offer some minimum return. And they must ensure that they always have adequate funds in their reserve accounts to meet cash demands, such as depositors' withdrawals.

The goals of profit, liquidity, and safety are often contradictory, since a high profit return usually means a more risky and less liquid investment. The bank's job is to balance these three objectives.

Commercial banks also try to match the relative liquidity of their assets with the liquidity of their liabilities. For example, if a bank holds many five-to-seven-year commercial term loans and depositors withdraw more funds than they deposit, the bank has to call in commercial loans to cover the depositors' demands for cash (or go bankrupt). For this reason, banks generally look for core deposits (or other liabilities) that are long-term and relatively stable and assets (or investments and loans) that are relatively short-term and liquid. Shorter-term investments, however, usually carry lower investment yields, so the bank has to balance its liquidity requirements with its target for earnings.

For this reason, municipal accounts are often very attractive to banks. They involve large amounts of core deposit money that are usually maintained in significant, stable balances.

When banks manage their assets they rank their management goals in order of the most pressing needs. They ensure that funds are sufficient to meet payment demands by maintaining adequate reserves and adequate balances at corresponding banks. They next ensure that they have enough short-term assets available to liquidate in the event of depositor withdrawal or other liquidity requirements. Then they use funds for corporate or consumer loans to the customers with the best risk or credit rating. Finally, they use remaining funds, which might result from a lack of loan demand in the community, for investment in corporate or government securities.

On the liability side, banks have competed for funds, within the limits of regulation, through aggressive advertising campaigns, a variety of retail and corporate services, bank branching, and specialized financial services including international banking and money market investment services. To attract funds, banks have also offered attractive terms for certificates of deposit, and they have formed bank holding companies that issue commercial paper.

Many banks aggressively seek government deposits not only for core deposits but because these depositors may make use of other modern financial services that banks offer. This competitive atmosphere puts local governments in an attractive position to use banking services at reasonable prices.

Other Types of Banks

Almost all of a municipality's banking needs are met by commercial banks. This section lists other types of banks that serve essentially the individual depositor or consumer home owner. Municipalities would be interested in these banks as possible alternatives for savings or time deposits.

Mutual savings banks are thrift institutions that are owned by their depositors. They receive their funds from deposits in savings accounts and consumer transaction accounts, and they place their funds mainly in home mortgages, U.S. government securities, and temporary short-term investments at commercial banks. Mutual savings banks exist in eighteen states, primarily in the Northeast and Far West.

Savings and loan associations invest an even larger percentage of their deposits than do mutual savings banks in residential mortgages, and they too receive their funds from individual savings accounts. Mutual savings and loan associations, like mutual savings banks, are owned by their depositors. Stock associations, however, raise their capital, and thus sell ownership, through the issuance of shares in the association. They were formed to encourage thrift and home ownership in America.

Bank Regulation 4.10

As discussed in the previous section, local officials must understand the business of banking in order to effectively manage banking relationships. A mutually beneficial relationship depends on each party having a fair and realistic understanding of his business partner's motivations and abilities. One of the most significant aspects of a bank's ability to provide service and ensure the safety of funds is federal and state regulation of banking practices.

Commercial banks are regulated in the United States under a *dual banking* system. That means that banks may be chartered and regulated by the federal government or chartered and regulated by state governments. For purposes of regulation and insurance, commercial banks in this country may be classified into four types: nationally chartered banks, state chartered banks that are also members of the Federal Reserve System, state chartered banks (non-Fed members) which are still insured by the Federal Deposit Insurance Corporation, and state chartered banks that are neither members of the Fed nor insured by the F.D.I.C. Most banks are state chartered, non-member, insured banks.

Of the 14,048 commercial banks in the country in 1973, 4,631 are nationally chartered banks, and therefore they are required by law to join the Federal Reserve System. Another 1,076 state chartered commercial banks also belong to the Fed. National bank members of the Fed are regulated and inspected by the Comptroller of the Currency and insured by the Federal Deposit Insurance Corporation. They are, to some extent, regulated by all three federal agencies (the Federal Reserve Bank, the Comptroller of the Currency, and the F.D.I.C.), although the Fed is primarily regulator, and the Comptroller of the Currency, the examining agency. State chartered banks that are members of the Fed are regulated and examined by the Federal Reserve Bank itself and are also subject to the examination and regulation of the state.

The bulk of commercial banks in the country, 8,137, are not members of the Federal Reserve System but are still insured by the F.D.I.C., which is, along with the state banking authorities, the major regulatory and examining authority for these banks. There are only 204 commercial banks, state chartered, that are not members of the Federal Reserve System and not insured by the F.D.I.C. They are subject only to state inspection and regulation.

Banking regulations are designed to protect depositors and provide a safe level of competition. They regulate both the structure of the industry, through laws on branch banking and capital requirements, and the practices of individual banks.

The following is a sample of Federal Reserve regulations that affect bank behavior and even the nature and price of services member banks offer:

- Regulation Q sets limits on the amount of interest banks may offer customers on time deposits (amounts over $100,000 pay market rates).
- Federal Reserve member banks may not pay interest on demand deposits. Any local government wishing to earn revenue on cash balances must then invest in interest-bearing securities.
- Federal Reserve member banks are not allowed to levy domestic exchange charges (charges for clearing out-of-town checks) on bank customers. Banks are not directly charged for this service but support this activity through reserve balances left at the Fed and through the purchase of Federal Reserve stock (mandated by Regulation I).
- Except for a few minor exceptions, banks are prohibited from investing in stocks, and stocks acquired as collateral for defaulted loans must be sold within a certain period of time.
- Bank mergers require the approval of the Comptroller of the Currency if the new, combined bank is a national bank; the Federal Reserve if it is a state chartered member bank; or the F.D.I.C. if it is a non-member insured bank.
- The Federal Reserve Bank requires that member banks hold a certain portion of their deposits in reserve at the Fed (the reserve requirement—Regulation D).
- Federal and state laws limit the amount and to some degree the nature of bank loans. For example, banks cannot lend over 10% of their capital and surplus to one customer, and Regulation O limits the credit banks may extend to their executive officers.
- Banks are permitted to buy only bonds, notes, and debentures that are of relatively high investment quality. Banks are automatically eligible to buy federal, state, and municipal bonds, and federal agency securities (Regulation E).
- Banks are prohibited from underwriting any issuance of securities except for state and municipal bonds (Regulation R).
- Regulation Y subjects bank holding companies to federal banking laws.
- Regulation A sets the terms by which member banks may borrow short-term funds from the Federal Reserve. Usually, the Fed demands strict terms and high rates. The rate the Fed charges member banks is called the *discount rate*.

All state banking laws, unless superseded by federal regulation, must be observed by all banks doing business in that particular state. The following are a few samples of state regulations:

- Directors of banks must be U.S. citizens, live in the community of the bank, own a portion of bank stock, and be of high character and reputation.
- State laws regulate the conditions, number, and location of bank branches.
- New banks must meet minimum requirements for capital structure, and they must prove that they meet the convenience and needs of the community.

Part 3

Short-Term Investing

Cash Forecasting 5

An effective cash management program consolidates cash balances for investments so that otherwise idle assets produce nontax revenues for community coffers. Cash forecasting is essential to those who manage their own short-term investments. The investor must know when and how much money will be available in order to make the most beneficial investment choices. This chapter introduces cash forecasts while chapter 6, on short-term investing, shows how a local treasurer uses forecast information to form an investment strategy, then buys and sells money market and other investment instruments.

Cash forecasting serves two purposes for local government treasurers. It helps them ensure that funds are on hand to meet disbursement demands, and it helps them plan an investment program. Section 5.1 introduces forecasting and explains its value to community cash management programs. Section 5.2 shows cash managers how to develop forecasts from municipal sources. It describes a simple method to analyze recurring cash receipts and payments, using past patterns to predict future cash flows. It is a sensible approach that limits the effort that local officials must make to collect useful information.

The value of a forecast depends on its format. Overly general forecasts are irrelevant, while overly detailed forecasts are too burdensome to prepare. Section 5.3 describes different cash forecasts and gives guidelines for choosing the proper level of detail, time horizon, and forecast divisions for communities of different sizes. Then sections 5.4 through 5.7 put the forecast together, arriving at the bottom line, and discuss adjustments that managers may make to keep forecasts current and accurate as circumstances change. Finally, section 5.8 shows how communities may keep their cash information current through reconciliation with bank records.

How to Forecast Cash Flow 5.1

Cash flow forecasting estimates when revenues will be collected and when salaries and bills will be paid. The cash manager then knows when to borrow short-term funds to offset cash deficits or, better yet, when to invest surplus cash. Cash forecasting projections show how much of a cash surplus or deficit may be anticipated, when it is likely to occur, and how long it is likely to last.

Cash forecasting offers local managers valuable benefits. If one cash management goal is to ensure that town coffers do not run dry, then cash forecasts warn of future cash shortfalls. Town officials may then plan to borrow money and notify short-term creditors, they may accelerate revenue collections, or they may rearrange disbursement schedules and plan a financial strategy to meet cash demands.

As important, cash forecasts are essential to an intelligent short-term investment strategy that maximizes investment return. A community can take advantage of higher-yielding instruments only if it knows how long funds will be available. A town that has $500,000 on hand for three months would most likely buy a 90-day investment, which would bring a higher yield than 90 overnight investments and save the brokerage fees and extra time that daily buying and selling of securities would require.

If a town develops a useful, simple forecast for its principal cash systems, such as central purchasing and capital budgets, it will not need to spend much time tracking cash flows. In most municipalities three-quarters of the information on cash flows, such as payroll disbursement information and property tax collection schedules, is readily available, and the remaining information is necessary only for fine tuning. With good forecasting, a town will know what cash is needed to run day-to-day operations, and it will have a good data base for planning an effective investment policy.

A professional cash forecasting operation provides other indirect benefits. Over the long run a town improves its credit worthiness. Only a professionally managed municipality could approach its banker six months in advance of a request to borrow short-term funds with a schedule of cash flows showing the amount and length of borrowing required and the timing and source of repayment. That option is more attractive than a town's frantic phone call when it discovers that it has run out of cash as the biweekly payroll comes due.

5.2 How to Identify Cash Flows

The first step in developing a cash forecast is to identify each cash flow. There are two kinds of cash flows: (1) recurring flows that pass at regular, predictable intervals, such as payroll payments, debt service redemptions, and property tax collections; (2) irregular flows that occur once or only a few times, such as unusual tax refunds or the sale of city assets. Of these irregular flows, expenditures for capital projects are the most difficult to predict, given unpredictable delays in building construction.

Exhibit 5.A lists some of the more common expenditures and revenues of local governments. Forecasting cash flows consists of two general steps. First, the cash manager uses past history of major collections and disbursements to identify recurring patterns. Then he adjusts these flows for predicted changes in the timing of the patterns and for anticipated rises and falls of amounts. The process becomes clearer if we examine the type of steps taken to forecast these flows. From an annual budget, a town's payment and collection records, department personnel discussions, and double checking with the treasurer on past cash flow patterns, a cash manager should be able to identify the municipality's major cash items.

Forecasting Disbursements

The community's records might show that the public works department plans to spend $350,000 in salaries for the upcoming year. Discussions with the department's

COLLECTIONS

Property Taxes

Characteristics
- Major portion of revenues
- Collected semi-annually

Projection techniques
- From historical collection information construct three-year history of tax collections
- From annual budget determine gross tax levy and reduce by abatement or overlay and uncollectible reserves
- Apply net tax levy to historical collection percentages developed in first step
- Adjust for anticipated changes in collection patterns

Potential adjustments
- Changes in anticipated abatement awards or uncollectable amounts
- Economic upturns or downturns
- Changes in the date bills are issued or bill payment terms

Sales and Excise Taxes

Characteristics
- Collected daily (excise) or monthly or quarterly (sales) when collected by local government. May be collected by state or county and remitted to local government quarterly, semi-annually, or annually.
- Heavy collection during times when bills are due or in peak shopping seasons.

Projection techniques
- Estimate timing of receipts from remittance agreements with state and county governments and collection records
- Apply estimate of current year amounts to historical percentages and adjust for any anticipated changes

Potential adjustments
- Changes in excise or sales tax rates
- Changes in state and county remittance agreements
- Changes in consumer buying

Federal and State Aid

Characteristics
- Significant portion of revenues
- Federal aid includes general revenue sharing, education and categorical grants
- State aid includes aid for education, handicapped persons, and welfare
- Collected as needed, quarterly, semi-annually, or annually

(continued on next page)

EXHIBIT 5.A / Glossary of Major Collections and Disbursements

Projection techniques

- Review annual budget to identify all reimbursable or chargeable programs and their estimated amounts
- Discuss with department personnel timing of program expenditures and claims processing (where possible, control collection by timely submission of claims)
- Determine nature of payments, whether cash advance, letter-of-credit, or claim reimbursement
- Discuss with federal and state payment agencies timing of anticipated payments

Potential adjustments

- Changes in federal or state programs
- Delay or acceleration of program expenditures
- Changes in amounts of program expenditures
- Changes in claim approval process or payment process by federal or state agencies

Agency Revenues

Characteristics

- Includes user payments for hospital, library, and water and sewer services
- Agencies may collect these receipts. If so, timing and amount of revenues depends on agency efficiency in billing and collection and remittance agreements with municipal collector

Projection techniques

- Using historical collection patterns, agency's annual budget, and discussions with agency personnel, construct collection history and apply amount of anticipated annual revenues

Potential adjustments

- Changes in fees or rates
- Increase or decrease in usage
- Changes in agency collection procedures

Other revenues

Characteristics

- Includes cash collections from parking meters, golf courses, and other services as well as licenses, fines, and subscriptions
- Small portion of revenues

Projection techniques

- If amounts are material (greater than $5,000 for any forecast horizon), take estimated annual amount and apply evenly throughout collection period. For any major amounts, apply in accordance with collection history

Potential adjustments

- Changes in rates, fees, or fines (assure that upcoming amounts are reasonable)
- Changes in usage or deliquency

(continued on next page)

DISBURSEMENTS

Salaries and Wages

Characteristics
- Approximately 70% of general fund budget
- Approximately 50% of capital projects budget

Projection techniques
- From annual budget and payroll records determine annual payroll disbursements
- Eliminate payroll deductions to find net cash outflow
- Divide annual net outflow into forecasting periods in accordance with payment due dates

Potential adjustments
- Changes in number of employees
- Increase or decrease in salaries and wages
- Seasonal or overtime payments
- Changes in group insurance, income taxes, and other deductions

Payroll Taxes

Characteristics
- Includes federal income taxes, state income taxes, FICA—including municipal portion of federal and state unemployment taxes
- About 30% of payroll expenditures

Projection techniques
- From the salaries and wages forecast determine annual payroll tax disbursements
- Estimate amount required on due dates by dividing annual taxes into quarterly or semi-annual payments

Potential adjustments
- See Salaries and Wages
- Changes in tax rates

Debt Service

Characteristics
- Payments determined by fixed schedule

Projection techniques
- From debt maturity and coupon redemption schedules determine amount due on redemption dates

Potential adjustments
- Additions of new debt issues or adjustments for refinancings in upcoming year

Capital Expenditures

Characteristics
- Irregular; plans often change

Projection Techniques
- Develop separate cash flow estimates for each project
- From construction contracts determine total construction costs
- From discussions with construction supervisors determine probability of cost increases, pace of construction, and likely payment patterns. Estimate the timing and amount of payments
- Deduct retainage from in-progress payments and add back to final payment

Potential adjustments
- Changes in construction schedules (develop advanced warning system with construction supervisor)

(continued on next page)

EXHIBIT 5.A / Glossary of Major Collections and Disbursements (continued)

Employee Benefit Plans

Characteristics
- Includes funded pension plans, health insurance, group life insurance, and disability income plans

Projection techniques
- As specified in contracts, estimate amounts due on each payment date

Potential adjustments
- Changes in insurance rates
- Changes in number of employees
- Changes in number and nature of plans in employee benefit package
- Changes in number of employees qualifying for benefits, such as new retirees

Materials and Supplies

Characteristics
- Usually minor portion of expenditures
- Includes office supplies, stationery, postage, printed forms, vehicle supplies, and textbooks and school supplies (usually purchased during the summer)

Projection techniques
- From annual budget and purchase contracts, isolate major items
- From discussions with department personnel, predict timing of outflow for major items
- Approximate smaller cash payments based on annual budget and past experience (if amounts are not significant, do not forecast)

Potential adjustments
- Usually only minor adjustments, but can be significant during budget cutbacks
- Changes in usage rates due to purchase cycles (example: textbooks or vehicles every two years)

Utilities

Characteristics
- Usually minor portion of expenditures
- Monthly, bi-monthly, or quarterly payments
- Includes telephone, electric, fuel, and water charges

Projection techniques
- Using contracts, historical results, and current rates estimate timing and amount of utility payments

Potential adjustments
- Rate changes or price increases
- Usage changes, particularly during conservation programs

Other Current Costs

Characteristics
- Includes travel expenditures, dues and subscriptions, per diem fees, insurance

Projection techniques
- From annual budget and discussions with department personnel estimate timing of nonrecurring costs

Potential Adjustments
- Changes in timing of payment or cancellation of plans

assistant director might reveal that 90% of these payroll expenses are usually spread evenly over a twelve-month period. The remaining 10%, personnel expenses for snowplowing, occur in December, January, February, and March. On the disbursements side, payroll accounts for approximately 70% of most local government budgets. Because of their importance, personnel expenditures should be identified first.

Personnel expenditures are relatively constant and therefore can be reliably predicted. A town manager would use payroll records or the upcoming budget to determine the yearly personnel costs. He then divides that amount by the number of pay periods (52 weekly payrolls) for the gross weekly payroll. The gross weekly payroll, however, is not the amount disbursed. The weekly gross, minus federal, state, and local income taxes and fringe benefits such as workers compensation and retirement, is the net weekly cash outflow.

Disbursements for withholding taxes and benefits are also significant. The forecasts for these items are calculated in approximately the same manner. As an illustration, assume that payments to the IRS for withholding federal income taxes occur monthly. The amount disbursed to the IRS on the due date equals the total federal taxes withheld for that quarter. This amount may be calculated by adding all the income tax deductions from weekly payrolls and multiplying by the number of pay periods falling within a particular month.

In forecasting personnel disbursements, a town treasurer should try to estimate the *actual* cash disbursement if it deviates from the budgeted or authorized amounts. Budgeted amounts change with supplemental appropriations, while authorized amounts change with the increase or decrease of available positions. This is true for all disbursements. Calculate carefully the effect of these changes (if any) on actual cash flows. The forecast should also include adjustments for seasonal or temporary workers and seasonal payments such as vacation advances in the summer months.

Once the payroll disbursements have been forecast, the cash manager should then forecast other cash payments. This might be performed by analyzing each departmental budget for nonpayroll items and then choosing *target* amounts first. Discussions with the department official familiar with expenditures should reveal the pattern of past cash disbursements for these items and the predicted pattern and amount of disbursement for the upcoming year. Care should be taken to ensure that these amounts coincide with the treasurer's sense of reasonable payments and past disbursement experience. Department officials may have incorrect impressions of their department's cash disbursements because they do not usually monitor the timing and volume of cash outflows.

Forecasting Collections

Local taxes and intergovernmental aid are the primary sources of funds. Property and sales tax collection patterns are drawn from historical flows. To identify these patterns, the cash manager usually develops a table that shows (1) the type of tax, (2) the amount of the levy or the total amount due, (3) the month when each portion of that tax levy was collected. If flows are traced back two or three years, enough

	July		Aug.		Sept.		Oct.		Nov.		Dec.	
	#	%	#	%	#	%	#	%	#	%	#	%
1. Property tax												
FY 77							1.676	32.7	482	9.4	405	7.9
FY 78							1.739	30.3	614	10.7	517	9.0
FY 79							1.778	30.0	658	11.1	527	8.9
Average							1.731	31.0	585	10.4	483	8.6
FY 80 (budget)							1.922		645		533	
2. Sales tax												
FY 77												
FY 78												
FY 79												
Average												
FY 80 (budget)												
3. Federal aid (revenue sharing)												
FY 77												
FY 78												
FY 79												
Average												
FY 80 (budget)												
4. Federal aid (CETA)												
FY 77												
FY 78												
FY 79												
Average												
FY 80 (budget)												
Total												
FY 77												
FY 78												
FY 79												
Average												
FY 80 (budget)												

The exhibit completes the property tax section to show how to construct a collection history. The forecaster takes the expected FY 80 net property tax collection and spreads it among each month according to the percentage usually collected in that month. In this case, the forecaster estimated receipts on the basis of the month's three year average, but it was also possible to use

EXHIBIT 5.B / History of Revenue Collections

Jan.		Feb.		Mar.		April		May		June		Total			
#	%	#	%	#	%	#	%	#	%	#	%	#	%	Budget	Variance
						1,794	35.0	523	10.2	246	4.8	5,125	100%	5,100	25
						1,871	32.6	654	11.4	344	6.0	5,740	100%	5,800	*60*
						1,896	32.0	681	11.5	385	6.5	5,925	100%	6,000	*75*
						1,854	33.2	619	11.0	325	5.8	5,597	100%	5,633	*37*
						2,058		682		360				6,200	
													100%		
													100%		
													100%		
													100%		
													100%		
													100%		
													100%		
													100%		
													100%		
													100%		
													100%		
													100%		

the most recent year's pattern, the emerging pattern to receive collections somewhat later after bills are issued, or some other pattern based on events not mentioned in this example. The method used depends on the forecaster's personal experience and judgment.

information should be available to produce a recognizable pattern. For property taxes the table might look like Exhibit 5.B.

If the town's May 1981 levy for property taxes is calculated at $1.9 million, and if 60% of the tax is usually received in May, then the town might expect $1.14 million in May 1981. This type of table is also useful for estimates of other regular revenues, such as sales taxes or motor vehicle excise taxes.

These historical patterns of cash flows are reassessed in light of the estimates of new events. There is naturally much uncertainty in these adjustments, but a manager should make a best guess based on experience. He is worse off by ignoring probable events simply because the timing and amount is difficult to predict.

Examples of some of the more predictable adjustments to historical cash flows are announced increases in federal revenue sharing or changes in the date that the state sends out local aid payments. Sometimes a large upswing or downturn in the economy affects collections, particularly of income tax and other collections that are sensitive to economic changes. For example, if economic forecasters anticipate a downturn in the local economy, perhaps a drop in local tourism due to the gasoline shortage, then a manager might reduce the amount of money that is expected from sales taxes. If the situation worsens, he might even forecast a lag in the receipt of property tax payments. In these cases, the forecaster might look at the operating history of a prior year that fell in the midst of an economic recession (1974–1975, for example) to get a feel for the size of the adjustment needed.

5.3 The Cash Forecast Format

Once the money manager has identified collection and disbursement cash flows, he designs the formats for the town's cash forecasts. The format should make forecasts relatively simple to operate, yet functionally useful for cash planning decisions.

Level of Detail

To determine the appropriate degree of detail of cash forecasts, the cash manager should remember that a less detailed forecast is easier to construct and operate. It requires less precision and less information from department heads and other operating people. A forecast must be detailed enough, however, to be useful in guiding investment decisions for short-term securities, which generally begin with denominations of $5,000 to $10,000. As a rule of thumb, most forecasts round to about 1/100ths of the total receipts or disbursements for the year. If receipts total $10 million, the forecast will be rounded at most to even $10,000 amounts. This level of detail meets the standard necessary for investment decisions, since investment denominations are not much smaller than $10,000.

Time Frames

The time horizon (the period that the forecast encompasses) and the subdivisions (the daily, weekly, or monthly divisions) of cash forecasts vary depending on the level of funds being managed and the purpose and use of the forecast. (Exhibit 5.C describes the uses of different forecasting formats.) In general, forecasts should be made on an annual time horizon and on a rolling basis so that the forecast is extended regularly every month or quarter. (Forecasts exclusively for a particular grant or project can be made at the outset for the lifetime of the grant or project.) For medium and large-sized communities, weekly subdivisions are preferable to monthly subdivisions, because they give the cash manager greater flexibility for time investment purchases and maturities. For large-sized communities—say, those with average daily cash receipts of $200,000 or more—daily forecasts should be prepared for the immediately forthcoming weeks. But monthly forecasts may be sufficient for small communities, so long as there are no large and unpredictable disbursements or collections that could create a severe cash shortage if they were suddenly moved from one month to another.

Forecast Horizon	Annual Forecast	Monthly (or Quarterly) Forecast	Weekly Forecast
Forecast subdivisions	■ Divided into months	■ Divided into weeks or days	■ Divided into days
Major purpose	■ Determines the amount available for investment in maturities greater than 30 days ■ Determines major cash shortfalls for any month in upcoming year	■ Monitors accuracy of annual forecast ■ Determines investment decisions for maturities from overnight to thirty or ninety days	■ Manages cash levels at lead bank ■ Determines investment decisions for maturities less than one week ■ Optimizes disbursement and collection management (including float creation) to keep maximum amounts invested
Issued	■ Before beginning of fiscal year	■ Before each month or each quarter	■ Beginning of each week
Revised and updated	■ Monthly	■ Weekly	■ Daily
Comments	■ Uses rough estimates ■ Monthly fixed transactions easy to predict ■ Collection patterns relatively reliable ■ Annual budget levels important ■ Economic trends may affect timing or amount of collections	■ Payroll clearance cycle easy to predict ■ Timing of major receipts and disbursements need to be more precise than annual forecast ■ Dates of fixed commitments (such as debt service) important	■ Use for major disbursing and collection accounts ■ Need to manage available bank balances ■ Check clearance (float) schedules important ■ Payroll clearance by day important ■ Expenditures/disbursements more erratic ■ Transfer timing important

EXHIBIT 5.C / Uses of Different Forecast Formats

Contents

Even the simplest cash forecasting systems begin with an annual cash forecast divided into monthly units (see Exhibit 5.D). A one-year span gives an overview of cash flows through the budget cycle. It highlights potential problems, such as the need to borrow short-term funds at certain times of the year, and it suggests times when surplus cash may be invested in securities with longer maturities.

To a lesser degree, an annual cash forecast shows the effective changes of collection or disbursement policies. For example, if state aid is delayed one month, the forecast shows the probable impact on borrowing or investment strategies.

The annual forecast should contain a section for the inclusion of each month's actual results. At the end of the month, the treasurer enters and actual cash results from that period (how much cash was sent for construction payments, how much was taken in from sales taxes, etc.) next to the forecasted amount for that item. If there are any large discrepancies, the treasurer finds out why those differences occurred and their effect on the present forecast. For example, if state aid in April was expected to be $200,000 but the town in fact received $250,000, then the treasurer might find that the state included $50,000 of May's state-aid payment in April. The cash manager would then adjust the cash forecast to reflect that change, deducting $50,000 from May's estimated receipts. That change might also dictate a change in investment strategy. The town would now be able to buy $50,000 worth of securities for at least one month.

The *actual* column, in addition to revising current forecasts, is useful in future years when local officials develop new forecasts. These past results provide data for making increasingly accurate forecasts.

From an annual forecast divided by month, the cash manager can develop more detailed monthly forecasts with weekly or daily divisions (see Exhibit 5.E). Monthly forecasts highlight weekly and daily investment opportunities, pinpoint borrowing deadlines, and provide an early warning system for adjustments to the annual forecast. To generate a monthly forecast, the line item for each month on the annual forecast is extracted and then used as the total receipts or disbursements in the monthly forecast. For example, the annual forecast might predict that the town will receive $10,000 in motor vehicle excise taxes in April. This $10,000 of excise revenue for April would then be allocated into the proper week, based on the estimated collection dates. In this case, assume that the state pays the town its portion of the excise tax on the fifteenth of every month. The April monthly forecast will show no excise collections in week 1 or week 2; it will show $10,000 revenue in week 3, and no motor vehicle excise revenue in week 4.

In smaller governments monthly forecasts suffice for most investment decisions. During the month investment decisions can be made after examining the prior week's actual cash flow and an informal forecast of the upcoming week. Treasurers may arrange for their bank to automatically invest any daily surpluses in overnight investments. That leaves all available funds invested, although probably not at the best achievable interest rate, and keeps the administrative chores of investing to a minimum. (Chapter 6 explains how to use local government investment pools to stay fully invested at high interest rates.)

	1st Quarter	2nd Quarter	3rd Quarter	4th Quarter	Total
	Est. Act. Var.[1]	Est. Act. Var.	Est. Act. Var.	Est. Act. Var.	Est. Act. Var.
Cash Receipts[2]					
Property taxes					
Sales taxes					
Excise taxes					
Federal aid and grants					
CETA					
CDBG					
etc.					
State aid and grants					
Education					
Welfare					
etc.					
Special revenues					
Bond Sales					
Other					
Rents					
Licenses & fees					
Tax titles					
Departmental revenues					
Recreation dept.					
Parking & traffic fines					
Parking meters					
School lunches					
Other					
Total cash receipts					
Cash disbursements[2]					
Payroll (net)					
Federal withholding taxes					
State withholding taxes					
Employee benefit plans					
Contracted services					
Debt service					
Capital expenditures					
Supplies & materials					
Insurance					
Other					
Total cash disbursements					
Net cash flow[3]					
Beginning cash balance					
Plus: investments maturing					
Less: note repayments					
Ending cash balance[4]					
Less: compensating balances					
Amount available for investment (required by borrowing)[5]					

Legend

1. Est. = estimated (or forecasted); Act. = actual; Var. = variance (the difference between estimated and actual results)
2. These cash receipts and disbursements categories are shown as examples. Each community should change the categories to reflect the actual items it processes.
3. Net cash flow = total cash receipts − total cash disbursements
4. Ending cash balance = net cash flow + beginning cash balance + investments maturing − notes payable
5. Amount available for investment = ending cash balance − compensating balances

EXHIBIT 5.D / Annual Cash Forecast

	Week 1 Est. Act. Var.[1]	Week 2 Est. Act. Var.	Week 3 Est. Act. Var.	Week 4 Est. Act. Var.	Total Est. Act. Var.
Cash receipts[2]					
Property taxes					
Sales taxes					
Excise taxes					
Federal aid and grants					
CETA					
CDBG					
etc.					
State aid and grants					
Education					
Welfare					
etc.					
Special revenues					
Bond Sales					
Other					
Rents					
Licenses & fees					
Tax titles					
Departmental revenues					
Recreation dept.					
Parking & traffic fines					
Parking meters					
School lunches					
Other					
Total cash receipts					
Cash disbursements[2]					
Payroll (net)					
Federal withholding taxes					
State withholding taxes					
Employee benefit plans					
Contracted services					
Debt service					
Capital expenditures					
Supplies & materials					
Insurance					
Other					
Total cash disbursements					
Net cash flow[3]					
Beginning cash balance					
Plus: investments maturing					
Less: note repayments					
Ending cash balance[4]					
Less: compensating balances					
Amount available for investment (required by borrowing)[5]					

Legend

1. Est. = estimated (or forecasted); Act. = actual; Var. = variance (the difference between estimated and actual results)
2. These cash receipts and disbursements categories are shown as examples. Each community should change the categories to reflect the actual items it processes.
3. Net cash flow = total cash receipts − total cash disbursements
4. Ending cash balance = net cash flow + beginning cash balance + investments maturing − notes payable
5. Amount available for investment = ending cash balance − compensating balances

EXHIBIT 5.E / Monthly Cash Forecast

	Day 1 Est. Act. Var.[1]	Day 2 Est. Act. Var.	Day 3 Est. Act. Var.	Day 4 Est. Act. Var.	Total Est. Act. Var.
Cash deposits[2]					
Property taxes					
Sales taxes					
Excise taxes					
Federal aid and grants					
CETA					
CDBG					
etc.					
State aid and grants					
Education					
Welfare					
etc.					
Special revenues					
Bond Sales					
Other					
Rents					
Licenses & fees					
Tax titles					
Departmental revenues					
Recreation dept.					
Parking & traffic fines					
Parking meters					
School lunches					
Other					
Total cash deposits					
Availability:[3]					
Day 1					
Day 2					
Day 3					
Day 4					
Day 5					
Day 6					
Day 7					
Total availability					
Cash disbursements[2]					
Payroll (net)					
Federal withholding taxes					
State withholding taxes					
Employee benefit plans					
Contracted services					
Debt service					
Capital expenditures					
Supplies & materials					
Insurance					
Other					
Total cash disbursements					
Clearing:[3]					
Day 1					
Day 2					
Day 3					
Day 4					
Day 5					
Day 6					
Day 7					
Total clearing					
Net cash flow					
Beginning cash balance					
Plus: investments maturing					
Less: note repayments					
Ending cash balance					
Less: compensating balances					
Amount available for investment (required by borrowing)					

Legend

1. Est. = estimated (or forecasted); Act. = actual; Var. = variance (the difference between estimated and actual results)
2. These cash receipts and disbursements categories are shown as examples. Each community should change the categories to reflect the actual items it processes.
3. Availablity and clearing schedules for each deposit or disbursement may be prepared separately (see the following table), then the total clearing amount entered into the expected day in the forecast.
4. Net cash flow = total availability − total clearing.
5. Ending cash balance = net cash flow + beginning cash balance + investments maturing − notes payable
6. Amount available for investment = ending cash balance − compensating balances

	Amt. disbursed today	Clearing today	Clearing in 1 day	Clearing in 2 days . . .
Payroll				
Federal withhold.				
State withhold.				
Employee benefit				
Total clearing				

EXHIBIT 5.F / Daily Cash Forecast

Medium and large communities can profit from dividing monthly forecasts into estimates of daily collections and receipts (see Exhibit 5.F). The interest income from daily forecasting exceeds the cost of daily cash forecasts only when cash balances are significant. If daily forecasting costs an additional $5,000 and this information allows an extra 0.1% yield, then a city needs an average daily investable balance of $5 million to break even.

These day-by-day forecasts estimate each day's available cash balances. When predicting the exact day that the city receives cash or releases funds from its account, these forecasts are necessarily sensitive to minor changes in timing. The delay of a state-aid payment by as little as a few days may require a significant change in a daily cash forecast and a subsequent change in the short-term investment plan.

A daily forecast differs from a weekly or monthly forecast in one crucial way: it can be designed to predict the *available funds*—funds that may be invested or disbursed, as opposed to the community's book balance—and can thereby ensure maximum investment. For example, funds are not disbursed from the city's bank account on the day that checks are released. After payroll checks are distributed to employees, the employee must deposit his check; not until the employee's bank presents that check to the city's bank are funds paid from the city's account. Until then, those funds in the city's account are available for investment. (Section 2.4 shows how to estimate the float.)

Daily forecasting of available balances makes it possible to predict the city's near-term cash position with precision and buy with confidence six- or seven-day investment instruments offering slightly higher interest rates than overnight investments.

Forecasts with daily divisions need not extend only one week. Some extend to two weeks or a month. The forecast's horizon should be chosen on the basis of the cash cycle of the largest disbursement items. For example, if the city's payroll is disbursed biweekly, the forecast should span two weeks.

In summary, the horizon and time division for cash forecasts should be chosen to provide the necessary investment information. Weekly forecasts with daily divisions are necessary for active day-to-day management of large pools of funds. Monthly forecasts divided into weeks are sufficient for medium-sized communities. Finally, any forecast should be economical. The extra income from more precise, more frequent forecasts should meet or exceed the extra cost of generating that information. That means that smaller governments, with relatively smaller available cash balances, should limit their efforts to an annual forecast with monthly divisions.

5.4 Putting the Forecast Together

After the cash manager has inventoried the town's receipts and disbursements and chosen the scope and detail of the forecast, it is time to put the forecast together. This exercise should give the cash manager a better understanding of what information is needed, how often, and in how much detail.

In the annual cash forecast, revenues less expenditures, plus the beginning cash balance will equal the cash surplus or shortfall. To find the amount of cash available for investment, or the amount to be borrowed, the cash manager should deduct compensating balances maintained to pay for banking services (see chapter 4).

For the relatively few governments that forecast cash flow on a daily basis, the forecast should also include an estimate of the net float on collections and disbursements (see section 2.4). The float is added to the cash surplus or shortfall. For instance, if a town disburses $100,000 worth of payroll checks on Friday, but those checks do not clear the bank account until Tuesday, the town's checkbook would show $100,000 disbursed on Friday. In fact, the town has that money until Tuesday, so it needs to add $100,000 worth of float to the ending cash balance on Friday, Saturday, Sunday, and Monday.

To check the reliability of the forecast, a cash manager may ascertain that the annual, weekly, or daily forecasts agree. The cash position at the end of the monthly week-by-week forecast (total receipts for the month less total disbursements, which is the cash balance at the end of the final week) should equal the monthly cash position on the annual forecast.

A cash manager could also match the annual cash forecast to the annual fiscal budget to ensure that the total collections and disbursements seem reasonable. An annual forecast will probably differ in some respects from the budget because most budgets usually include collections that the treasury will not receive until the following year, and they do not include present cash flows from the past year's budget. Fiscal budgets may also include reserves and other commitments that do not necessarily result in cash outflows. Given these differences, an annual cash forecast should approximate but not equal the fiscal budget.

Adjustments to Forecasts 5.5

Undoubtedly adjustments will be made to a community's cash forecast system after it has been implemented. The following adjustments might be expected:

- *Permanent increases or decreases in cash,* such as changes in the tax rate, final payments on loans, and supplementary budgets.
- *Periodic effects,* such as a shift from a weekly payroll to a biweekly payroll.
- *One-time effects,* such as the sale of an asset, the receipt of a federal grant, an abatement award, or the issuance of a note. In particular, cash flows for construction projects are notoriously hard to forecast accurately.

Adjustments to forecasts should be made only if the change or cumulative change is large enough to affect a cash investment or borrowing decision. Minor changes can often be ignored.

5.6 Forecasting for Large Governments

The following schedule shows how forecasts would be used by a large city that operates anual, monthly, and weekly cash forecasts. A large city was chosen for this illustration because its description shows how information on all forecasts fit together (Exhibit 5.G flowcharts this process).

At the beginning of the fiscal year, a money manager:

- Generates an annual cash forecast, month-by-month, for the upcoming year.
- Takes the monthly segments of the annual forecast and generates the upcoming month's forecast, week-by-week.
- Generates the upcoming week's forecast, day-by-day, from the weekly forecast in the monthly forecast and from estimated check clearance times.
- Determines an investment strategy for the upcoming year based on the new cash forecasts and on predictions of market conditions.

The money manager then begins the day-to-day operation of forecasts, which includes the comparison of forecasted to actual results. At the end of each day, a manager:

- Enters the actual daily collected balance onto the weekly forecast.
- Calculates the variance between the actual and forecasted collected balances and, after examining the remaining forecast for the week, determines the probable available cash for the next day and adjusts the weekly forecast for any major deviations.
- Makes buy or sell decisions for short-term investments to meet upcoming cash needs.

At the end of each week, the money manager compares the actual results to the forecast and adjusts the investment strategy to meet changing needs. The money manager:

- Enters the week's actual cash results in the monthly forecast.
- Generates next week's forecast, day-by-day, from the variance of actual and forecasted cash results and the upcoming week's prediction on the monthly forecast.
- Adjusts the monthly forecast for any major deviations in actual results from forecasted.
- Re-examines 30-day and 90-day investments in light of current cash results and forecasts.

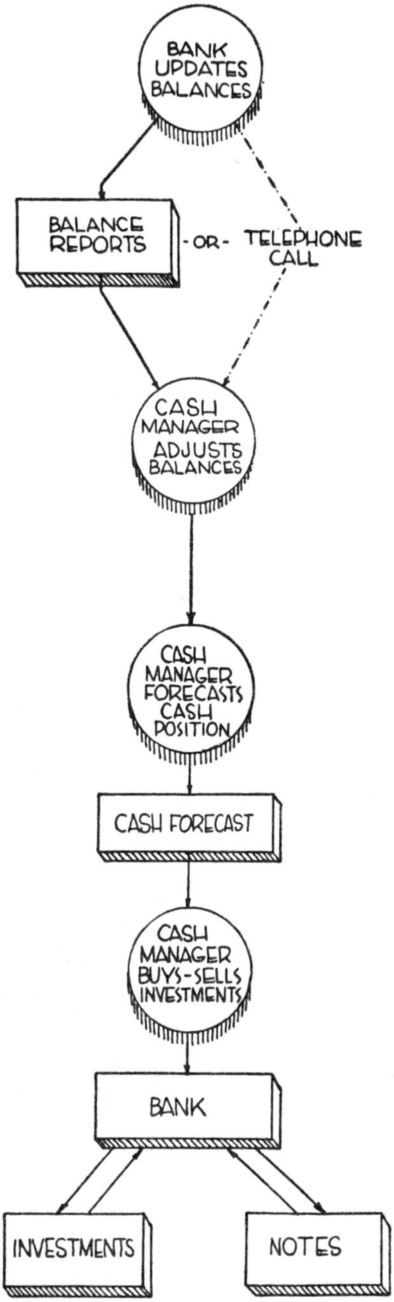

- Bank computers update government accounts daily for checks presented for payment (debits) and funds collected (credits).

- Bank communicates account balances to cash manager by computer-generated reports or by telephone. Cash balances reported as either bank ledger balances or available balances.

- Cash manager assesses cash balances in each account. On the basis of that data, CM adjusts balances of each collection and disbursement account to meet minimum compensating balances. This process includes:
  - the transfer of all excess funds from collection accounts to the central account (by wire or DTC),
  - the replenishment of funds (debit authorizations) in disbursement accounts to bring accounts to compensating balance levels (by wire)--note: these steps may be automatic after specific arrangements have been made with the bank.

- Cash manager forecasts tomorrow's cash needs from information on current balances and estimates of tomorrow's collections and disbursements:
  - estimates tomorrow's collections from estimated availability of new deposits and wire transfers
  - estimates tomorrow's disbursements from clearing schedule of items disbursed.

- On the basis of the forecast, CM initiates further transfer orders to buy or sell investments, borrow short-term funds, or repay short-term loans. Makes decisions before banks and money markets close (usually 3 p.m. or 3:30 p.m.). The ending cash position ensures that:
  - adequate cash is available to meet upcoming payments and compensating balance requirements, and
  - the maximum amount of funds are invested.

EXHIBIT 5.G / Daily Forecasting Cycle

At the end of each month the money manager updates the annual forecast and, if necessary, changes the investment and borrowing strategies. The money manager:

- Enters the actual month's cash results in the annual forecast.
- Generates next month's forecast, week-by-week, from the variance between forecast and actual cash results and the upcoming month's forecast.
- Adjusts the annual forecast for any major deviations.
- Re-examines the investment strategy for 30 days and longer and may buy or sell longer-term securities.

5.7 A Few Tips on Forecasting

Err on the side of conservatism. The best forecasts are the most accurate ones, so cash managers should attempt to predict the most likely outcomes in the upcoming fiscal year. However, in areas of uncertainty, they should err on the side of conservatism. It is much worse to run out of cash than it is to lose pennies because every investment is not extended to its fullest maturity. The government adage is true here: "One failure is worth a thousand successes."

Concentrate on forecasting major items. If payroll items make up the bulk of a town's expenditures, town managers should concentrate on understanding those payments and not worry so much about the timing of recreation fees.

Keep forecasts simple. Cash officials should not do any more than is necessary to develop a usable forecast. If major expenditures occur on a weekly basis, it is probably not necessary to focus on a daily forecast. The forecast should not round amounts to any less than $1,000. It is unlikely that a town would find an investment instrument in a denomination of $139. The accurate approximation of forecasts depends on the experience of the cash manager.

Retain the documentation for the forecasts. The town should keep whatever calculations were used to forecast cash flows available for referral. These worksheets should not be discarded, for they are used to make adjustments in later forecasts. For example, if a town forecasted the receipt of $500,000 in state aid for the month of March but received only $200,000, the town manager needs to know what portion was not received. Then the town may approach the department or state officials to find out when the funds will be received and how much the town may expect.

5.8 The Reconciliation System

A town needs to reconcile its cash management records with its actual investments and cash balances. This should be done at least monthly so that errors are caught before correction becomes difficult and before mistakes cause errors in cash management decisions.

To reconcile the books, the town needs an inventory of all investments, which is provided by the bank or by the institution in which the town stores its securities. It also needs an inventory of all cash on hand, copies of bank statements, and the check register that records all checks disbursed and all deposits mailed.

The formula for reconciling the books is fairly simple:

$$\frac{\text{Ending cash balance}}{\text{(cash management records)}} = \begin{array}{l}\text{Cash in treasury} + \text{(Cash per bank statements} \\ - \text{Outstanding checks} + \text{deposits in transit)} \\ + \text{Investment principal}\end{array}$$

Any discrepancies are resolved by reconciling the difference between cash and investments and the book balance to the outstanding checks or the deposits in transit. Like reconciling the home checkbook, this procedure is necessary to detect recording errors, unauthorized payments on the town's account, or mistakes committed by the bank. Many banks provide an account reconciliation service, but if a town uses more than one bank, it should ensure that all the banks follow the same procedure.

Short-Term Investing 6

The local treasurer who has consolidated all idle funds invests these funds to earn nontax revenue for the community. This chapter discusses short-term investments and money markets, then shows how to develop and execute a strategy for the investment of idle cash balances.

The first part of the chapter discusses the names and trading characteristics of different money market instruments and the factors, such as yield and liquidity, used to assess an instrument's value as an investment. The section explains each money market instrument, how it is created, its terms, its risk, and its attractiveness to those managing municipal portfolios.

With these facts available, a community can then develop its own investment strategy, using in particular the cash forecast described in chapter 5. Section 6.2 shows how to plan an investment strategy, when to buy and sell, how to incorporate predictions of market interest rates into an investment plan, and how to execute orders through banks and brokerage houses.

Some communities have the option of investing in a *money market fund,* which is a pool of cash from more than one investor used to purchase short-term instruments. Section 6.3 describes money funds, their advantages and disadvantages, and their procedures for investment.

Using the concept of money market funds, some state governments have created *local government investment pools* (LGIPs). These are pools of cash from local governments invested in short-term instruments. Section 6.4 describes the mechanics of LGIPs for the eleven states currently running these pools.

Communities in states that allow money market fund or LGIP investment have the option of placing funds in a mutual fund or running an investment program themselves. Mutual fund investment saves communities the effort of generating detailed forecasts, planning an investment strategy, executing buy/sell orders and performing many accounting chores. The final section of the chapter offers a simple analysis that shows when in-house management is more economical and when money fund investment is more economical.

Money Market Instruments 6.1

Money managers who invest idle cash for short periods of time invest in money market instruments or interest-bearing accounts offered by local banks. For those unfamiliar with short-term investment opportunities, or how to put idle cash to work, this section describes money markets and introduces short-term investment vehicles.

The *money market* is an electronic market place where billions of otherwise idle dollars are invested hourly in instruments with maturities from one day to a year.

Essentially, investors buy high quality, short-term IOUs offered by the U.S. government, federal agencies, banks, and large companies. Money market instruments are just various short-term loans.

In fact, there is not one money market exchange that acts as an intermediary to trade short-term instruments, as the New York and American stock exchanges do for private equities. The money market comes to life when money market instruments are traded by telephone connections between investors, brokers, and issuers. The largest investors in money markets are commercial banks, state and local governments, larger nonfinancial businesses, individuals through money funds, foreign banks, and nonbank financial institutions such as insurance companies.

Within the money market there are several "markets" that channel the trading activities of various instruments. There is not so much one money market as there are specialized markets for treasury bills, for certificates of deposit, and for other instruments.

Each market is subdivided into primary and secondary markets. Primary markets are those in which securities are sold when they are issued. After issue, secondary markets trade these instruments among investors until the security is redeemed by the issuer.

In primary markets, borrowers issue their IOUs (securities) directly to the public in an initial offer. An advertisement for an initial offering of a security, for example, would mention the selling price of the security, the maturity dates of the new issue, the announced interest rate (if any), any legal provisions, and the agent or place where the issue may be purchased. A strong primary market for an instrument means that there are many willing buyers at the time the instrument is issued.

After investors purchase a security in a primary market, they may need to sell it for cash before maturity (the time when the issuer would redeem the instrument for cash). They may sell these instruments to other investors in the secondary market. In secondary markets, holders of securities may sell their investments at any time to other buyers; in other words, they may purchase investments after they are issued or they may sell them prior to maturity. Some instruments sold to investors are not traded after issue, so the investor may receive cash only when the instrument is retired. These insruments have nonexistent or weak secondary markets.

Whenever the demand for a previously issued security is high, the secondary market is strong; whenever the demand is low, the secondary market is weak. In other words, in a strong market there are many willing buyers, and that particular instrument is considered *liquid*.

An instrument's secondary market affects the security's attractiveness as an investment for local governments. If its market is weak and the instrument is difficult to sell before maturity, then buyers risk being unable to convert that asset into cash if unforeseen needs develop. That risk, or lower investment liquidity, forces lenders to raise the yield offered to buyers. If, according to the town's cash forecast, there is a strong probability that cash will not be needed in the near future, instruments with weak secondary markets that offer higher returns may be reasonable.

Some instruments, such as Treasury bills, have strong secondary markets; others, such as commercial paper, do not. When it is fairly certain that investable funds will be available for the term of the security, local governments may invest in instruments with weak secondary markets if there is the opportunity to reap a higher return.

Characteristics of the Security 6.1.1

The value of a money market instrument to its holder depends on the terms or characteristics of the security. This section explains short-term investment characteristics and their implications for managers of local government portfolios. Each security is characterized by its maturity, liquidity, risk, denomination, and yield. It is unlikely that one instrument will offer the most attractive opportunity for all these features. Higher yielding securities, for example, carry higher risk. The local manager's challenge is to choose the most important investment characteristics given the community's investment goals, and then to choose the instruments that have those characteristics and offer the best return.

Maturity is the date on which the principal of the instrument is redeemed for cash at the par value (face value). Sales of money market instruments before maturity may result in the loss of some of the expected interest. In some cases, where secondary markets are weak, it is difficult to redeem securities at any price before maturity. Ideally, a government money manager maintains a mix of securities with different due dates so that the town may meet upcoming or unforeseen cash needs without suffering from premature sales.

Liquidity is the possibility of selling a security before maturity with a minimum penalty in the form of a price discount. When the number of willing buyers of securities on the secondary market is high, liquidity is high. Local government money managers should not invest in instruments with weak secondary markets unless they are certain that the invested funds will not be needed until the due date.

Risk is the probability that a town will lose all or some of the interest or principal of an instrument. In general, the greater the price fluctuations the greater the risk.

There are three types of risk: default risk, price risk, and liquidity risk. Default risk is the probability that the principal or par value of the security will not be redeemed at maturity. U.S. Treasury bills are considered the short-term investment least subject to default risk. Since money market instruments are almost exclusively issued by governments and blue chip companies, the default risk for other instruments is almost zero. (Still, some banks and corporations have failed with money market obligations still outstanding.)

Although a community must choose its own acceptable level of risk, most state laws confine the potential degree of risk with legal lists that restrict the range of possible investments. States have used legal lists for a variety of reasons, but primarily in the case of money market instruments to eliminate the chance that communities could lose funds on speculative investments, such as investments in foreign currencies.

Denominations are the dollar amounts in which securities are sold, such as instrument face values of $5,000, $10,000, or $1 million. In general, the larger the denomination, the higher the yield. Because an investor must risk, however slightly, larger amounts of money, larger denominations earn a higher yield.

The *yield* of a security is the annual rate of return on an investment. For maturities less than one year, the yield is the actual return for the instrument during the period that it is held, extended (or prorated) to a full year.

Yield on short-term instruments is calculated in one of two ways, depending on how an investment pays its return. An investment pays its return (1) by selling at a price less than face value (the buyer later earns money when the instrument is redeemed at face value) and/or (2) by paying interest.

In the first way, investors make money by selling the instrument at a higher price than they paid for it. If the instrument cost $982 dollars and is sold or redeemed for $1,000, then the investor reaps an investment gain of $18. When investments are redeemed at a profit, a *premium* is earned, and when they are sold at a loss, a *discount* is suffered. In other words, instruments selling at a price greater than their par value are at a premium; those selling below par are at a discount.

Some instruments, such as Treasury bills (T-bills), do not pay any interest, so the entire investment yield is earned by selling it at a higher price. T-bill prices are quoted as a percentage of the par value, which is considered 100.00 or 100% of par. All sales of T-bills are made at values less than par, since sale at a discount is the only way investors can make a profit. For example, if a T-bill quote is 98.22 asked (the buying price), then it is selling for 98.22% of its par value. That is, if the instrument's denomination is $1,000, it is selling for $982.20.

The effective annual yield for investments that are sold only at discount can be calculated with the following formula.

D = discount from par value
P = par value
Y = yield (or rate of discount)
T = days to maturity
360 = days in year
(See Exhibit 6.A.)

$$Y = \frac{D}{P} \times \frac{360}{T}$$

This is a *simple interest* calculation, which means that the effective yield will be slightly higher if the yield from this investment plus the principal are reinvested for the remainder of the year (*compound interest*).

Unlike instruments that are offered only on a discount basis, some money market instruments are interest bearing. Investors earn a return not only from the discount or premium on the face value of the instrument but also from its stated interest rate. Interest rates are paid to investors in two ways. If the instrument is registered, that is, if it is listed in the name of the holder, the paying agent for the issue merely sends the interest payment to the registered party. If the instrument is in bearer form, which means that it is redeemable when due upon presentation by the bearer, then it has coupons attached. The coupons are redeemed when the interest payments are due. For example, a security that has a par value of $1,000, an interest rate of 5%, and interest payments every six months will pay the holder $25 twice a year.

The yield of instruments that pay interest and mature in less than one year can be computed with the following formula.

Y = yield (or rate of return)
PD = adjustment for premium or discount on the face value of the instrument; the adjustment equals the par value minus the initial investment
I = dollar amount of the interest earned on the investment
B = amount of the initial investment
D = number of days the instrument is held
365 = days in year
(See Exhibit 6.A.)

$$Y = \frac{PD + I}{B} \times \frac{365}{D}$$

In general, the yield of an instrument rises when (1) the maturity is longer, (2) the liquidity is limited, (3) the risk is greater, (4) the denominations are larger, and (5) the yield is taxable.

A word about taxability. The yield on short-term instruments of state and local governments (municipal securities) is tax exempt, so those investments offer lower yields to investors. No tax on the interest and capital gain means that a lower yield on a municipal security offers to the taxpaying investor the same or better yield as taxable securities. Since state and local governments do not pay taxes, it is unwise for them to buy the securities of other state and local governments, as they would earn lower yields.

Money Market Instruments 6.1.2

Exhibit 6.A lists the characteristics of different short-term investments and their relative advantages and disadvantages for the municipal investor. This section briefly explains the nature of each investment.

Instrument	Issuer	Original Maturity	Denominations	Primary Market
U.S. Treasury Securities:				
Treasury Bills	U.S. Treasury	91, 182, 270, 360 days	$10,000-$1 million	Weekly auction
Treasury Notes	U.S. Treasury	1-10 years	$1,000-$1 million	Periodic auction
Treasury Bonds	U.S. Treasury	10-30 years	$1,000-$1 million	Periodic auction
Federal Agency Securities:				
Banks for Cooperatives Debentures	Banks for Cooperatives	180 days-3½ years	$5,000 min.	Monthly
Federal Home Loan Bank Discount Notes	Federal Home Loan Banks	30-270 days	$5,000 min.	Monthly
Federal Intermediate Credit Bank Debentures	Federal Intermediate Credit Banks	Usually 9 months	$5,000 min.	Monthly
Federal Land Bank Notes	Federal Land Banks	Months-20 years	$1,000 min.	Irreguler
Federal National Mortgage Association Notes	FNMA	1-20 years	$1,000 min.	4 times per year
FNMA Discount Notes	FNMA	30-270 days	$25,000 min.	Daily
Government National Mortgage Associaton (PCs)	GNMA	Few months-8 years	$5,000 min.	No longer issued
GNMA Pass-throughs	GNMA	12 year expected life	$25,000 min.	Varies
Negotiable Certificates of Deposit	Commercial banks	Min. 30 days	$100,000 min.	On demand
Non-negotiable CDs	Commercial banks and Savings and Loan Inst.	Min. 30 days	$1,000 min. (usually $100,000)	On demand
Bankers' Acceptances	Commercial banks	Up to 6 months	$25,000-$1 million	Daily
Repurchase Agreements	Commercial banks	Min. overnight	$100,000 min.	On demand
Time Deposits	Commercial banks and Savings and Loan Inst.	Min. 30 days	No min.	On demand
Commercial Paper: Finance Cos.	Finance company	5-270 days	$100,000-$5 million	Daily
Commercial Paper: Industrial Cos.	Industrial company	5-270 days	$100,000-$5 million	Daily
Federal Project Notes	Local agency	Up to 2 years	$25,000 min.	

1. Yield Basis

A = Discounted; 360-day year
B = Interest-bearing; 360-day year
C = Interest-bearing; 30-day month
D = Interest-bearing; 365-day year
X = Established with each agreement

2. Taxability

F = Taxed by federal government
S = Taxed by state government
L = Taxed by local government

EXHIBIT 6.A / Money Market Instruments

Secondary Market	Yield Basis[1]	Security	Taxability[2]	Comments
Very Active	A	Full faith & credit of U.S. government	F	Highest safety; short issues not always available
Very Active	D	Full faith & credit of U.S. government	F	Highest safety; short issues not always available
Very Active	D	Full faith & credit of U.S. government	F	Statuatory limit of 4.5% on coupon rate
Very Active	B and C	Obligations of member banks	F	Next to U.S. Treasury issues, highest safety
Very Active	B	Obligations of member banks	F, S	Next to U.S. Treasury issues, highest safety
Very Active	B and C	Obligations of member banks	F	Next to U.S. Treasury issues, highest safety
Very Active	B and C	Obligations of member banks	F	Next to U.S. Treasury issues, highest safety
Very Active	B and C	Guaranteed by FNMA	F, S, L	
Very Active	A	Guaranteed by FNMA	F, S, L	
Very Active	B and C	Full faith & credit of U.S. government	F, S, L	
Active		Full faith & credit of U.S. government	F, S, L	Early retirements & mortgages shorten maturity to 7 years on average, raising effective yield
Active	B	Guaranteed by issuing bank	F, S, L	
None	D	Guaranteed by issuing bank	F, S, L	
Active	A	Guaranteed by accepting bank plus collateral	F, S, L	Bid price is usually ⅛% higher than offered price
None	X	Collateral: U.S. Treasury and agency issues	F, S, L	Yield usually close to federal funds rate
None	D	Insured to $100,000 by FDIC	F, S, L	Limited interest rate; penalty for early withdrawal
None	A or B	Guaranteed by issuing corporation	F, S, L	Issuers often buy back paper at lower rate; dealers may negotiate buy-back agreements
None	A or B	Guaranteed by issuing corporation	F, S, L	
Very Active		Full faith & credit of U.S. government	F	Notes of local agencies secured by contract with federal agencies

U.S. Treasury Obligations

The United States Treasury monetizes the national debt by issuing Treasury bills, notes, and bonds. In other words, it raises funds to pay for the federal government's budget deficits by issuing these instruments. Treasury bills have maturities less than one year; Treasury notes, from one to ten years; and Treasury bonds, greater than ten years.

Treasury bills (T-bills) are considered the safest investment on the money markets because of the large volume of outstanding issues and because their backer is the federal government. If the government goes out of business, a lot of other investments are in trouble, too. Therefore, next to tax-exempt state and local government notes, T-bills carry the lowest yield.

T-bills are sold on a discount basis, and the offering price for bills is set at auctions run by the Federal Reserve System. With the face value of bills equal to 100.00 points, bills are awarded to the highest bidders (example format of bids: 98.25 and 97.625). Purchases in round lots (denominations of $1 million) earn higher yields than odd lot purchases and often carry lower transaction fees. T-bills of three months and six months (90 and 180 days respectively) are usually auctioned weekly, whereas bills of nine months and one year (270 and 360 days) are sold monthly.

T-bills may be purchased in one of three ways. First, an investor may buy them with no brokerage fee by sending a certified personal check or a cashier's check to the Bureau of the Public Debt, Securities Transactions Branch, Washington, DC 20226. The difference between the sale price and the face value is returned to the customer. Second, T-bills may be purchased directly at a Federal Reserve bank. Third, investors may buy T-bills from commercial banks, investment brokers, or investment dealers. Because of their large demand, T-bills sell quickly. (Remember, neither the Treasury Department nor the Federal Reserve Banks set the price for T-bills; prices are set by market conditions at auction.)

T-bills are highly liquid, and maturities begin at 30 days.

Treasury notes, obligations of one to ten years, pay interest in semiannual installments. The interest rate (or "coupon" rate) is determined by the lowest bid at auction, so the price of the note at issue is fairly close to or the same as the face value and the coupon rate is adjusted to the lowest offer. Face values of these notes begin at $1,000. They may be purchased in bearer form or, to ensure better security, in registered form.

Treasury bonds, obligations of longer than ten years, also pay coupon interest, which is determined by competitive bids. Federal law sets the maximum coupon rate of these bonds at 4.25%, far below market rates, so they are issued only when Congress gives permission to suspend the ceiling, which is not often.

Treasury bonds are traded in the secondary money markets when their current maturity (the time from the present to maturity) becomes one year. Investors buy T-bonds at a discount (less than the face value) to take advantage of yields of interest and capital gains for short periods of time.

Note: all Treasury obligations are eligible for wire transfer.

Federal Agency Securities

Most federal agencies that issue short-term investments were created by Congress to provide financial aid to targeted segments of the economy. Many issue money market securities to raise funds that are later loaned to sectors of the economy needing credit. Some agencies also borrow from a branch of the U.S. Treasury, the federal financing bank, which in turn borrows funds from financial markets. The largest federal agencies support housing and farming.

Many of the securities issued by federal agencies are excellent short-term investments for local governments. They are extremely secure, only slightly more risky than T-bills, since most carry the expressed or implied support of the full faith and credit of the U.S. government. Federal agency bonds, notes, and discount paper (all called *agencies*) are issued through fiscal agents who sell to dealers at negotiated prices. Dealers in turn sell agencies to investors.

Federal agency issues are attractive to some investors, although not to municipalities, because most are exempt from state and local taxation. They are also attractive because they are liquid and they carry a slightly higher interest rate than T-bills and notes and are almost as safe.

Federal Agency Securities: Loans for Mortgages

Federal Home Loan Bank (Home Loans). As the Federal Reserve Bank is owned by member commercial banks, the Federal Home Loan Bank is owned by member savings and loan institutions. The FHLB lends funds to S&Ls who then lend that money as mortgages to homeowners. To get the money to lend to S&Ls, the FHLB issues consolidated bonds (bonds issued by all twelve regional FHLBs that have a maturity greater than one year) and short-term discounted notes. These issues are backed by collateral at member S&Ls but not explicitly by the federal government, although it is difficult to believe that the government would let this part of the savings market fail.

Federal National Mortgage Association (Fannie Mae). Fannie Mae smoothes the cycles of the supply of mortgage money for government insured mortgages, such as those guaranteed by the Federal Housing Administration, the Veterans Administration, and the Farm Home Administration. When the supply of funds for these mortgages is low, Fannie Mae buys them on the secondary market, thereby increasing mortgage funds. When mortgage money is plentiful, it sells back the mortgages. To finance its operations, Fannie Mae issues discount notes. The notes are backed by the full faith and credit of Fannie Mae, a federally chartered organization owned by the dealers of Fannie Mae securities who have considerable bank and U.S. Treasury lines of credit.

Government National Mortgage Association (Ginnie Mae). Ginnie Mae, a government owned agency within the Department of Housing and Urban Development, increases the supply of home mortgage funds in areas such as low-income housing that would not otherwise be profitable by buying mortgages from private lenders and forming those mortgages into a pool. It sells shares of the pool to investors. It also buys these normally unprofitable mortgages, guarantees their payment, and resells them at a lower price to private mortgage lenders. These private mortgage lenders then sell shares (or certificates) in their pool of Ginnie Mae mortgages to private investors. These certificates have the full faith and credit of the U.S. government. Because interest payments go directly from the government to investors, less a profit for dealers, they are called *pass-through securities*.

Federal Home Loan Mortgage Corporation (Freddie Mac). Freddie Mac is the profit making branch of the FHLB. It increases the supply of mortgage money by buying mortgages from banks and S&Ls, pooling them into a single fund, adding its guarantee, then selling shares in the pool at a profit to investors.

Federal Agency Securities: Loans for Farming

To support the supply of funds for farm loans, the Farm Credit Administration supervises the Bank for Cooperatives, the Federal Intermediate Credit Bank, and the Federal Land Bank in each of twelve districts across the country. These agencies offer credit to different parts of agribusiness and raise money for these loans through the issuance of securities sold by a single agent in New York. These issues are generally backed by collateral in the form of cash, U.S. Treasury securities, or notes or obligations of those who borrow agency funds.

Banks for Cooperatives (Co-ops) make seasonal loans to farm cooperatives.

Federal Intermediate Credit Banks (FICBs) provide short-term financing for producers of crops and livestock.

Federal Land Banks lend money to farmers for mortgages.

Repurchase Agreements (Repos)

Repos are agreements between a bank that holds a money market instrument and a lender. The agreement says the holder of the money market instrument (the bank) will sell the instrument to the lender, for whatever period of time; then the lender will sell the instrument back to the holder at the same price with additional interest. Repos mostly have overnight maturities.

For example, suppose that a commercial bank, which needs cash, offers to sell a T-bill to the town of Happydale, which has a short-term cash surplus, for overnight. (The bank may need cash to meet its reserve requirement with the Fed.) To buy this agreement, the bank offers Happydale an interest rate that is competitive with current money market yields, usually a few basis points lower than the instrument's yield because of the lower risk. The next day, the bank buys back the T-bill and pays Happydale the agreed interest. The net result is that the government lends the bank overnight funds with interest. The money market instrument, in this case the T-bill, serves as collateral.

Repos may be outstanding for any period of time and may be renewable on a day-to-day basis. They are an excellent way of earning interest on funds that will be needed soon. When the bank offers instruments that are not guaranteed by the U.S. government, the interest rate on the repo is a little higher.

Repos are sometimes more attractive to local governments than direct trading of T-bills because they keep the funds they lend or invest in local banks, which in turn may maintain their loans to local business.

Bankers' Acceptances

Bankers' acceptances (BAs) arise from a series of trade transactions, but the net result is that BAs are traded like money market instruments that are bought or sold at a discount or premium (such as T-bills).

BAs emerge through an international trade transaction. For example, assume that an American company that imports foreign goods cannot pay for a foreign purchase at the present time. To receive the goods, the importer's bank writes him a letter of credit, which he gives to his foreign seller. To collect his money, the foreign merchant creates a *draft* (a check written by the seller rather than the buyer) and deposits the draft in his bank. The merchant's bank then presents the draft to the American importer's bank. If the American bank accepts the draft, it stamps "acceptance" and pays the foreign bank the funds. As with the purchase of T-bills, it does not pay the foreign bank the full face value of the draft but something less in return for this payment prior to the due date of the draft. At this moment, the BA is created.

The American bank can keep the BA as an investment. The holder of the BA makes money when the BA comes due; the bank is paid more money from the importer than the bank paid for the BA originally. Or the bank may sell the acceptance for cash. In either case the importer is required to place the proper amount of funds with the bank on the date the BA matures. If he does not, the bank must make the payment.

Thus a banker's acceptance is a loan that a corporation (in this example, the American importer) must repay on a specified due date. The lender repays the full face value of the acceptance. If not, the lender's bank must make the payment. Acceptances are sold at a discount, so when the instrument is redeemed at face value, the holder earns a profit. Banks and money market dealers sell BAs.

BAs are safe (guaranteed by major banks) and liquid. Because they arise from purchases of foreign goods, they often come in small and odd denominations.

Commercial Paper

Instead of borrowing short-term funds from banks, large corporations can borrow from money market investors by selling *commercial paper*. Commercial paper is a short-term promissory note guaranteed by the issuing corporation (usually well-known finance companies, such as the General Motors Acceptance Corporation). It is an unsecured transaction, although issuers often support sales of commercial paper with bank lines of credit, and thus investors in commercial paper should investigate credit ratings through the analyses published by Standard and Poor's or Moody's Investment Service. Because of this higher risk, commercial paper offers a higher yield.

Commercial paper is sold at discount, so yield is calculated in the same manner as that of T-bills or BAs. It is issued in one of two ways. A small number of large finance companies issue paper by direct placement with large investors. Other issuers, such as industrial companies, sell their paper to dealers who then sell it to investors. Local governments can buy commercial paper from the issuing corporations, from banks, or from money market dealers.

Commercial paper is attractive because it offers high yields, but since it has a weak secondary market investors usually buy commercial paper only when funds will be available until the paper matures.

Certificates of Deposit

Banks also borrow short-term funds from money markets by selling certificates of deposit (CDs). The Federal Reserve's *Regulation Q* allows banks to offer competitive interest rates on amounts exceeding $100,000 (interest rates on amounts less than $100,000 are limited by Congress). Banks issue CDs for a minimum of 30 days, in 30-day increments thereafter, although the strong secondary CD market allows sales prior to maturity. CDs pay interest; therefore their yields are calculated using the interest formula in the first section. These negotiable CDs (CDs that can be sold or traded) can be purchased from a bank or a dealer, although a bank can tailor the maturity to the customer's specifications.

Nonnegotiable CDs (CDs that have no secondary market) are also issued by banks and S&Ls. Maturities and interest rates may be set by borrower and lender, but liquidation before maturity may involve penalties.

Other Investment Opportunities (Outside the Money Market)

Commercial Bank Savings Accounts. Savings accounts at commercial banks usually offer the lowest yields of any investment opportunity. In early 1979, when money market rates reached 10%, savings accounts paid 5¼%. Maximum rates on savings accounts are set by Congress, so rates are unable to respond to economic changes. At most commercial banks, amounts up to $100,000 are insured by the Federal Deposit Insurance Corporation for government units (1) that are created by federal or state statutes and (2) that use the account only for their own purposes. If town funds are deposited in commercial savings accounts, they should be adequately insured. *Time deposits* are special commercial savings accounts that pay a slightly higher interest rate but stipulate that funds may not be withdrawn before a specified period of time (commonly 30 days). Time deposits also require an advance notice to withdraw funds, and premature withdrawal results in an interest penalty. Poor liquidity and low rates usually make time deposits unattractive investments to municipalities.

Savings Bank Savings Accounts. Savings bank savings accounts have the same advantages and disadvantages of commercial bank savings accounts, except that savings bank rates are ¼% to ½% higher. The Federal Savings and Loan Insurance Corporation insures government accounts up to $100,000.

Mutual Savings Banks. Mututal savings banks are savings banks that are owned by their depositors, but they offer the same investment opportunity as savings banks. They are insured either by the FDIC or by their state's insurance agency. Some are not allowed to receive deposits from anyone other than individuals and nonprofit institutions. Governments are not allowed to use negotiable order of withdrawal (NOW) accounts (checking accounts that pay interest), which mutual savings banks offer individual depositors or nonprofit institutions.

In-house Investment Management 6.2

The investment management of short-term funds is the effort that bears the fruit of an efficient money management program: extra income from invested funds. This section of the chapter describes a fairly simple process to plan and execute a local investment program. Smaller communities may not have to manage short-term investments if their state allows money fund investment or operates a local government investment pool (the economics of that decision are described in section 6.4) This section describes the decision process for communities who manage their own investments.

Before a community implements investment decisions, it must first define an investment policy that gives preference to certain investment characteristics. This policy determines the type of short-term investments that the community later purchases.

In ranking the most preferable investment characteristics, some might assume that high yield is the most important objective of investment policy. However, that is not always the case. Government financial officers more often identify objectives in the following order of importance.

1. To preserve the amount of the initial investment (capital preservation).
2. To ensure high liquidity so cash is available to meet disbursement needs (liquidity).
3. To earn the highest return on invested funds (yield).

The first two objectives are almost synonomous. No community will buy an investment that risks its funds or fails to produce cash to meet payments. This list means that a town's portfolio manager (usually the town treasurer) narrows the choices to investments that are safe. Then he picks investments that mature at the time when the town is likely to need the cash. Among these final options, he finds investments with the highest yields.

Capital preservation is possible with almost any type of money market investment, since money markets accept instruments only from the U.S. government, federal agencies, banks, and blue-chip companies. Some investors prefer to lower that risk

	July Est. Act. Var.	Aug. Est. Act. Var.	Sept. Est. Act. Var.	Oct. Est. Act. Var.	Nov. Est. Act. Var.	Dec. Est. Act. Var.
Total cash receipts[1]	1280	960	960	6720	3200	2880
Total cash disbursements[1]	2400	1400	1400	3200	3300	3300
Net cash flow[2]	(-)1120	(-)440	(-)440	3520	(-)100	(-)420
Beginning cash balance	360	440	750	310	1830	1730
Plus: investments maturing	1200	750				
Less: note repayments				(-)2000		
Ending cash balance[3]	440	750	310	1830	1730	1310
Less: compensating balances	250	250	250	250	250	250
Amount available for investment (required by borrowing)[4]	190	500	60	1580	1480	1060

	Jan. Est. Act. Var.	Feb. Est. Act. Var.	Mar. Est. Act. Var.	Apr. Est. Act. Var.	May Est. Act. Var.	June Est. Act. Var.	Total Est. Act. Var.
Total cash receipts	1280	960	960	6720	2880	3200	32,000
Total cash disbursements	2000	2000	2000	2800	3200	3000	30,000
Net cash flow	(-)720	(-)1040	(-)1040	3920	(-)320	200	2,000
Beginning cash balance	1310	590	(-)450	(-)1490	2430	2110	360
Plus: investments maturing							1,950
Less: note repayments							(-)2,000
Ending cash balance	590	(-)450	(-)1490	2430	2110	2310	2,310
Less: compensating balances	250	250	250	250	250	250	
Amount available for investment (required by borrowing)	340	(-)700	(-)1740	2180	1860	2060	

Notes:

This is a cash forecast for a community with a $30 million annual budget.

1. See Exhibit 5.D for a detailed history of these forecasted cash receipts and disbursements.
2. Net cash flow = total cash receipts − total cash disbursements. In this example, the community collects property taxes in October and April. Other collections and disbursements are forecast as shown.
3. Ending cash balance = net cash flow + beginning cash balances + investments maturing − note repayments. This example assumes that investments maturing in July and August will provide available cash amounts of $1,200,000 and $750,000 respectively. It also assumes that a $2,000,000 tax anticipation note comes due at the end of October.
4. Amount available for investment (required by borrowing) = ending cash balance − compensating balances. The community has agreed to leave $250,000 of compensating balances at a local bank to pay for banking services. The amount available for investment or required by borrowing is graphically displayed and discussed in Exhibit 6.C.

EXHIBIT 6.B / Annual Cash Forecast

even more by buying only government or agency issues, which still offer attractive and competitive yields.

To ensure that cash is available to meet disbursement needs, local officials first identify and anticipate cash needs using the forecasting techniques described in chapter 5. In a cash forecast, a town manager takes receipts less disbursements to arrive at a cash surplus or deficit. Exhibit 6.B shows a cash forecast that arrives at net investable balances. If the forecast predicts a cash deficit, then the town should plan to borrow rather than invest.

With a cash surplus, the town subtracts the amounts of its compensating balances with banks. Since these balances remain in bank accounts to pay for banking services, they are not availble for investment. The town also subtracts a cash reserve or

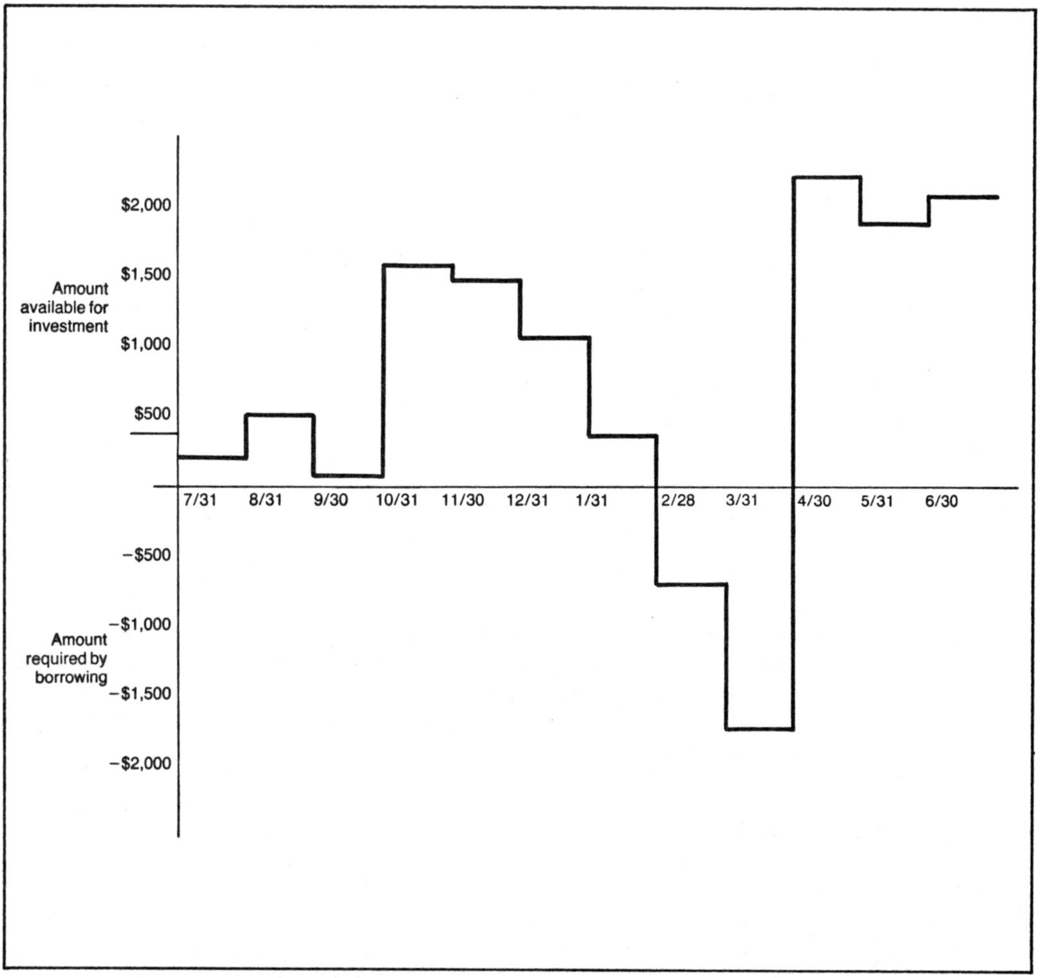

EXHIBIT 6.C / Graph of Investable Balances

cushion. The cushion ensures that the town will have enough free cash available to meet an upcoming, unforeseen need. As long as no need develops, the cushion can be invested nightly in repurchase agreements. The size of the cushion will vary with the certainty of the forecast. If the forecast is made with great certainty about the timing and amount of collections or payments, then the cushion can be smaller than the cushion needed if a forecast is made with less certainty. Some towns keep between one-half week's and one week's disbursements in this cushion.

The cash surplus less compensating balances and a reserve cushion is the cash available for investment. To visualize the amount and duration of available funds, the town treasurer may plot cash available for investment on a graph that spans six months to one year (see Exhibit 6.C). If the town's forecasts are divided into monthly segments, then the graph shows how much is available each month for investment.

With this information, the town manager buys the highest-yield securities from among those that the town has previously approved for investment. This approved list should ensure that the town's investment is safe. The forecast ensures that enough cash is on hand to meet town needs, so the town manager can choose money market investments that offer the highest yield.

There are two rules of thumb that help investors attain high yields. First, investments with longer maturities and higher denominations usually pay higher returns. By using the graph in Exhibit 6.C, a town manager can see that the town might have a certain amount of money available for an extended length of time. For example, the town might have $100,000 for six months. In normal circumstances the town does best to invest those funds for the entire six months in an instrument with a $100,000 denomination. Investment of that money in three-month or one-month intervals or $10,000 instruments will probably yield a lower return. It is emphasized that for a town to schedule its maturities to pay high returns, it needs to develop a cash forecast.

The second rule is that the investment manager should have some sense of whether interest rates are likely to rise or fall in the near future. Exhibit 6.D shows the history of short-term interest rates since 1930. If interest rates are expected to rise, the town manager should buy investments with shorter maturities. That way, cash will not be tied up in lower-yielding investments with long maturities, and the town will have cash to buy instruments when interest rates are higher. If interest rates are about to fall, the town should buy investments with the longest possible maturities to *lock in* high interest rates. Again, to implement an effective investment strategy, the town needs a cash forecast to know how much money will be available and for how long.

Some communities require that a governing board, such as a city council, approve each security acquisition before purchase. This effectively prohibits day-to-day investment, so Exhibit 6.E shows a model investment resolution that, when adopted, gives local treasurers authority to make short-term investment decisions.

6.2.1 Understanding Money Market Rates

One important goal for investors is to pursue the highest possible yields from investments. Investors maximize their yields by buying instruments with short

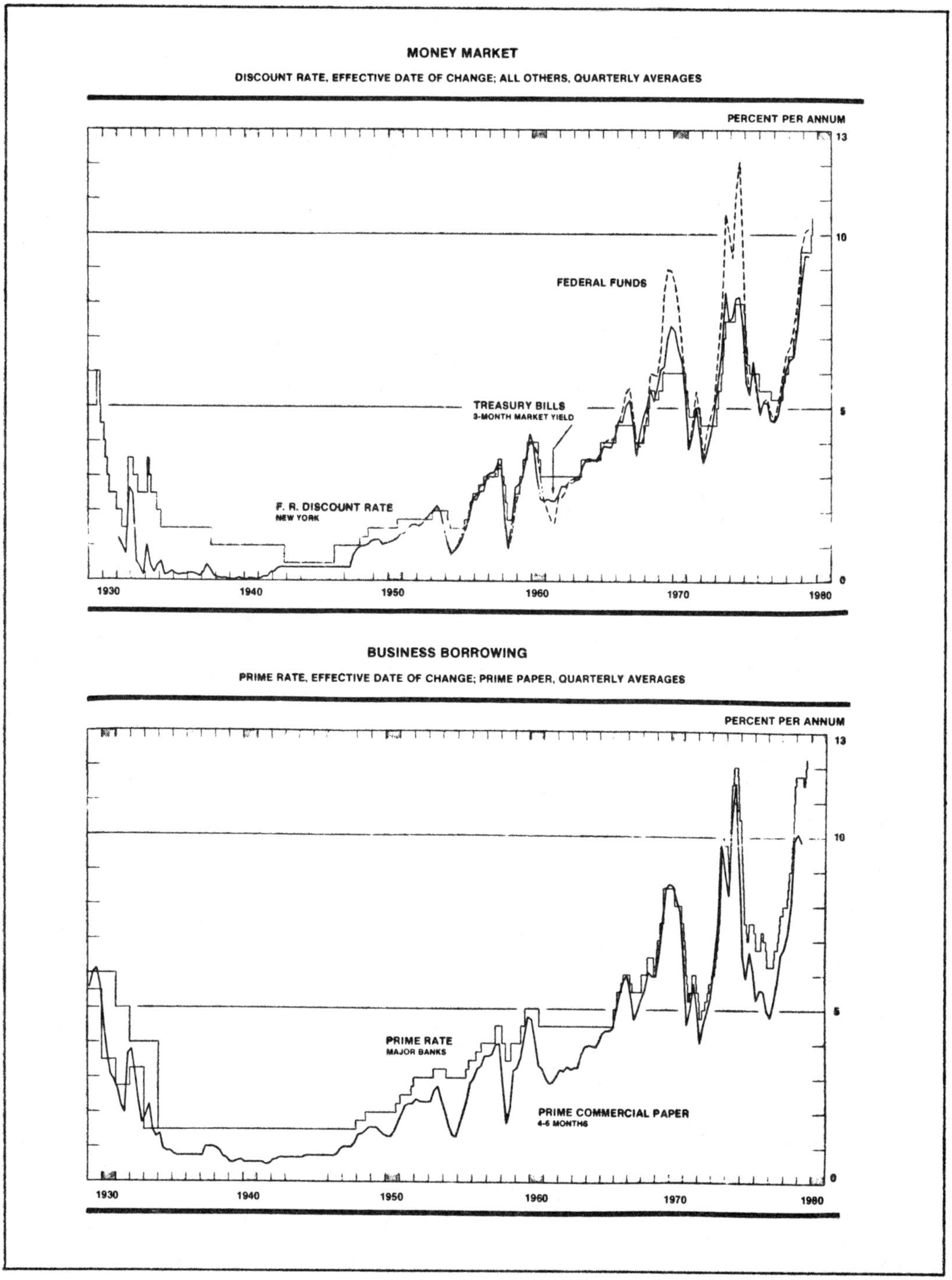

EXHIBIT 6.D / Short-Term Interest Rates

WHEREAS it is in the public interest of the citizens of ___A___ to invest and reinvest any money of ___A___ which is under the control of ___B___ in bonds or other obligations for the payment of principal and interest of which the full faith and credit of the United States of America are pledged, or in obligations of the Federal National Mortgage Association, Federal Land Banks, Federal Intermediate Credit Banks, or Banks for Cooperatives, issued pursuant to Acts of Congress or in banker's acceptances that meet investment policy requirements or in repurchase agreements or to deposit said moneys in any bank or banks in ___C___ in interest-bearing time deposits and/or savings accounts; and

WHEREAS it is appropriate to designate one of the legal officers of ___A___ to make such investments and reinvestments of such money; and

WHEREAS such investment and reinvestment of such money is presently authorized under the laws of ___C___, ___D___;

NOW, THEREFORE, BE IT RESOLVED by ___B___ of ___A___:

Section 1. That the ___E___ of ___A___ be, and he is hereby authorized and empowered to invest and reinvest any money which is under the control of ___B___ in the following:

(a) Bills, certificates of indebtedness, notes, and bonds of the United States of America, and any agreement to purchase and resell these securities on an overnight basis (repurchase agreements); or

(b) The bonds or debentures issued under the authority of the Federal Farm Loan Act, as amended (U.S.C. title 12, section 851-921); the Federal Home Loan Bank Act, as amended (U.S.C. title 12, section 1421-1449); the Home Owners Loan Act, as amended (U.S.C. title 12, section 1461-1468); or

(c) Obligations issued, assumed, or guaranteed by the Federal Land Bank or Federal Intermediate Credit Bank, pursuant to the provisions of the Act of Congress known as the Federal Farm Loan Act (U.S.C. title 12, section 641-1012) (as amended, or by or for any bank for cooperatives pursuant to the Act of Congress known as the Farm Credit Act of 1933 (U.S.C. title 12, section 636 et seq.).

Section 2. That ___E___ be, and he is hereby authorized and empowered, in addition to any other investment rights and powers he may hold or possess, to invest and reinvest money which is under the control of ___B___ in certificates of deposit issued by banks and savings banks incorporated under the laws of ___C___ and in offices in ___C___. Such investments shall be in such amounts, and for such terms as ___E___ deems proper. The placement of such investments shall be on a competitive bid arrangement and shall include no less than two solicitation requests.

Section 3. That ___E___ be, and he is hereby authorized and empowered, in addition to any other investment rights and powers he may hold and possess, to invest and reinvest any money which is under the control of ___B___ in banker's acceptances issued by banks incorporated under the laws of ___C___ and in national bank associations. ___E___ shall purchase banker's acceptances only from banks meeting all financial ratio requirements outlined in (resolution number) ________ approved by ___B___ on ___(date)___.

Section 4. That ___E___ be, and he is hereby authorized and empowered, in addition to any other investment rights and powers he may hold and possess, to invest and reinvest any money which is under the control of ___B___ in commercial paper issued by corporations incorporated in any State or Commonwealth of the United States of America. ___E___ shall invest in commercial paper rated at the price of purchase within the two best classifications established by not less than two standard rating services and which matures not more than 270 days from the date of purchase. Not more than ________% of any fund's total investments shall be invested in commercial paper at any time. The purchase of commercial paper of any one corporation shall be limited to 5% of that corporation's total outstanding commercial paper or $3,000,000, whichever is less.

EXHIBIT 6.E / Sample Investment Resolution

Section 5. That __E__ be, and he is hereby authorized and empowered, in addition to any other investment rights and powers he may hold or possess, to invest and reinvest any money which is under the control of __B__ in interest-bearing time deposits and/or savings accounts in banks and savings banks and associations incorporated under the laws of __C__ and in national banking associations having their principal banking offices in __C__. Such interest-bearing accounts shall be in such amounts for such rate and for such terms as may be agreed upon from time to time by __A__ and participating banks or savings associations.

Section 6. That __E__ be, and he is hereby authorized and empowered, in addition to any other investment rights and power he may hold or possess, to invest one or more combined investment funds administered by the state treasurer with the advice of the Investment Advisory Council for the purpose of investing funds of __C__, trust funds, and funds under the custody of agencies, authorities, commissions, boards, political subdivisions and other public units within __C__.

Section 7. That __E__ be, and he is hereby authorized and empowered to sell any of the securities acquired pursuant to authority granted in Sections 1, 2, 3, 4, 5, and 6 of this Resolution, and he is further authorized and empowered to protect the interests of the funds so invested including the exercise of exchange privileges which may be granted with respect to maturing securities in cases where the securities offered in exchange meet the requirements for initial investment.

Section 8. All interest derived from investments under this Resolution shall become a part of the funds invested and in cases where funds have been commingled to obtain the maximum return on investment, the fund is to receive a pro-rata share of the earnings based on factoring the original investment by fund and applying this factor to the total earnings received on the investment.

Section 9. This Resolution shall be in full force and effect from and after its passage, approval, and publication according to the law.

BY ORDER OF __B__

OF __A__

Legend:

A The jurisdiction, such as Centerdale City, Kansas.
B The governing board, such as the city council, county commissioners or board of aldermen.
C The State of the jurisdiction, such as the State of Kansas.
D The State code or law that regulates local investments, such as Article 53, Section 12.
E The local official responsible for invesment management, such as the Director of Finance or Town Treasurer.

maturities when interest rates are likely to rise and instruments with long maturities when interest rates are likely to fall.

Essentially, the yield or rate of investments is the price that borrowers are willing to pay for the short-term use of funds. This short description of money market rates does not explain all the factors that cause interest rates to rise or fall. Although some of the factors influencing interest rate fluctuations can be explained, much judgment is involved. If future money market rates were known with certainty, then investment policy and operations would be uniform and simple.

What economic factors cause interest rates to change? Market rates for money rise and fall with the supply and demand for short-term funds. As with other commodities, interest rates rise when demand for short-term funds increases or the supply of those funds decreases. Likewise, interest rates fall when demand slackens or supply expands.

Business cash demand. The effect of loan demand on short-term interest rates is seen as business varies its needs for funds. During business expansions, companies need funds to finance working capital, so they borrow funds from banks or issue other forms of financing such as commercial paper. When many people want to buy the same amount of goods (in this case, money), the cost (in this case, the interest rate) rises. The reverse happens during industrial production lags or during a business contraction, when fewer short-term loans are needed because inventory is liquidated to provide funds. The reduced demand lowers interest rates. Some of the standard indicators of business' demand for short-term funds are the number of new orders for durable goods, contracts and orders for plant and equipment, the rise or fall of inventory levels, industrial production, and the current levels of commercial and industrial loans.

Money market rates also rise when the supply of funds contracts (during *tight* money). Rates rise during inflation because more borrowers bid for fewer funds, and because investors seek a higher rate of return to compensate for the declining value of their cash.

The Federal Reserve. The Federal Reserve Bank changes the supply of money in three ways: by buying and selling short-term investments, changing the discount rate, and adjusting reserve requirements. The most effective and direct method is through the Open Market Trading Desk in New York City where the Federal Reserve Bank directly buys and sells securities in the financial markets. When the Federal Reserve buys securities, say from commercial banks, it gets the security and gives the banks funds which the banks may lend. This increases the supply of loanable funds and thus decreases the interest rates. To reduce the supply of funds, the Fed sells securities; then interest rates rise.

The Fed also affects the supply of funds through its discount window and its reserve requirements. Banks may borrow money from the Fed's discount window. To reduce the supply of funds, the Fed raises the interest rate at the discount window or restricts the amount that banks may borrow. As a result, fewer banks borrow from the Fed, thereby curtailing the supply of loanable funds and causing interest rates to rise. As important, changes in the discount rate signal changes in Federal Reserve policy, and financial markets react to these changes. If the discount rises, markets assume the Fed is pursuing a *tight money* policy (reducing the supply of funds), so rates will rise.

The Fed further reduces or increases the money supply by raising or lowering the reserve requirement. If it raises the reserve requirement (section 4.9), it increases the amount of funds that banks must keep on hand at the Fed and thus reduces the supply of funds available for investments. Raising the reserve requirement raises the interest rates.

Market tone. Interest rates are affected not only by business conditions, Federal Reserve policy, and the like, but also by the way that money market participants perceive the effects of those conditions and policies on short-term rates. So much of the market tone depends on the psychology of its participants: their interpretation of changes in governmental monetary policy, fiscal policy, debt management and international policy, as well as political and social events, may have a major impact on trading. For example, a signal by the Federal Reserve that it plans to reduce the supply of money may cause interest rates to rise even though actual policy has yet to affect supply or interest rates. The market is merely anticipating that effect. Technical analysis, as well as the expectations and anticipations of market participants, changes market tone.

Economic conditions. Interest rate volatility accelerates or decelerates with the condition of the national economy. During periods of national stability, such as the 1950s, interest rates fluctuate little. The reverse was true of the 1970s. Many national statistics measure the health of the economy: gross national production, international balance of payments, unemployment, inflation. Until recently, high unemployment meant a reduced demand for short-term funds by business, which in turn lowered interest rates. The same was true of inflation. Information and comment on the economic outlook is available in the economic sections of newspapers or business magazines.

These are the major factors that analysts watch to predict the course of interest rates. No busy municipal treasurer will be able to keep apace of this type of information, but given this background information, and analyses of professional economists, and the treasurer's own financial intuition, he should have a rough idea of where interest rates might go.

Trading Money Market Instruments 6.2.2

Communities may buy or sell money market instruments in one of two ways. First, they may bargain directly with the institution issuing the security. For example, banks may borrow money by offering new repurchase agreements or certificates of deposit directly to local governments. In buying these investments, communities may avoid paying transaction fees charged by intermediaries. In other cases, communities may also purchase Treasury bills and notes issued by the Federal Reserve Bank.

Second, communities may arrange sales through a third party: either a broker or a dealer. A broker buys and sells securities for a client's account and charges a commission for performing each transaction. If a local official wanted to buy money market instruments, for example, he could phone the municipality's broker with instructions to purchase $300,000 worth of T-bills maturing on 10/30/81. The broker would then call a willing seller and arrange the transaction. For this service, the broker charges a commission or transaction fee that is a percentage of the dollar amount traded. Since it takes the same amount of research and time to process a transaction for $1 million as it does a transaction for $100 million, brokers' commissions decrease with larger orders. That is, transaction costs are lower per dollar of investment with larger orders.

Brokers offer clients a full range of services, including investment advice. A local official is likely to call a broker and say, "I have $300,000 to invest for thirty days. What investments do you suggest?" That advice helps local officials decide what to buy or sell. Exhibit 6.F shows a typical daily money market report produced by banks or brokerage houses. Local officials can use this form to tabulate current investment opportunities. Both banks and investment houses serve as brokers for money market investments. Since it is impractical for brokers to charge each customer for the use of advisory services, brokers charge higher commissions above the transaction costs on all purchases and sales, whether or not investment advice is sought or used by the client.

The alternative is to use *discount brokers,* who offer no advisory services but merely process buy and sell orders. Their transaction fees are lower than those of brokers; they are used by investors who perform their own market and investment analysis.

Some investors have had bad experiences with brokers who advised the client to buy and sell securities frequently. This practice, called *churning,* increases the investor's transaction costs (and the broker's income) with little gain, and sometimes a loss, to the investor.

Investors may also purchase securities through dealers. Dealers buy and sell securities for their own account, so their profit comes from selling a security for more than the amount they paid. A broker trades using client money, but a dealer uses his own money to buy securities. In the extreme, investors should be wary of firms that act as both brokers and dealers. Unless there is a high level of investor sophistication, brokers might advise the client to buy a security that the firm is selling from its dealer inventory. This is an apparent conflict of interest because the firm is selling the client a security that it makes money on as a dealer. A broker's only interest should be the wisest investment advice for his client.

6.2.3 Using Banks as Brokers

Banks offer a wide range of investment services, including savings accounts and the sale of CDs and repos. In addition, a bank can serve as a local government's broker in the secondary CD market and the purchase and sale of Treasury obligations.

	1 Mo.	2 Mo.	3 Mo.	4 Mo.	5 Mo.	6 Mo.	9 Mo.	12 Mo.
U.S. Treasury securities Bills Notes								
U.S. Government agency issues Banks for Cooperatives Federal Home Loan Bank Federal Intermediate Credit Bank Federal Land Bank FNMA discount notes GNMA pass-throughs								
Repurchase agreements Cityville Bank & Trust Co. Union Street Bank Hoover National Bank								
Certificates of deposit Cityville Bank & Trust Co. Union Street Bank Hoover National Bank								
New York City (1MM) (100 MM)								
Secondary CD's								
Commercial Paper Direct Dealer								
Bankers' Acceptances Cityville Bank & Trust Co.								
Term fed funds								
Other repurchase agreements								
Fed funds EST Open Open								

EXHIBIT 6.F / Table of Money Market Rates

Since local governments keep their cash accounts in banks, banks are convenient brokers. A single telephone call enables local treasurers to transfer funds among accounts or authorize the acquisition of a CD or a repo. Confirmations of transactions are prepared by the bank and sent to the local treasurer, as are summaries of all account activity. Banks will also store purchased securities, which dramatically reduces the risk of having investments lost or stolen (see Exhibit 6.G for a sample bank custodian agreement).

To evaluate the investment opportunities of banks, communities should ask the following questions:

- What fees does the bank charge for buying U.S. Treasury obligations for local governments?
- What fees does the bank charge for buying or selling an investment instrument on the secondary market?
- What interest rate does the bank offer on CDs and repurchase agreements, and how willing is the bank to provide these types of investments?
- What denominations of CDs and repos does the bank offer?
- What maturities does the bank offer for CDs and repos? The shorter the maturity, the more possibility to invest, although at slightly lower yields than those of longer maturity.
- Is there any lapse of time between the date of redemption for CDs and repos and the date that the funds become available for municipal use? If so, is any interest lost?
- Do the bank's investment instruments yield interest on the basis of a 360-day year or a 365-day year? The 360-day basis produces higher daily interest.
- How willing is the bank to experiment with the community in devising investment packages and procedures that enable the municipality to earn the most interest at the greatest possible convenience?
- Does the bank offer any technical advisory services?
- How does the bank charge the municpality for various investment services? If it requires the maintenance of minimum balances, how much investment income would be lost?

6.2.4 Using Brokerage Firms

Currently, a relatively small proportion of local treasurers make extensive use of brokerage services. Like banks, brokerage firms can act as a local government's agent in acquiring U.S. Treasury obligations, arranging repos, and making transactions on the secondary market for CDs and other instruments. Look under "Investment Securities" in the yellow pages.

Date

Cityvale Bank & Trust Company
One Center Plaza
Centerville City, Kansas

Dear Sirs,

Centerville City (the City) expects to purchase and sell U.S. Treasury bills, issues of federal agencies, certificates of deposit, repurchase agreements, banker's acceptances, or other securities from time to time through or from Cityvale Bank & Trust Co. (the Bank). The following conditions will govern any purchases or sales.

1. All orders for purchases or sales of securities shall be confirmed by the City in writing and signed by the Director of Finance.
2. On the delivery date, the Bank shall charge the City's master bank account (account number 030-428-97) for the cost of the securities purchased or credit the account for the proceeds of sales or collections at maturity.
3. The Bank shall hold securities purchased by the City in custody for the City's account. The Bank shall acknowledge the receipt of these securities in writing to the Director of Finance within one working day after the delivery date.
4. The Bank shall not deliver, assign, hypothecate, pledge, or otherwise encumber or dispose any securities held by the Bank in custody for the City's account unless authorized in writing by the Director of Finance. However, the Bank may deliver securities against payment at maturity, or upon instructions of the Director of Finance to a purchaser after a sale, without further authorization of the Director of Finance.
5. The City's Director of Finance and independent auditor have the right to inspect at any time any securities held by the Bank in custody for the City's account.
6. This letter shall apply to any securities now held by the bank in custody for the City's account, and it supersedes any previous instructions with respect to any such securities.

If these conditions are acceptable to the Bank, please sign the acceptance section of the enclosed copy of this letter and return the copy to us.

Very truly yours,

____

Director of Finance
Centerville City, Kansas

Accepted for Cityvale Bank & Trust Co.

By ________________________________

Title ________________________________

Date ________________________________

EXHIBIT 6.G / Sample Custodian Agreement

Investment Position

Security	(1) Delivery date	(2) Maturity date	(3) Par value	(4) Price paid	(5) Number of instruments purchased	(6) Amount invested	(7) Interest rate	(8) Effective yield	(9) Price sold or redeemed	(10) Number of instruments sold	(11) Amount sold	(12) Interest earned
Total												

Maturities

Security	Principal Maturing On											Total
	Date	Date	Date	Date	Date	Date	Date	Date	Date	Date	Later Mat.	
	$	$	$	$	$	$	$	$	$	$	$	$
Total												

Summary of Cash and Securities

	Amount	%
Cash		
Bank A		
Bank B		
Bank C		
Total cash		
Securities		
Maturing in		
Maturing in		
Total securities		
Total cash and securities		100%

How to use the investment control form

Investment Position form (continuous)

1. Enter descriptive information on each security upon purchase. Column (6) = column (4) × column (5).
2. Enter selling information including price and interest earned, upon sale (enter split sales on separate lines). Column 11 = column 9 × column 10.
3. Keep running total of investment position on bottom line.

Maturities form (periodic)

Spread investment amounts of each purchase to the date of expected maturity or sale. The total shows how much and when investment principal will come due.

Summary of cash and securities form (periodic)

Enter current amount of securities and cash available. Form shows current liquidity and overall invested position.

EXHIBIT 6.H / Investment Control Form

Investment performance can be measured against internal or external standards. This example shows a simple method that communities can use to evaluate net investment return (the amount of income earned from investment operations).

There are three factors that affect net investment return: the amount available for investment, the efficiency of investment, and the yield earned on investment. They determine the amount of investment income:

$$\text{Amount available for investment} \times \text{Efficiency} \times \text{Yield} = \text{Net investment return}$$

Amount available for investment (AAI) is the average cash balance that is available for investment each day in interest-bearing accounts or securities, less compensating balances and other requirements. The estimate of the upcoming AAI is the bottom line of cash forecasts.

Efficiency (EFF) is the percentage of available daily cash balances that the city invests in income-earning securities. Mathematically, efficiency is expressed as follows:

$$\text{Efficiency rate} = \frac{\text{Average daily investments}}{\text{Average daily investments} + \text{Average daily cash balances}} \times 100$$

Yield (YLD) is the rate of return that the muncipality earns on its investments. The estimate for the upcoming year's yield depends on the community's prediction of interest rates and the type and maturity of proposed investment purchases (see Appendix A for a discussion of yield considerations).

An example

To show investment evaluation in action, the following example describes the investment performance of Centerdale City for the 198X fiscal year.

	AAI	×	EFF	×	YLD	=	Net return
Estimated	$4,572,300		95.00%		12.2%		$529,930
Actual	$4,322,650		96.30%		10.8%		$449,573
							$ 80,357 U

At the beginning of the fiscal year the Centerdale City treasurer predicted that the Centerdale Investment Program would produce $529,930 of nontax income for local coffers. At the end of the year, however, results were disappointing. Centerdale earned only $449,573, $80,537 less than predicted ("U" means an unfavorable variance), and the City Council and news media wanted to know why. Generally, the treasurer could see that less cash was available for investment and interest rates were lower than predicted, but how and why did these factors affect the net investment return?

An explanation of the variance

The following method, which may be used annually for external reports or quarterly for internal performance reviews, helps explain the variance between the estimated and actual investment results. It does not provide answers, but points to areas that require further investigation. There are many different ways to calculate variance; this one is standard.

The first variance calculation shows the amount of the $80,357 investment shortfall that is due to less cash being available for investment.

$$(\text{Act. AAI} - \text{Est. AAI}) \times \text{Est. EFF} \times \text{Est. YLD} = \text{Variance due to lower AAI}$$

or

$$(\$4{,}322{,}650 - \$4{,}572{,}300) \times (.9500) \times (.122) = \$28{,}934 \text{ U}$$

(continued on next page)

EXHIBIT 6.1 / How to Evaluate Short-Term Investment Performance

Almost $30,000 of the $80,000 variance is due to lower available balances, which could be explained in a number of ways. For example, net payment levels could have increased from either spending that exceeded or revenues that fell short of budgeted amounts. Also, there could have been late payments of uncontrollable receipts from the state or federal governments. Finally, the management of controllable receipts and disbursements could have lagged behind expected performance, which gives the treasurer an opportunity to examine current systems for better cash management procedures.

The second calculation shows the amount of extra funds the community earned due to increased investment efficiency.

(Act. EFF − Est. EFF) × Act. AAI × Est. YLD = Variance due to efficiency

or

(.9630 − .9500) × ($4,322,650) × (.122) = $6,856 F

The favorable variance (F) means that the city earned an extra $7,000 due to the increased efficiency of its investment program. This is good news; however, the treasurer should see that the increased efficiency did not occur because too much cash was placed in investments while balances at banks were left below compensating levels or overdrawn.

The last calculation shows the amount of the variance that is due to lower investment yield.

(Act. YLD − Est. YLD) × Act. AAI × Act. EFF = Variance due to yield

or

(.122 − .108) = ($4,322,650) × (.9630) = $58,278 U

The largest variance is due to a disappointing yield. This could have happened if interest rates did not reach their forecasted levels. That would be apparent when actual yields are compared with forecasted yields for each type of investment.

A lower yield could also come from a lag in portfolio performance, which has three causes. First, the city could have purchased the wrong maturities. It could have bought six-month investments when cash was needed three months later, thereby forcing the city to sell investments prematurely.

Second, the mix of investments might have caused a lower yield. For example, the city could have placed funds in a savings account at 5.25% rather than in U.S. T-bills at 9%.

Third, the city could have miscalculated market timing. If it purchased a one-month investment at the beginning of the year at 11% instead of a twelve-month investment at 10%, it would have earned a lower yield if rates later fell to 8%.

These three variance analyses help explain what portion of the investment process was responsible for an increase or decrease in actual results.

Variance due to lower AAI	$28,934 U
Variance due to greater EFF	6,856 F
Variance due to lower YLD	58,278 U
Net Variance	$80,357 U

The variance analysis is an internal comparison. Local governments can also compare investment performance with other local communities, although accounting problems can affect the analysis. They can also compare their performance with the return of their state LGIP, a specific money fund as listed weekly in the *New York Times,* or the Donoghue Money Fund average as published weekly in Donoghue's *Money Fund Report.* In these comparisons, local officials should compare apples with apples. The gross investment income earned by the community should be reduced by the cost associated with earning investment income, such as transaction fees and management expenses (see Exhibit 6.K). The net investment return should serve as the basis for comparison.

In general, brokerage firms charge fees competitive with those of banks, although with brokerage firms slightly more effort is required to arrange for the payment and receipt of funds. Growing investment activity among government units and large institutions has sparked action on the part of some brokerage houses to offer services geared to the requirements of such investors.

If local governments manage their own short-term investment portfolios, they are most likely to buy or sell securities through banks or investment houses.

Other Investment Mechanics 6.2.5

Local officials can track investment activity with an Investment Control Form (see Exhibit 6.H). The form records each purchase and sale, shows upcoming maturity dates, and, when combined with current cash balances, summarizes the community's liquid assets position. The form can be a control summary of investments or a planning tool for investment decisions when generated in conjunction with the community's cash forecast.

On a regular basis, perhaps every six months or once a year, communities should assess investment performance. Evaluations of cash management operations against internal objectives show areas that need improvement, and evaluations against external standards, such as the yield from money market funds or local government investment pools (see sections 6.3 and 6.4), compare in-house management with other investment opportunities. Exhibit 6.I describes a process for calculating and assessing investment results.

Money Market Funds 6.3

For many smaller local government investors, there is a much more attractive way to invest in the money market than buying and selling instruments directly: through money market mutual funds, called *money market funds*.

Money market funds are pools of cash from individual and institutional investors that are used to buy money market instruments. Money market funds are like mutual funds that invest in long-term securities, except that those funds pool cash to buy stocks or bonds. Investors, strictly speaking, do not make deposits to money funds; rather, they buy shares.

Money funds offer investors several attractive advantages:

1. With pooled investor cash, money funds may buy large denomination instruments that smaller investors could not have afforded. This opens up new investment opportunities in securities that are not offered in smaller sizes. Money funds also have access to national markets.
2. The purchase of larger denominations also offers higher yields. In general, the yield of money market investments increases with larger denominations.

3. With larger denominations, transaction costs are a smaller percentage of the investment. For example, it would cost less to buy or sell one investment of $1 million than it would to buy or sell 100 investments of $10,000.
4. The larger amount of money that is in the fund allows for greater diversification. Because the fund owns more investments from different sources, it reduces the impact of failure or loss in any one investment.
5. Money funds are highly liquid. Cash may be withdrawn as needed through wire transfers or free check-writing privileges. This gives local officials the flexibility to withdraw funds at unforeseen times without losing interest or principal.
6. Money funds calculate interest daily, so overnight investments earn interest.
7. Since many withdrawals from money funds are offset by new investments, money fund managers can buy longer maturities than a single local government that may experience only short periods of surplus cash. In general, longer maturities earn higher yields.
8. Money funds are extremely safe. Some funds only buy U.S. government or federal agency securities.
9. Money funds are professionally managed. The investor does not need to become an economic or security expert. This saves a local financial officer time, effort, and worry.

From the point of view of local governments, money funds have one disadvantage: they are not insured. Since money market instruments are so safe, this is less a practical than a legal consideration. Most states prohibit investment in private money market funds, although some states are making efforts to lift such outmoded restrictions. Many other states are offering state-run investment pools, also known as local government investment pools or LGIPs (see section 6.4). LGIPs are money market funds that accept investments only from local and state governments.

Most money funds required a minimum investment of $5,000, some as little as $1,000.

The Mechanics of Money Market Funds

To establish an investment in a private money fund, the town treasurer should contact each fund that looks attractive. William E. Donoghue's *Money Fund Directory* publishes a list of the 60-plus funds across the country. The directory also includes their addresses the phone numbers, and their relative net yields. (The directory may be purchased by writing to P&S Publications, 770 Washington Street, P.O. Box 540, Holliston, Massachusetts 01746; phone number 617/429-5930.) Upon contacting the funds, the investor receives a prospectus that details the mechanics of investment and withdrawal of funds and a simple form to open an account.

To invest in a money fund, an investor usually deposits cash in the money fund's bank. Once the funds are collected from the investor's bank, the funds are considered invested. Most larger investors wire transfer funds into the account to reduce delays in collecting funds. Many funds have free check-writing privileges, although they may limit the number of checks that can be written against the account. Most investors use money fund checks to pay bills or withdraw funds, since doing so takes advantage of collection float. Investments continue to earn interest until the check is presented to the money fund for payment. In some funds the minimum size check is $500; in others it is $100.

Money funds do not charge a front-end fee or a sales commission for joining. The funds are compensated by charging clients approximately 1% of each investment. The 1% equals a management fee of 0.5% plus a charge for transaction costs of 0.5%. The funds usually declare dividends daily, and an investor buys into the fund on the basis of the day's net asset value of the fund's investments.

Local Government Investment Pools (LGIPs) 6.4

Local government investment pools are merely money market funds run or supervised by the state government for local governments within the state. Currently there are eleven state-run LGIPs. Some are managed by state-hired personnel, others by the same professionals that manage private money funds. For example, the LGIP in Massachusetts, the Massachusetts Municipal Depository Trust, is managed by the Fidelity Management and Research Company.

LGIPs have the same advantages as private money funds (see section 6.3), although the terms vary from state to state. They are designed specifically for local government investment, so all instruments are legal investments. In fact, many pools are allowed to buy investments not otherwise available to municipalities, thus expanding local government investment opportunities and the potential for higher yields.

A potential disadvantage to LGIPs is the lack of availability and product competition. Naturally, if a state does not offer a state-run fund, then its municipalities cannot participate in LGIPs. A town in Washington cannot invest in Oregon's investment pool. But another potential problem is the lack of other investment pool options for states with LGIPs. LGIPs are the only investment pool, and although many have competitive yields and terms with private money funds, there is no guarantee that they will remain competitive.

Features of LGIPs

Although the features of LGIPs vary from fund to fund, most have similar characteristics. Participation in all funds is voluntary. Exhibit 6.J lists the features of all LGIPs. Most local governments invest in LGIPs by wire, transferring funds to the LGIP's bank. As with money funds, the community's account gets credit only when funds are

	CALIFORNIA	CONNECTICUT	FLORIDA	ILLINOIS	MASSACHUSETTS
FUND CONTACT:					
Name	Mr. James Sargent	Mr. Terry Helming	Mr. Carmen Heier	Mr. Donald Smith	Mr. David E. Maynard
Title of official	Investment Director	Investment Officer	Investment Specialist	Chief Fiscal Officer	Program Manager
Fund name	Local Agency Investment Fund	State of Connecticut Short Term Investment Fund	Local Government Surplus Trust Fund	Illinois Public Treasurer's Investment Pool	Massachusetts Municipal Depository Trust
Address	915 Capital Mall State Treasury Office/ Attn: Investment Division Sacramento, California 95814	20 Trinity Street Hartford, Connecticut 06115	P.O. Box 5318 State Capital Tallahassee, Florida 32301	State Treasurer's Office 219 State House Springfield, Illinois	c/o Fidelity Management Research, Inc. 82 Devonshire Street Boston, Massachusetts 02101
Phone number:	(916) 445-0428 (916) 322-5471	(203) 566-3804	(904) 488-7311	(217) 782-221	(617) 726-0200
ADMINISTRATION					
State agency	State Treasurer's Office	State Treasury	State Board of Administration	State Treasury	Private contract: Fidelity Management Research, Inc., supervised by State Treasurer Investment Advisory Council
State investment Board	Yes - Pool Money Investment Board	Yes	(Same as above)	No	
Local government advisory council	Local Agency Advisory Board	No	No	No	
Voluntary	Yes	Yes	Yes	Yes	Yes
Commingled with state funds	Yes	Yes	Only at time of investing	No	State funds are in it. Generally no.
PROCEDURES:					
Daily transactions	Yes	Yes	Yes	Yes - Requires prior day's notice for deposit and withdrawal	Yes
Wire transfers	Yes	Yes	Yes	Yes	Yes
Advance notice of large withdrawals	24 hours/$5 million minimum	Previous business day	24 hours	No	24 hours/$1 million minimum
Interest earned	Daily	Daily	Varies	Daily	Daily
Interest paid	Quarterly	Quarterly - May/Aug/Nov/Feb Special interest dist. 5/31	Quarterly — as earned	Monthly	Monthly
Direct deposit of state aid and taxes	No	No	No	No	Yes
Check writing privileges	No	No	No	Only for withdrawal	Yes
OPERATIONS 1978-1979:					
Average pool balance	545 million	738 million	300 million	52 million	125 million
Authorized administration costs	25% of earnings	.005% of average balance 5% of averge income	36%	4%	3%-100 mill. ave. bal.
Effect on yield	(Same as above)	(Same as above)	Practically no effect	(Same as above)	.25%
Net yield, 1978-1979	7.60%	9.48%	8.5%	'76 - 5.4% '77 - 5.55% '78 - 7.289% '79 - 11.849%	'78 - 7.59% '79 - 10.72% 1/80 - 13.47%
DEPOSIT REQUIREMENTS:					
Minimum transactions	$1,000 increments Yes - $5,000	Even dollar amounts	Yes - $10,000	$1,000 increments	No
Method of earnings	Dollar days on distribution	Guaranteed rate for each calendar month	NA	NA	Amortized costs

EXHIBIT 6.J / Local Government Money Market Pools (As of Spring 1980)

MONTANA	NEW JERSEY	OREGON	UTAH	WISCONSIN	WEST VIRGINIA
Mr. Richard Kain State of Montana Board of Investment Short Term Investment Pool Room 236 Mitchell Building Helena, Montana 59602	Mr Ronald MacHold Director of the Division of Investment Cash Management Fund State of New Jersey Department of the Treasury 349 W 8th Street Trenton, New Jersey 08625	Ms Cheryl Griffith Pool Manager Local Government Investment Pool Department of the Treasury Room 159 State Capital Salem, Oregon 97310	Mr Ken Done Investment Officer Utah State Treasury Investment Pool State Treasury State Capital Salt Lake City, Utah 84101	Mr Peter J Nelson Assistant State Treasurer Local Government Investment Pool 111 West State Capital Madison, Wisconsin 53702	Mr Forrest Kee Political Subdivision Coordinator State of West Virginia Consolidated Pool Room E-120 State Capital Charleston, West Virginia 25305
(406) 449-2656	(609) 292-5106	(503) 378-4155	(801) 533-5781	(608) 266-1716	(304) 348-8916
State Board of Administration	Department of the Treasury	Oregon State Treasury	Utah State Treasury	State Treasury Department	State Treasury
Yes	Yes - State Investment Council	Yes - Oregon Investment Council	Yes - Utah State Money Management Council	Yes	Yes
No	No	Yes	No	No	No
Yes	Yes	Yes	Yes	Yes	Yes
Yes	Yes	Yes	No	No	No
Yes	Yes	Yes	Yes	Yes	Yes
Yes	Yes	Yes	Yes	Yes	Yes
24 hours	No	24 hours for more than $1 million	24 hours - no minimum	10 A.M. phone call - no minimum	24 hours/$1,000 minimum
Daily	Daily	Daily	Upon Maturity	Quarterly	Daily
Semi-annually or upon withdrawal	Daily	Monthly	Upon Maturity	Monthly	Monthly
No	No	Some	No	Choose beforehand	No
No	Yes — no third party payments, - custodian bank First Jersey National	No	No	No	No
89 million	671 8 million	310 million '79 —	about 10 million	24 million	8 million
N/A	1% non state charged	1% of earnings	None at present -- but will probably change	15%	5%
N/A	1%	1% max	No	varies w/quarter	(Same as above)
N/A	8 88%	'78 - 7 43% '79 - 10 21%	N/A	first quarter '79 - 7 0% second quarter '79 - 6.9% third quarter '79 - 7 94% fourth quarter '79 - 8.66%	'79 —
$1,000 increments	No	No	Yes - $5,000	No	Yes
Simple Interest	Price to market, every day unit price of $1 00	NA	Simple Interest	NA	

collected, so funds that are wired are collected immediately. Some LGIPs require a minimum advance notice, for example by 10 a.m. of the day of transfer, of investments greater than $100,000 to allow the fund time to choose a higher-yielding investment. A few states directly deposit state-aid payments and taxes into the community's LGIP account, saving several days of lost float.

Investments are withdrawn from pools by wire or by check. Most LGIPs limit the number of checks per year and the minimum amount per check. Sometimes the limitation of the number of checks is informal, but the clear intention of check-writing privileges is to allow participants to move investments in and out of the pools, not to provide a free checking account for every minor disbursement. A few LGIPs, such as the Oregon and California pools, require a minimum transaction of $5,000.

With significant amounts of money, such as those exceeding $5,000, town treasurers should consider wiring funds into the pool and withdrawing funds by check. If wiring funds saves three days otherwise lost in mailing time, and the pool currently yields 9%, then by the profitability calculation in section 2.5.3 the minimum amount needed to pay for the cost of the wire is

$$M = \frac{(\$3) \times (365)}{(.09) \times (3)}$$

$$M = \$4{,}056$$

The town earns money if it transfers by wire rather than by mail all amounts exceeding $4,056.

Communities should remove funds from LGIPs by check, not by wire, to take advantage of mail and collection float. For example, Arlington, Massachusetts draws all payments exceeding $25,000 directly on its account with the Massachusetts LGIP. When the state delayed for more than a week the cashing of Arlington's $3 million assessment check, the town earned over $5,000. For each day the funds remained in the LGIP, the town earned $875. Clearly it is best to invest by wire and withdraw by check.

LGIPs usually send communities written notification of each deposit, mailed on the day after the transaction. Monthly account statements, similar to statements sent by banks, show all account transactions, balances, and interest earned. Almost all funds compute earned interest on a daily basis and credit the investor's account at the end of the month. For the exact method of computing interest, a local manager should contact the state LGIP. Pools compute interest from day of deposit to day of withdrawal. That means that once collected, the money in the pool earns interest until the checks clear the account.

The yields on LGIPs are competitive with other investments. A study by the Advisory Commission on Intergovernmental Relations (ACIR) found that LGIP yields almost always exceeded the rates for 90-day Treasury bills and almost always exceeded the returns obtained by individual local government portfolios.

Low Participation in LGIPs

Despite the attractiveness of LGIPs, the ACIR study and other independent reports on individual state pools show that the rate of participation is still low. Less than one-quarter of all eligible communities maintain accounts in their state-run pools. Taken together, the explanations for low participation appear contradictory. Yet any one reason may block local investment. Here is a sample of the more common explanations, with comments:

1. *Officials of smaller towns lack the time to manage an investment program.*

   Understandably, managers of smaller communities are busy overseeing the day-to-day operations of collecting taxes and paying bills. Often they have only part-time assistance. Yet this is precisely one of the advantages of LGIPs. Investment only takes a phone call, and because funds may be withdrawn at any time, local managers do not need detailed forecasts or information systems.

2. *Some fear that an investment in an LGIP draws money out of local banks, which in turn harms the local economy.*

   This is more fear than reality. A detailed report by the international accounting firm Deloitte Haskins & Sells, released in September 1978, found that local investment in Oregon's LGIP had no effect on local commercial loans or mortgages.

   Because of the short-term nature and the wide fluctuations of local deposits, it is difficult to find a direct link between changes in bank deposits and changes in local investment in the economy. On the other hand, there is little reason that earnings on idle funds, which belong to the taxpayers, should accrue to banks.

3. *In response to LGIPs, more banks are offering competitive investments.*

   Of course, if banks offer competitive rates on CDs or repos, then these investments should be considered. LGIPs usually outperform these securities because LGIP economies-of-scale reduce transaction costs per dollar of investment, and LGIPs require less professional time on the part of the local official. Investment in CDs means local officials must maintain a minimum cash forecast to ensure that funds are available for 30 to 90 days. The ACIR study found that LGIP yields almost always exceeded 90-day CD rates.

4. *Some communities fear withdrawal of funds will upset banking relationships.*

   Some communities are anxious about their banking relations. They fear that banks will not buy their short-term notes (their tax and bond anticipation notes) if the community withdraws funds from banks to invest in an LGIP.

   The best response is that it almost never happens. In many cases in which municipalities have improved cash management practices, any reservations that banks had at the time of announced withdrawals of idle municipal deposits were later forgotten. Even with withdrawals, banks still see governments as attractive customers for services, since municipalities, like all other customers, will pay fair prices. With regard to the sale of short-term notes, banks seek financially sound

For communities that have the option between pooled investments (LGIPs or money funds) and in-house investment management, should the community invest in a pool or do it themselves? This exhibit examines the relative costs, yields, and conveniences of each option.

The following calculation finds the average daily portfolio size where pooled investment fund fees equal in-house investment expenses. When a pool's fees exceed in-house expenses, then in-house management becomes more attractive financially. Initially, the analysis assumes that an in-house investment team and a pooled investment fund will achieve the same gross yield on investments. Here are the expenses of both options.

	In-House	Pooled Fund
Pooled fund management fee and expenses @ 1% of portfolio		$(.01)x
In-house expenses:		
5% of director of finance @ $40,000/year	$2,000	
100% of cash manager @ $20,000/year	$20,000	
25% of clerical @ $14,000/year	$3,500	
Transaction fees:		
Daily repo fees @ $20/day × 254 days	$5,080	
Weekly trading fees @ $20/week × 52 weeks	$1,040	
	$31,620	

x = break-even size of average daily portfolio

$$(.01)x = \$31{,}620$$
$$x = \$3{,}162{,}000$$

At $3,162,000 the expenses of the in-house investment team and the pooled investment fund are equal, so very few communities have a portfolio large enough to achieve in-house cost savings. If a portfolio exceeds $3.2 million, then the in-house management team is less expensive; however, communities should consider other important factors.

Advantages of pooled investment funds

1. Pools offer greater convenience, in part because they allow accounting separation for funds that require independent control. They also relieve treasury officials from the duty of supervising in-house management.
2. Pools offer professional management. It is difficult for busy treasury personnel to keep abreast of rapidly changing financial markets.
3. Pools may offer a higher yield because they have more flexible maturity requirements and larger amounts for purchases with high minimum denominations.
4. Pools may offer a lower risk because they spread investment risk over a greater number of securities (investment diversification).
5. Minimum investment denominations can prevent an in-house management team from fully investing balances in higher yielding investments. For example, assume that a community had $104,000 to invest and maintained a $10,000 compensating balance. If it invested in a pooled fund, it would achieve a 91.2% rate of efficiency [104,000 ÷ (104,000 + 10,000) × 100]. If it invested on its own, it could only invest $100,000 (minimum denominations are $5,000), which is an 87.7% rate of efficiency [100,000 ÷ (104,000 + 10,000) × 100]. Pooled investments also allow a community to keep a lower cash cushion since funds may be withdrawn daily.

Advantages of in-house investment management

In some states, local government investment has outperformed state-run LGIPs. On the other hand, the reverse may be true. A community should factor the difference of investment returns into their expense analysis to produce a net yield comparison.

EXHIBIT 6.K / In-House vs. Pooled Investment

investments. If a community's notes are attractive, banks will still want to buy those notes.

5. *LGIP investments are not federally guaranteed nor secured.*

   Although they are not federally guaranteed, there is almost no chance of losing principal with LGIP investment. LGIPs buy only securities issued by the U.S. government, federal agencies, and blue-chip companies and banks. Some LGIPs limit this risk even further by choosing only U.S. government and guaranteed agency securities. Even in the event that an investment in the LGIP portfolio defaults, the loss is distributed equally to each share in the pool, so the effect on any one participant is minimal.

6. *A few local governments are suspicious of sending local cash deposits to an agency controlled by state government.*

   Some communities feel that their funds, if not directly under their control, may somehow be expropriated by state governments.

   States have no more legal right to withdraw a town's investments from LGIPs than to withdraw the town's funds from local bank accounts.

7. *Some communities think they can earn more themselves than in an LGIP.*

   If a community can earn more than its state pool, and it is willing to invest the extra professional time, then local investment management makes sense. The calculation described in Exhibit 6.K compares LGIP and in-house investment management and shows when the extra income from in-house management exceeds the extra costs.

Accounting for Pooled Investments 6.5

If a treasurer decides to invest in an outside investment pool or form his own investment pool, he should understand the basics of pooled investment accounting. Specifically, he should understand the method of quoting the pool's yield and the method of evaluating each participant's share of the fund. At first glance, yield and share value appear to be easy to determine, but a closer look indicates that they are complex subjects that may cause a great deal of confusion if not fully understood.

The accounting approach used for a particular investment pool should reflect the goals under which the pool operates. For example, state sponsored local government investment pools are designed to operate like open ended money market funds, insofar as their participants can place essentially unlimited amounts of funds in the pools for an unpredetermined period of time and can change their level of investment without notice. (It is possible to impose some informal or formal constraints on participants, in terms of advance notice and size of deposits and withdrawals, without seriously eroding the appeal of the pool as a flexible investment tool.)

For these pools, the accounting systems must be capable of providing accurate data every day on the prior day's deposits and withdrawals and changes in the value of the pool's portfolio. Open-ended money market mutual funds keep their accounting records on computer so that the prior day's activity can be updated automatically overnight, regardless of the volume of the activity. These pools also value their investments daily, often with the aid of computerized pricing systems that collect data on the closing prices of traded securities and compute the value of untraded securities on the basis of prevailing interest rates.

An in-house investment pool that is designed exclusively to accept a limited number of accounts, all of which are managed by a city treasurer, need not have such an elaborate accounting system. The accounting can be kept very simple if the pool manager follows several guidelines regarding participant activity and investment decisions. (1) Record all investments at book value. (2) Schedule deposits and withdrawals to match up with investment purchases and maturities. At the time of maturity, allocate interest income only to the participants in that particular investment. (3) Try never to sell an investment prior to maturity. Keep maturities short to minimize the danger of a premature sale. If a premature sale results in a capital gain or loss, charge that gain or loss to the participant(s) whose withdrawal(s) caused the sale to take place.

Open-ended money market funds, such as state sponsored investment pools, are especially attractive to city treasurers because they relieve the treasurers of virtually all accounting tasks, yet allow them to obtain the maximum possible investment return. Still, it is important to understand how pool managers account for the yield on the pool's portfolio and how participant shares are valued. What follows is a summary of how yield and share values are accounted for.

For illustrative purposes, assume that investors have placed $300,000 into a pool holding three securities and that market values of the securities are recorded daily as follows:

(in 000s)

Day	6% Repo	6.5% Six-Month Treasury Bill	7% Two-Year Treasury Note
1	$50.00	$100.00	$150.00
2	50.01	100.00	150.00
3	50.02	100.00	150.00
4	50.02	100.00	150.00
5	50.03	100.00	150.00
6	50.04	100.00	150.00
7	50.05	98.00	147.00
8	50.06	98.00	147.00
9	50.07	98.00	147.00
10	50.07	98.00	Sold
11	50.08	98.00	Sold

From the above chart we can see that on the first day of the month a $50,000 repurchase agreement ("repo") was acquired yielding 6%. The book value of the repo is increasing each day because interest is paid daily and adds to the par value of the subsequently purchased repo. A $100,000 six-month Treasury bill was purchased yielding 6.5% and a \$150,000 two-year Treasury note was also purchased, both at par value. On day seven, interest rates rose sharply. The market value of the pool's Treasury bill and note fell.

Yield: Mark to Market Method

Of the alternative methods for determining the yield on this model investment pool, the so-called "mark to market" method is probably the most common among open-ended money management funds. The Securities and Exchange Commission encourages all mutual funds open to the public to utilize this method. This method records all the gains and losses, realized and unrealized, on the day they occur. The basic formula is:

$$\frac{(360 \times \text{Accrued Interest}) + Ap - Dp}{\text{Market Value}}$$

360 = the investment year for portfolio calculations
Ap = Appreciation of portfolio's value
Dp = Depreciation of portfolio's value

The mark to market method determines yield by adding the sum of accrued interest to changes in portfolio value, then dividing the total by the market value of the portfolio. Accrued interest is calculated by first determining accrued interest for each security on a daily basis, then recomputing accrued interest in a uniformly annual basis. Accrued interest for one day is determined by dividing the amount of interest to be earned on a security by the number of days in the term of a security. For example, the six-month Treasury bill provides interest earnings for a year of 6.5% times \$100,000 divided by 2, or \$3,250. Treasury bill yields are computed on a 360-day year. Therefore to calculate accrued interest for one day one divides \$3,250 by 180, to get \$18.05. This daily accrued interest is totalled with that of other investments and multiplied by the portfolio's investment year (in this example, 360 days), to calculate annual investment income.

Appreciation of a security is the increase in the market value of a security from one day to the next. Likewise, depreciation refers to the decrease in the market value of an investment. (In our example, the two-year Treasury note experienced a \$3,000 depreciation in value on day seven.) The numerator of the "mark to market" formula therefore equals the total accrued interest on all securities times 360 (so that the yield is on an annual basis) plus total appreciation of the portfolio.

In our example, the "mark to market" yield for day one would be determined as follows:

Repurchase Agreement	(\$50,000 × .06)/365	=	\$ 8.20
Treasury Bill	(\$100,000 × .065÷2) / 180	=	18.05
Treasury Note	(\$150,000 × .07) / 360	=	29.17
Total Accrued Interest			\$55.42

Appreciation of Securities = 0
Depreciation of Securities = 0

Yield (day 1):

$$\frac{(360 \times 55.42) + 0 - 0}{300{,}000} = 0.67 \text{ or } 6.7\%$$

On day seven, the accrued interest would be essentially the same except for a slightly larger amount of interest earned on the repurchase agreement. There was no appreciation, but the depreciation was substantial. The Treasury bill decreased in value by \$2,000 and the Treasury note by \$3,000. The numerator would therefore be \$19,951.20 (360 × \$55.42) less \$5,000 or \$14,951.20. The denominator, market value of the portfolio, would be \$295,050, resulting in a yield of 5.1% But on the following day, there being no further depreciation in value, the numerator would return to \$19,951.20, and the yield (\$19,951.20 divided by \$295,060) would climb to 6.8%.

The principal advantage of using the mark to market approach is that it reflects both the interest being earned and the change in value in the pool's assets on a day-to-day basis. But critics claim that the method is too erratic and, moreover, fails to reflect the true yield of the pool. They argue that market changes of a portfolio's value are not important unless an asset is to be sold prior to maturity either as a trading tactic or as a means to fund an unexpectedly heavy amount of withdrawals from the pool. In practice, public investment pools rarely sell securities prior to maturity. They maintain a portion of the portfolio in repos and other very short-term securities sufficient to meet cash demands. Therefore, critics contend, the yield should reflect changes in the portfolio's value only when that change is realized by the sale of a security. They recommend generally that the "amortized cost method" be used to calculate yield.

Yield: Amortized Cost Method

To apply this method, the following formula is used:

$$(360 \times \text{Accrued Interest}) + \frac{\text{Realized Gain} - \text{Realized Loss}}{\text{Book Value of Securities}}$$

RG (realized gain) or RL (loss) is the difference between the purchase price of a security and the price for which it is sold.

Notice that this method utilizes the book value as the denominator. The book value is the price at which the investment is purchased. The amortized cost method would offer the same yield quote as the mark to market method for the first six days. However, on the seventh day, when the market values fell, the yield would stay the same assuming that none of the pool's assets were sold.

Suppose the Treasury bill was sold on day 10. The yield would be 6.7% up to the 10th day. For day 10 the quote would be determined as follows:

$$(360 \times \$26.25) + 0 - \$3{,}000 = 6{,}450 = 4.3\% \text{ of } \$150{,}070$$

(See Exhibit 6.L)

The next day the yield would rise to 6.3%. If all participants attempted to withdraw their shares from the pool at this point, the fund would not have enough assets to return each individual's initial investment plus the yield that had been quoted. This is a disadvantage of this method when used by an open ended money market fund.

This method also arbitrarily allocates gains and losses according to who is in the fund at the time of sale. A participant can deposit money in the fund on a day the asset is liquidated and be forced to share in a loss that occurred prior to his participation. This method might entice participants to leave the fund when the value of assets is falling (for example, during a period when short-term interest rates are rising), thereby triggering a spiral of premature sales of investments at losses and further withdrawals. This built-in instability makes the fund difficult to manage.

Yield: Mixed Method

A third method, sometimes referred to as "total payout," reduces the negative effects of the preceding two methods by combining them. The Massachusetts Municipal Depository Trust (MMDT), sponsored by the Commonwealth of Massachusetts, has adopted the following among many possible variations on the mixed method. The MMDT quotes two yields, a daily yield and a yield for the preceding month. The formula for the daily yield is simply:

$$\frac{360 \times \text{AI}}{\text{Book Value of Securities}}$$

Gains and losses as a result of portfolio trading are distributed into a "reserve fund." At the end of the month one-twelfth of the reserve fund balance is distributed to participants

	Method		
Day	Mark to Market	Amortized	Mixed
1	6.7%	6.7%	6.7%
2	6.7	6.7	6.7
3	6.7	6.7	6.7
4	6.7	6.7	6.7
5	6.7	6.7	6.7
6	6.7	6.7	6.7
7	5.1	6.7	6.7
8	6.8	6.7	6.7
9	6.8	6.7	6.7
10	6.4	4.3	6.3
11	6.4	6.3	6.3

Day 7: Market value of portfolio declined by $5,000
Day 10: Note sold for $147,000 ($3,000 loss)

EXHIBIT 6.L / Comparison of Yields Determined by Three Alternative Methods of Quoting a Yield

Money Market Funds

The following quotations, collected by the National Association of Securities Dealers Inc., represent the average of annualized yields and dollar-weighted portfolio maturities over the seven day period ending Friday, May 15, 1981. Realized and unrealized gains or losses aren't taken into account.

Fund	Avg. Mat. (Days)	Avg. Yld. (Pct.)	Fund	Avg. Mat. (Days)	Avg. Yld. (Pct.)
Alliance Capital	23	15.08	Lex Money Mkt	26	15.56
AllianceGvt Res	25	13.75	LiquidCaptl Inc	24	15.80
AmGn Resrve b	22	16.11	Liquid CashTrst	1	17.20
AmLiquid Trust	26	15.34	LordAbbet Cash	30	15.70
Babson MonMkt	z	z	LuthBrMonMt c	27	14.77
Capitl Preserve	21	15.26	MIF NtwMnM c	28	14.82
CapitlPresrve 2	4	16.67	MassCash Mngt	28	14.27
CardGovt SecTr	15	14.63	MerrLGovtFd bf	10	15.06
CarngieGov Sec	15	15.64	MerrLInstFd bf	22	14.85
CashEquivalnt f	22	15.04	Midwst Incm Tr	22	15.13
Csh MgtTrAm b	22	16.00	MoneyMktMgt f	28	14.57
Cash RsvMgt bf	23	15.60	Money Mkt Trst	37	14.63
Centennial Cap	27	14.86	MnyMar Asst bf	28	15.01
Col Daily Inc bf	29	14.79	Morgan Keegan	24	14.39
Comp CashM bf	23	14.80	MuniFundInv e	60	6.15
Current Interest	25	15.67	MtlOmMnyM c	23	15.78
Daily CashFd 1	21	15.58	Natl Liquid Res	z	z
DBL Cash Fd a	26	15.98	NEL CashMgt c	24	15.24
DelaCashRsrv f	23	16.64	NRTA AARP f	36	14.15
DollarReserv a	21	16.35	Oppn Mny Mrkt	25	15.83
DreyfsLiqAsst f	22	15.15	PaineWb Cash f	31	15.18
DrMMkGvSc af	26	14.25	Plimoney Fd b	37	15.46
DrMnyMkSer af	18	15.42	PutnamDlyDiv b	29	15.33
EatonHow Cash	20	15.41	Reserve Fund	27	16.09
Equit MMktAc f	21	14.83	RowePrPrRes f	14	15.22
FedMaster Trst	25	15.35	St Paul Money	27	16.86
FedrtTaxFree e	76	6.56	ScuddCashInv f	15	15.88
FidelCash Resv	19	15.34	ScuddrTaxFr ef	185	6.45
FidelDlyIncm c	24	14.95	Secur CashFd a	18	15.04
FidMM Domstc	23	15.06	Select Mny Mkt	27	15.06
FidMM Govmnt	10	15.49	ShearDailyDiv f	21	15.45
FidTxExempt e	72	6.30	ShearGvtAgen f	20	14.07
FnclDlyInc Shr	15	16.47	ShortTermYld b	20	14.65
FstInvCshMgt f	18	15.09	Stdmn FedSec b	25	12.60
First Variable	31	15.27	SteinRoe CshRs	20	15.17
FrnklnMnyFd b	27	15.26	TempInvest Fd	30	15.31
FrnklMnFd2 ab	33	14.01	Trust CashRes f	28	14.85
FundGovt Invst	7	15.89	TrShtTr FedFd	25	15.00
GovtInvstTrst b	21	15.82	TrShtTFed TFd	24	15.04
Gradison Cash	25	14.77	TrShTer US Gvt	48	14.81
IDS Cash Mgt f	28	15.18	TrstUSTrea Obl	39	14.52
INA Cash Fund	29	15.47	Union Cash Mgt	18	16.70
InterCap LiqAs	33	15.30	UnitedCshMgt b	28	15.72
JohnHanc Cash	23	15.33	USAA MutlMM	z	. z
Johnston Cash	z	z	ValueLineCsh b	24	16.19
JonesDly Pssp f	29	14.43	Vangrd MnMk f	z	z
KemperMonM f	25	15.00	VangMunMM ef	z	z
LeggMasn Csh f	28	14.82	VangdMunST ef	z	z
Lehman CashM	18	16.48	WebstrCshPre f	20	15.32

a-Yield increased by temporary subsidization of expense. b-Actual yield may vary due to net realized/unrealized gains/losses. c-Actual yield may vary depending on account size. d-Change in net asset value during period. e-Invests primarily in Federally tax-exempt securities. f-As of previous day.

on a prorated basis, which is a function of the participant's average daily balance for a particular month. The monthly yield on the reserve fund is calculated as follows:

$$\frac{1/12 \times \text{Reserve Fund}}{\text{Total Average Daily Balance}}$$

The monthly distribution of the balance in the reserve fund can be a dividend if the reserve fund has a positive balance or a levy if the reserve fund has a negative balance. In practice it has always been a dividend. The MMDT investment managers purposely built up a positive balance in the first months of the MMDT by selling some securities for a gain as soon as the opportunities presented themselves.

The advantage of this third method is that it generally produces a steadier, more predictable yield (see Exhibit 6.L).

Reporting Yield

No matter what accounting method is chosen, it is important when reporting a yield to quote a running average. Often a fund will state the average yield for the last 5 or 7 days of operation. The advantage of averaging is that it smooths out abbreviations and offers a more realistic view of the fund's performance.

Accounting for Shares

Once a method for accounting for yield is chosen, the fund manager must establish a technique for calculating each participant's share in the pool. There is a clear consensus as to the best method for accomplishing this. Many government-sponsored funds value a participant's share in terms of units with constant value. A participant in the MMDT in Massachusetts purchases "units of participation" at one dollar per share. Users of Wisconsin's investment pool purchase "shares" in denominations of $1,000. No matter what the deposit is called, the value of the share or the unit of participation is always valued constantly and at a parity with a specific dollar amount. Interest income can be automatically reinvested in the form of new shares. If the value of a fund's portfolio and reserve fund balance (to handle gains and losses) falls below the par value of the shares, participants would be required to make capital contributions to the fund by relinquishing a portion of their shares on a prorated basis. This will ensure that the par value of all units of participation outstanding is never greater than the value of securities and cash on deposit.

Penny Rounding

Many money market fund participants and fund managers prefer to ignore very minor fluctuations in share values caused by gains and losses in sales. Sometimes a reserve account is not available to handle these minor gains and losses. These fluctuations are particularly bothersome for funds that use the mark to market method of accounting, since very small day-to-day changes in interest rates result in gains and losses on purchased securities. Consequently, a "penny rounding" rule is used to determine when daily fluctuations should be reported. The rule, stated in its most simple form, permits fund managers to ignore for accounting purposes gains or losses so long as they do not equal or exceed one-half of one percent of the book value of the portfolio.

Part 4

Long-Term Investing

Introduction to Long-Term Investing 7

The long-term investment of funds is a complex task in any economic environment. When inflation was low, it was relatively easy to project long-term obligations such as pension benefits; to fund them it was often sufficient to put most of the available funds into long-term bonds, with perhaps a small amount in the equity market. Long-term bonds seemed to carry a "real," i.e., inflation adjusted, rate of return of 2% to 3% per year. From the end of World War II to the late 1960s the stock market seemed to return better than 10% per year.

The rules of the game changed in the late 1960s. Inflation accelerated, and suddenly bond rates were not keeping pace with inflation. Even the stock market began to behave erratically; returns, even when positive, were often below the inflation rate. Experts began to doubt the conventional wisdom that had declared stocks the best hedge against inflation.

The long-term investment problem is now much more complex. There is no sure way to protect the value of long-term assets against inflation. Indeed, it is easy not only to lose purchasing power but to suffer capital losses in both the stock and the bond markets. The buy-and-hold strategy in either market looked like a certain way of guaranteeing a decline in at least the real value of the assets. Treasury bills alone have offered protection from inflation and capital losses: they are essentially risk-free and their historical yields have been close to the rate of inflation.

The investment task is further complicated by the increasing scrutiny and defacto regulation from federal agencies, local agencies, professional groups, and the general public. This is especially true in the case of pension funds, which probably account for 90% of the long-term assets invested by state and local authorities. The attention focused on pension funds is in part the result of the very magnitude of the funds—estimated at $200 billion, and growing by $20 billion or more annually. In addition, interest in the security of retirement funds has increased as the population has begun to age.

The United States Congress enacted the Employee Retirement Income Security Act of 1974 (ERISA) to regulate the administration of private sector pension funds. While this act did not apply directly to government funds, it prompted proposals to enact a Public Employee Retirement Income Security Act (PERISA). Such an act, narrower in focus than ERISA, may be passed in the 1980s. Whether it is passed or not, the spotlight is on the administration and management of retirement funds, both private and public, and it is not likely to be lifted. Indeed, attention will intensify as the funds continue to accumulate.

Finally, the investment task has been complicated by the development of the new investment techniques and approaches and even new investment vehicles. In the past the pension officer had to know only about stocks and bonds, and often he knew relatively little about stocks because purchases of them were severely limited by law.

Now he needs to know about a whole range of alternatives including options, real estate, and Ginnie Maes.

In the late 1960s new investment techniques were developed by academics and were put into practice by a few adventurous investment managers in the private sector. The new investment approaches used sophisticated statiscal techniques to help investors measure potential risk and returns for individual investments and total portfolios. The object of most investors was to maximize returns for a given level of risk or to minimize risk in obtaining a given level of return. These new investment techniques, which have been applied to investment in common stock for some time and which are now being applied to investment in bonds, go under the general name of *modern capital market theory*.

7.1 What Should You Know?

Anyone responsible for pension fund investing—executives and trustees alike—should be acquainted with *all* the topics covered in this chapter. However, this chapter is not an inclusive guide. It is a primer. The authors assume that the reader has access to qualified actuaries, legal counsel, and investment managers, and encourage the reader to rely upon these professionals to furnish expert advice. Neither this chapter nor any other book on pension management can substitute for competent, professional consultation.

The state or municipal officer charged with investing long-term assets needs a broader base of knowledge than his predecessor of a few years ago. Indeed, where once the investment task may have been assigned as an afterthought to an investment amateur, today a higher level of investment expertise is required. The investment officer who has no investment training when appointed must quickly become familiar with the investment world.

Initially the investment officer should develop and articulate long-range investment goals and objectives. The investment officer should become familiar with the major long-term investment vehicles and their attributes. These include common stocks, corporate bonds, government bonds, mortgages, Ginnie Maes and mortgage-backed securities, common stock options, real estate, convertible bonds, private placement of securities, and perhaps even financial futures. All have advantages and disadvantages. Each has its own level of risk and its expected range of returns.

The officer must also understand how these instruments may be combined in a portfolio to reduce the overall riskiness of the portfolio while enhancing the return. To that end the investment officer must be familiar with the workings of the capital markets.

In addition, he should understand how to study (with his actuary) the *cash flow requirements* of a pension fund. He must know these requirements in order to decide upon an appropriate investment policy. The forecasted cash outflow of pension payments must be matched by cash inflows from contributions and from investment portfolios. Today's investment policy will affect in subtle ways the degree to which

The following is a quiz to determine if you need to improve your knowledge of long-term investment practices.

1. The long-term historical real (net-of-inflation) return on common stocks has been (check one)

   ☐ 2.0% ☐ 4.1% ☐ 6.7% ☐ 8.3% ☐ 10.2%

2. The long-term historical real total return (annualized) on long-term corporate bonds has been (check one)

   ☐ 1.7% ☐ 2.0% ☐ 4.1% ☐ 7.0% ☐ 8.5%

3. The long-term historical real total rate of return on government bonds has been (check one)

   ☐ 1.1% ☐ 2.1% ☐ 4.3% ☐ 6.0% ☐ 6.7%

4. True or false? The total rate of return and the net effective yield of an investment are usually identical.

   ☐ True ☐ False

5. True or false? All investment brokerage concerns charge basically the same brokerage commissions for similar sized transactions.

   ☐ True ☐ False

6. True or false? Municipal bonds are generally a good investment medium for state and municipal pension funds.

   ☐ True ☐ False

7. True or false? It is possible to have a capital loss on government-guaranteed bonds.

   ☐ True ☐ False

Answers to Questions

1. 6.7%
2. 2.0%
3. 1.1%
4. False. Net effective yield does not include the unrealized gains or losses incurred on the investment, and therefore is rarely the same as the total rate of return, which incorporates such gains and losses.
5. False. Commission rates are now negotiable.
6. False. Municipal bonds are tax exempt and therefore carry a lower interest rate than the equivalent corporate bonds. Since pension funds are tax exempt and therefore gain nothing from the tax exemption on the municipal bond, corporate bonds with their higher returns are a better investment.
7. True. While government-guaranteed bonds are guaranteed against default, they are not guaranteed against capital losses caused by changes in the interest rate. If you hold 7% government-guaranteed bonds and interest rates rise to 8%, the market value of the 7% bonds has fallen and you will suffer a capital loss if you wish to sell them before they mature or before interest rates fall again to 7%.

EXHIBIT 7.A / Do You Know Enough?

pension managers can afford to withdraw cash from investment portfolios now, and years in the future, to honor pension obligations.

The investment officer must be familiar with the *legal concept of prudence,* which governs most investment law, and with many legal restrictions imposed by the state or locality. Most government entities impose some maximum level of investment in the stock market, and almost all impose restrictions on the quality of securities that may be bought.

The historical legal definition of prudence is that a trustee should conduct himself faithfully and exercise "a sound discretion. He is to observe how men of prudence, discretion and intelligence maintain their own affairs, not in regard to speculation, but in regard to the permanent disposition of their funds, considering the probable income, as well as the probable safety of the capital to be invested."

This "prudent man rule" first stated in a nineteenth-century court case, *Harvard College v. Amory,* became the model for the prudence rules adopted by eighteen states and for the prudence definition stated in the Employee Retirement Income Security Act of 1974. While ERISA does not apply to public employee funds, a similar definition of prudence is likely to be included in any PERISA that may be enacted in the 1980s and is also likely to be cited in court cases arising from the investment of employee benefit assets. It is therefore a standard worth knowing.

ERISA's definition can be broken down into five key rules. The fiduciary or trustee shall discharge his duties with respect to the fund (1) solely in the interests of the participants and the beneficiaries, (2) for the purpose of providing benefits to participants and beneficiaries and defraying the reasonable expenses of administration, (3) with the care, skill, prudence and diligence, under circumstances then prevailing, that a prudent man acting in like capacity and familiar with such matters would use in the conduct of an enterprise of like character and aims, (4) by diversifying investments to minimize large losses, and (5) in accordance with documents and instruments governing the fund.

The third rule is the core of the traditional definition, but the other rules are very important. The definition specifies that the trustee is to administer the funds solely in the interests of the participants and beneficiaries. No longer can some state project be rescued by using state pension funds with little regard for the welfare of pension beneficiaries. The trustee must also diversify the holdings and administer the fund in accordance with written policies.

7.1.1 Funds Under $500,000

Not all observations and suggestions contained in this chapter are applicable to very small funds—those under $500,000. These funds cannot afford to pay for full-time professional management. In addition it is difficult to diversify the investments of funds of that size. It is therefore more appropriate for small funds to be invested in a pooled account, either with a bank or an insurance company or, where allowed, in mutual funds. In a pooled account, as the name implies, the assets of many funds are combined for the purposes of efficient buying of stocks or bonds. Brokerage houses give volume discounts, so large pools save on brokerage commissions. Perhaps even more important, large pools permit better diversification.

Most experts believe that the minimum number of stocks for a safe level of diversification is twenty to thirty stocks representing diverse economic sectors, though some believe that it is higher. If a $500,000 fund was to be 25% equities, and twenty-five stocks were to be bought, each position would be only $5,000, or 500 shares of a $10 stock or 50 shares of a $100 stock. If the balance of the fund was to be in fixed income securities, and twenty-five bonds were to be bought, each position would be $15,000, or 15 bonds valued at $1,000. Small positions such as these mean high costs for buying and selling.

Pooled funds can give an investor more "bang for the buck." Even some very large pension funds use pooled funds for at least part of their investments. Many of the corporate clients of Morgan Guaranty Trust, for example, use that bank's pooled accounts.

The Revolution in Investment Practices 7.2

The investment community has experienced a revolution in concepts, terminology, and professional standards in the past twenty years. Nowhere has change been more dramatic—and difficult to assimilate—than in the area of measuring and evaluating risk and return. This section gives a taste of the intellectual ferment present in today's investment community.

Are stocks riskier than bonds? If they are, no one would invest in them except with the expectation of potentially higher returns. Researchers have shown that stocks over the long term are indeed riskier, in that their prices fluctuate more violently. But in addition they provide a better long-term return than bonds.

According to studies by Roger Ibbotson and Rex Sinquefield, common stocks returned 9.2% per year compounded annually over the 1926 through 1976 period. Adjusted for inflation, the compound annual return over the same period was 6.7%. Long-term corporate bonds, on the other hand, returned only 4.1% per year compounded over the same period. The inflation-adjusted return over the same period was only 2.0% per year. Government bonds (long-term) returned 3.4% compounded annually, and only 1.1% per year adjusted for inflation.

Between 1970 and 1980, however, corporate bond returns have been better than common stock returns. For the ten years ending March 31, 1979, corporate bonds, as measured by the Salomon Brothers high-grade bond index, had a compound annual return of 5.5% compared with a common stock return over the same period of 4.1% per year.

So, if stocks appear to outperform the market in the long term but from time to time underperform bonds, it is possible to always stay ahead by shifting between stocks and bonds at the right time. This sounds easy only with 20-20 hindsight. It is also possible to improve upon the average stock's performance by selecting exceptionally rewarding stocks. Many institutional investment managers try to concentrate full time on the equity market, hoping to select stocks that outperform the market as a whole.

Some researchers, probing more deeply into the historical yields on investments, have concluded that efforts to consistently select stocks so as to outperform the average stock is a form of chasing rainbows. They contend that over the past ten years the average equity manager has significantly underperformed Standard & Poor's 500 index. For example, according to *Pension and Investments' Performance Evaluation Report,* the average bank equity commingled funds had a return of only 2.2% per year over the past ten years compared with 4.1% for the S&P 500. This figure is consistent with the findings of other performance surveys. Indeed, the surveys show that only about 20% of the equity managers have equaled or bettered the S&P over the period.

All these findings—some of which are hotly disputed—raise some perplexing questions about risk and return from investing. Stocks appear to outperform bonds in the long term. But they are more volatile; hence the risk of exceptionally high losses (as well as gains) are higher. In addition, it appears that investment managers who invest in stocks are in no way assured of outperforming the market as a whole: in fact, many appear to have underperformed the market. Some professionals today recommend a strategy of investing in stocks, in view of the prospects of long-term gain, and choosing a portfolio modelled after a reliable index of the market as a whole. This strategy is intended, in the modern terminology of Wall Street, to reduce "nonmarket risk" to zero.

7.3 The Investment Process: An Overview

The investment process is a series of interrelated decisions. They are presented graphically in Exhibit 7.B. The first question is, what is the appropriate investment goal for this fund? Should the fund stress preservation of capital and relegate growth to a second place, or should it stress growth and take more risk? The answer to this question is determined in part by the nature of the plan, the basis upon which benefits are determined and actuarial assumptions are made regarding future employee wages (particularly wages immediately prior to retirement), investment returns, the nature of investment risk, inflation, and the efficiency of the capital markets.

Once appropriate goals and risk levels have been determined, the fund investment committee must decide how to pursue the goals. The committee can opt for internal management of the assets and build a staff of experienced investment people, or it can hire outside investment managers to make the buy and sell decisions. A third, very popular yet fundamentally inferior, approach is to gather together some outside advisors who (for a fee or on a *pro bono* basis) gather research, decide what should be bought, and then recommend the appropriate transactions to an internal staff who either make the transactions, if they are acceptable, or authorize an outside manager to do so.

Once these basic investment decisions have been made, and before the appropriate

1. Determine short-term cash flow needs and long-term growth needs of pension plan.
2. Determine risk tolerances of plan and plan sponsor.
3. Determine appropriate investment objectives given plan needs.
4. Determine how assets will be managed (internal, external with partial discretion, external with full discretion).
5. Establish an investment policy which states asset allocation, liquidity, diversification and investment quality requirements relevant to the needs and risk tolerances established above.
6. A. Hire and fund investment managers, whether internal or external.
   B. If internal, adopt investment strategy (e.g., when bonds or stock will be bought or sold).
7. Establish and implement review process for all steps above (annually for 1–5; quarterly for 6A).

EXHIBIT 7.B / The Investment Process for Pension Plans

investment structure is put into place, an investment policy guideline must be prepared. This guideline specifies clearly the long-term return expectations and the risk tolerance of the fund. It also specifies the appropriate asset allocation ranges for stocks, bonds, and other investment vehicles and the appropriate quality levels.

If the trustees choose internal management of the assets, then the policy statement must delineate the lines of investment authority. It must specify who has the ultimate buy and sell responsibility for all classifications of securities. It must also specify the responsibilities of outside advisory firms employed, and custodians.

If outside investment managers are to be hired, then the limits of their responsibilities and obligations must be clearly defined, as should the terms of their employment. For example, how often must they submit to review and what is expected of them in those review sessions?

Once the guidelines have been established and the management structure put into place, the tactical decisions have been made. If internal management has been chosen, then much more remains for the trustees to do. The primary sources of economic and investment input have to be chosen. A great deal of economic and market research will flow in from brokers hoping for the fund's business, but some of the best research will be bought from specific sources. Who should these sources be? How should they be paid? How much should they be paid? The available information includes economic forecasts, market forecasts, analyses of the prospects of individual stocks and bonds, services that measure the risk and reward profiles of individual stocks and bonds, services designed to help a manager select an optimum portfolio in terms of risk versus return, and services designed to help diagnose the causes of investment returns.

The internal investment organization must also select the brokers for executing the transactions and the bank or banks for custodian services. Finally, it must establish a review procedure and controls to ensure that the desired transactions are carried out, that the securities are acquired or sold on a timely basis, and that recordkeeping is accurate.

If the trustees opt for external management, the problems are somewhat simpler, but the decisions are no less important. First, they must determine the number of managers and the kinds of managers that they need. Then they must select those managers and establish a procedure for monitoring and reviewing them. In addition, they may hire a bank to act as master trustee or custodian for the assets. They must also be prepared for the possibility that they will want to replace one or more of the investment managers in the future.

Periodically, each step of the investment management process should be reviewed to determine whether the investment structure is still appropriate for the evolving needs of the plan.

7.4 Cash Flow Requirements and Investment Goals

The first step in the investment process is to determine the cash flow needs of the retirement plan. The fund's actuary, in conjunction with the plan sponsor, estimates the annual inflow required to honor benefit obligations. Future annual investment returns are also estimated.

A simplified description of how these forecasts are made, and how they influence investment policy, is presented below. The actuary, by examining the demographics of the plan, or similar plan if it is a new one, estimates the long-term obligation of the plan. He examines the growth of the work force covered by the plan, the age composition of the work force, the historic turnover rate, the historic salary growth rate, the national inflation rate, cost of living adjustments, and the mortality rate for the plan workers.

Then the actuary calculates the amount of money the fund will need to meet its obligations over the next thirty or forty years. He then prepares an investment return forecast. Referring to a model portfolio divided into asset groups—stocks, corporate bonds, government bonds, etc.—the actuary studies the long-term investment returns available for the capital markets and determines the return the fund, on average, can reasonably expect to attain on a long-term basis. The estimated return on a portfolio made up entirely of government bonds will differ from the estimated return on a portfolio 50% dedicated to stocks.

The investment return naturally reduces the amount that the plan sponsor has to contribute each year to fund the plan, assuming that the return is positive. However, sponsors must resist the temptation to persuade the actuary to set a higher interest assumption so that the sponsor's contributions can be reduced further. Most actuaries will resist, since they are charged with using their best estimates, but a few might give in. A victory in persuading the actuary to raise the interest assumption will be a hollow one if the actual return falls below the interest assumption, for the plan sponsor must then increase contributions in later periods to make up the difference.

Actuaries often submit a conservative estimate of investment return. According to William A. Dreher of Peat, Marwick, Mitchell & Co., "the actuarial investment return assumption may be artificially low, probably to compensate for other assumptions that are understated, the most likely of which is the forecast of future salary increases. Under these circumstances, the actuary's real expectation for investment return is several points higher than the nominal rate being assumed. Thus, the publicly disclosed assumption bears no relationship to the investment return that will be required if pension costs are not to rise substantially in the future."

Statement of Objectives 7.4.1

The next step is to prepare a statement of investment objectives, focusing on meeting a realistic investment return goal. Trustees should ask their advisors to answer the following questions:

- How important is preservation of capital? That is, if a capital loss is sustained, will benefit payments be jeopardized, or will political and economic difficulties arise?
- How must capital appreciation does the plan need? If the current yield—dividends and interest—is consumed in benefit payments, and contributions are not to bear the whole burden of keeping the assets growing and combating the effects of inflation, some capital appreciation will be needed.
- What level of current income will the plan require? Once again, the answer will depend largely on the level of benefit payment.
- How much variation in year-to-year performance can be tolerated? How will the trustees and their political constituencies react to investment performance that is below average periodically, or even negative?
- How important is liquidity of investments? That is, how marketable must the fund's assets be in the short run? This decision depends on the likelihood of financial surprises. Most state and local pension funds should not need a high degree of liquidity unless they are very poorly funded so that assets must be sold to meet benefit payments.

The trustees may ask their advisors to weigh the importance of each of these factors on a scale of one to five. The averaged weightings will clearly signal the trustees' collective view of the relative importance of these factors.

If the fund is a relatively mature one but also a relatively well-funded one, the trustees might order the criteria as follows: (1) capital preservation, (2) consistency of return, (3) income, (4) capital appreciation, (5) liquidity. They might state clearly the relative importance of the criteria as follows:

> The trustees of the plan regard preservation of capital to be of primary importance in the management of plan assets. Consistency of investment return is also important, and the plan needs a reliable income flow each year for payment of benefits. Capital appreciation and liquidity are of less importance.

This statement sets a basic guideline for the investment managers. They now know that their investment strategy should be relatively conservative and that it should aim at generating steady income. But they need more specific guidance. What, for example, is the minimum long-term rate of return expected of them? In the past some funds specified impossible total return targets, for example "beat the Standard & Poor's index in up and down markets by 15%." Research has shown that such a target is virtually impossible to achieve consistently over a long period. So, what returns are reasonable?

7.5 Forecasts of Investment Returns through The Year 2000

Ibbotson and Sinquefield made some assumptions about the twenty or so years from 1977 through 2000 and projected the long-term investment returns that might be expected. They expected the inflation rate, as measured by the consumer price index, to average 5.4% over the period, with a 5% chance of being as high as 8.8% and a 5% chance of being as low as 2.6%. (The forecast was made prior to the period of double digit inflation and, of course, it was made for the rest of the century.) They expected common stock returns to average 12.5% per year (compounded) over the period, with a 5% chance of being as high as 20.9% and a 5% chance of being as low as 5.1%. Long-term government bonds were predicted to return 7.1% per year with a 5% chance of reaching as high as 8.9% or as low as 5.3%. They expected long-term corporate bonds to return 7.6% per year, with a 5% chance of them being as high as 9.8% or as low as 5.5%

However, they projected much lower *real* returns, after forecasted nominal returns are reduced by the forecasted rate of inflation. Common stocks are expected to average 6.8% per year with a 5% chance of being as high as 16.1% or as low as −1.4%; for government bonds, only 1.5% per year, with a 5% chance they will be as high as 6.0% or as low as −2.3%. These real return figures assume, of course, that inflation will not continue at its current high level, a reasonable expectation based on history.

Most pension executives set their investment return objectives in terms of nominal returns rather than real returns. The impact of inflation should not be ignored. Both nominal and real return objectives should be included in investment planning.

7.6 Specifying the Investment Return Objective

Investment return targets should not only be realistic, but they should also be stated in adequate detail. A simple but inadequate way to set an investment return objective is to specify a single target for the entire portfolio. Say, for example, the actuaries assume an investment yield of 6%. The trustees might set a target at 7.5% and allow the investment managers to choose their own asset mix to achieve that rate of return.

One glaring flaw with this approach is the failure of the trustees to express the relative amount of risk they are willing to tolerate. Stocks are four times riskier than bonds. Some stocks are much riskier than other stocks. Those who set investment goals should also define risk limits, for example by restricting bonds to A rated or higher quality. For many public pension plans, risk limits may be specified by law. The target return should be appropriate for the risk limitations imposed.

Another problem with this approach is that it fails to distinguish between types of investible assets. The projected risk and return associated with government bonds, corporate bonds, stocks and other types of assets vary signficantly (see section 7.5).

Pension executives who fail to distinguish between types of assets in setting investment return objectives are effectively subjecting themselves and pension plan members to unnecessary uncertainty. They have not advised the manager how much risk to incur. They are giving free rein to their investment managers to decide how much risk the pension should incur. They are additionally making it more difficult to evaluate the performance of the manager.

It is also important to define the time horizon within which the investment return target is to apply. Five to eight years may be an appropriate time horizon. The target can be updated at the time of each actuarial study. Of course, investment results should be monitored frequently, perhaps quarterly, and managers should be evaluated annually.

Let us see how these suggestions can be applied in a case study of setting investment return objectives. What follows is a highly simplified example of investment policy-making, designed to show how pension executives can analyze risk and return in different asset types to develop objectives.

The executives in the above case may wish to assume more explicit responsibility for investments by specifying asset allocation. That is, they might decide how much of the fund's assets should be in stocks and how much in bonds at any particular time. If they assume this responsibility, then they can set a return objective of, say, 7.5%, and then set the investment manager's return objectives consistent with the expected long-term returns likely from different investible assets. For example, the equity manager or managers might be told that their return target is 12.5% per year over the long term. The goal might be set lower if adverse economic and market conditions such as those existing in 1979 are expected to persist. It may be optimistic, and it may even be dangerous, to expect a 12.5% return over the next three to five years. The goal must depend in part on expectations of the economic future.

The pension executives might strive to achieve the goal of 7.5% per year over an 8-year time horizon with an asset allocation of 20% common stocks, 20% government bonds and 60% long-term corporate bonds. If each of the investment vehicles achieved the returns projected by Ibbotson and Sinquefield, then the expected long-term annual return for such an asset allocation would be 8.4%, sufficiently in excess of the goal to provide a margin for unusual economic or market conditions.

This checklist will help you determine whether there is potential for improving the management of your long-term investments

☐ Yes ☐ No 1. Does your fund have a written statement of investment policy and objectives?

☐ Yes ☐ No 2. Is the investment return objective specified in terms of total rate of return (income plus realized or unrealized appreciation and minus realized or unrealized depreciation)?

☐ Yes ☐ No 3. Does it specify the risk limits that are acceptable in achieving the target rate of return (for example, occasional accumulations of unrealized losses in the portfolio)?

☐ Yes ☐ No 4. Does it specify a time horizon (e.g., 1, 5, 10 years) over which that return is expected to be achieved?

☐ Yes ☐ No 5. Does it specify quality (e.g., Moody's ratings) and quantity (e.g., percentage of portfolio) restrictions on types of investments?

☐ Yes ☐ No 6. Does it specify responsibility for specific buy and sell decisions?

☐ Yes ☐ No 7. Does it specify the proportion of the investments that may be in different types of fixed-income investments, for example, how much can be put into federal securities?

☐ Yes ☐ No 8. Does it prohibit investment in tax-exempt securities?

☐ Yes ☐ No 9. Is there a thorough, formal review of the investments, the investment strategy, and market and economic conditions conducted periodically?

☐ Yes ☐ No 10. Is a thorough, formal review of the performance of the investment manager, whether internal or external, conducted once a year?

☐ Yes ☐ No 11. For internal managers, is a thorough, formal review of the sources of investment research conducted annually to determine whether they should be changed?

☐ Yes ☐ No 12. Is there a quarterly review of holdings and transactions to ensure that investment guidelines and restrictions are being observed?

☐ Yes ☐ No 13. Is there a review of pension plan actuarial assumptions at least every three years to ensure that the investment goals being pursued are still appropriate?

☐ Yes ☐ No 14. Does a review of investment policy follow automatically after the actuarial review?

If the answer to any of these important questions is "no" there is room for improvement in the administration of your fund. At the very least, changes will result in better control over the fund and fewer unpleasant surprises, and they may result in better investment returns over the long run.

EXHIBIT 7.C / Can Management of Your Long-Term Investments Be Improved?

A 7.5% goal with a 6% actuarial assumption is a very conservative objective. The 7.5% return, according to the Ibbotson and Sinquefield projections could almost be achieved by a 100% investment in long-term corporate bonds. It would be unwise, however, to use such an approach for, if inflation over the period is higher than Ibbotson and Sinquefield projected (so far, it has been), interest rates will probably be higher, outstanding bond prices lower, and total returns will suffer. While the forecasters projected a 95% chance that an all-corporate bond portfolio would return 7.6%, they placed a 5% chance it would be as low as 5.5% or as high as 9.8%. (Forecasts of investment returns are very crude and do not contain the precision level suggested in these estimates.)

A fund sponsor might wish to give a larger margin of return over the interest assumption to provide a cushion against the impact of inflation on benefit levels. This could be done by raising the return objective to, say, 9% per year. While this seems very high in historical terms, and especially in terms of recent investment results, it is still well within the Ibbotson-Sinquefield projection of the average expected return on common stocks between now and the year 2000. Indeed, it might be achieved, based on their return expectations, with a still conservative asset allocation of 60% corporate bonds, 30% common stocks, and 10% government bonds. Such an asset allocation would be expected to provide a return of 9.02% with a 95% probability over an 8-year time horizon.

This is, granted, a highly simplified example of how to set investment return objectives. Many investment counseling firms and banks offer more sophisticated approaches, using tables that show the expected return, and the expected variability of the returns, for virtually every combination of stocks and bonds. Consulting organizations such as Peat, Marwick, Mitchell & Co., Rogers, Casey & Barksdale, Inc., Hewitt Associates, Wilshire Associates, and Barra (Barr Rosenberg Associates), offer sophisticated computer models that use the various plan assumptions together with the risk and return objectives to produce the most efficient asset allocation schedule based on the expected market outlook. Indeed, the assumptions about the capital market outlook can be varied to test their impact on the return expected from the fund and the risk to which it is exposed. In this way the trustees can test their assumptions under a whole range of economic and capital market scenarios.

Internal vs. External Management 7.7

Internal management of investments is used by a greater percentage of public funds than of corporate plans, but more corporate plans are changing to manage at least part of their assets internally, while leaving the remainder with outside managers.

What are the advantages of internal management? First and foremost, the trustees have direct control over the assets. Since the trustees have the ultimate responsibility for the success or failure of the investment process, many believe that they should be involved on a day-to-day basis. Internal management may offer more efficient communications between the trustees and the investment officers. On the other hand, internal managers, like other employees, may become overly involved in office politics and sacrifice their objectivity and professionalism.

Second, for large-sized funds internal management should offer cost advantages. The very largest funds should be able to set up a high quality internal system for less than they would have to spend for a diversified collection of outside managers. However, these funds may find it difficult to reproduce the diversity of styles and resources available in outside managers.

Internal management has disadvantages too. Perhaps the greatest is the potential for political interference. Too often politicians see the pension fund as a political playground where they can earn recognition by "reforming," "improving," or otherwise interfering.

The Twentieth Century Fund report on public employee funds in 1976 cited several examples of political influence in public employee plans. For example, a former governor of Oklahoma was convicted of bribing the secretary of state and chairman of the state retirement fund's board, to direct fund assets into a particular investment prospect.

Another example of political interference involves the Arizona public employee pension fund. This fund was internally managed for many years, and during those years was generally able to report good investment yields. High reported yields bolstered political careers and encouraged the passage of more liberal pension

These are some of the investment management consulting firms who will help set objectives and select managers:

Bache, Halsey, Stuart, Shields, Inc., 100 Gold St., New York, NY 10038; (212) 791–1000

A. G. Becker, Inc., 20 S. Clark St., Chicago, IL 60607; (312) 630–5000

Buck Pension Fund Services, Inc., 2 Penn Plaza, New York, NY 10001; (212) 279–4400

Callan Associates, 601 California St., San Francisco, CA 94108; (415) 986–1213

Collins Associates, 567 San Nicolas Dr., Newbort Beach, CA 92660; (716) 644–5771

Evaluation Associates, Inc., 25 Sylvan Rd., Westport, CT 06880; (203) 226–7864

Fund Monitoring Services, Inc., 6 East 45th St., New York, NY 10022; (212) 661–5560

A. S. Hansen, Inc., 150 N. Wacker Dr., Chicago, IL 60606; (312) 621–9800

Hewitt Associates, 100 Half Day Rd., Lincolnshire, IL 60015; (312) 295-5000

Meidinger Associates, 2440 Grinstead Dr., Louisville, KY 40204; (502) 499–1240

Peat, Marwick, Mitchell & Co., 345 Park Ave., New York, NY 10022; (212) 758–9700

Rogers, Casey & Barksdale, Inc., 1 Federal St., Stamford, CT 06905; (203) 356–9400

Frank Russell Co., Inc., 1100 One Washington Plaza Bldg., Tacoma, WA 98402; (206) 572–9500

Wilshire Associates, Inc., 100 Wilshire Blvd., Santa Monica, CA 90401; (213) 451–8728

EXHIBIT 7.D / Investment Management Consultants

benefits. However, in the mid-1970s when the fund changed to external management it was discovered that the investment returns were not what they seemed. What had been reported was income from dividends of common stocks and the interest from bonds. It took no account of any losses realized when stocks or bonds were sold or of unrealized losses on securities still held.

When the Arizona plan adopted external management and a total return approach, it was found that the fund had accumulated substantial unrealized losses which had to be amortized over many years. The new outside investment managers provided better than average total returns in the difficult investment environment of the next few years but the yield as previously calculated was lower.

Another disadvantage of internal management is that it does not offer diversity of investment management style. Diversification is a key method of reducing risk. Often a particular type of equity investment management may be out of style while another is producing excellent investment returns. For example, in 1971 growth stocks flourished, and growth stock managers turned in returns far above the market in general. While the overall market might have been up only 14.3%, growth stock managers were often up 20% or more. But in the middle of 1973 the markets turned against growth stocks. Indeed, one growth stock, Avon, fell from 140 to 40 in less than a year. It is difficult for a single investment manager to recognize such market turns all the time, though a few do it relatively frequently. And it is difficult for an internal management system to cover all styles.

Another disadvantage of internal management can be cost. For the small-sized fund, external management firms take funds in the $500,000 range and provide individualized service for 1% of the assets per year. It would be difficult to replicate the quality of investment reporting, much less management, for $5,000.

Even for funds of intermediate size internal management can be more costly than external management. If a fund is planning to manage equities and bonds internally, then, at the very least, it should have an experienced equity portfolio manager and an experienced fixed-income manager. Rarely can one person be familiar, let alone expert, in both areas. It would probably be advisable to have an equity analyst to evaluate the research reports and to make recommendations to the portfolio manager. It would also be advisable to have an in-house trader to execute the buy and sell orders given by the portfolio managers. Qualified people in these areas do not come cheaply. A good portfolio manager can earn more than $70,000 a year in an investment counseling firm and $50,000 a year at a bank. A good securities analyst can earn even more, as can a good trader. While it is possible to get portfolio managers, analysts, and traders for less, they will probably be less able or experienced.

One advantage of external management is that the trustees can look for the best talent available, and they can generally buy more of that talent per dollar than they would with internal management in the smaller and medium-sized funds. Investment management consulting organizations, such as Peat, Marwick, Mitchell; Hewitt Associates; Callan Associates; Rogers, Casey & Barksdale, Inc.; Meidinger & Associates, and Collins Associates, have experience in evaluating the talent and the organization of investment management firms and can help sponsors set investment objectives and find suitable investment managers.

It is easier to fire an unsatisfactory outside investment management organization than it is to fire a public servant or civil servants. Firing one outside manager will cause the fund must less disruption than replacing a key member of the internal organization.

Finally, hiring a team of outside managers and giving them full investment discretion, with the trustees retaining the right to monitor their progress toward the objective and their observance of the investment guidelines provided, reduces the political temptation to interfere with the investment of the funds.

7.8 In-house Management: Small Funds

The trustees of small funds, say with $1 million or less in pension assets, may wish to manage investments in house even if they cannot afford to hire a professional investment manager. They should recognize the fact that they have chosen to take a difficult path toward investment survival. Below are a few suggestions on how they can improve the odds of achieving adequate investment yield.

Perhaps the simplest way for such a fund to get adequate investment diversification, together with access to good investment talent, is to buy shares of no-load mutual funds. If these are allowed by the state or county regulation and the provisions of the plan, the trustees could buy shares in two fixed-income funds and two or three equity funds with different approaches. If they wished to move into cash because they did not like the investment climate, they could even buy shares in a money market fund, if they are legally empowered to invest in one.

Mutual funds are an excellent, often overlooked investment tool. Some have excellent long-term investment records, their records are easily available, they have talented investment managers and analysts, and they are diversified.

If mutual funds are not possible because of legislative or regulatory restrictions, the trustees should provide the internal manager with the best in investment research. They should also provide whatever support systems they can afford. It is not enough to rely on the local brokerage houses for research and recommendations and for execution of trades. The quality of research varies enormously from institution to institution. Some are better at analyzing the market or economic environment than at selecting stocks. Others are better at picking stocks than reading the investment outlook.

The manager should learn how to select brokerage firms to make transactions. Different brokerage firms quote different commissions for transactions of the same size since brokerage fees are now negotiable. And different trading desks can vary in their ability to make the most advantageous trades. A series of poorly executed trades can wipe out the gain from a correct investment move. The best way to find the trading capability is to ask professional investors.

In-house Management: Medium-sized Funds 7.9

The in-house management task for the medium-sized fund is still difficult, but it gets easier. A fund in the $1 million to $5 million range can afford more services and has more options. For example, it is much easier to adequately diversify a fund in this size range than one with $1 million or less, because it is easier to take positions in the twenty-five to thirty stocks which are regarded as the minimum for good diversification. However, it is still difficult for the fund to afford good investment talent. In most cases it must still rely on a staff member who has other responsibilities as well.

Only when the fund exceeds $10 million does it become feasible to hire an investment professional. At this level, if the trustees are willing to allocate 1% of asset value to management, they can hire a couple of managers and equip them with the necessary support services. But a top quality in-house management team probably cannot be put together for less than $250,000 in total costs. This size of budget would be appropriate for funds of $25 million or more. It would provide for the salaries of several quality managers, and for support services including computer-based analytical systems.

In-house Management: Large Funds 7.10

A fund that has accumulated assets greater than $25 million can afford to hire a team of investment professionals. The larger the fund, the larger the team can be. An equity portfolio manager (if equities are allowed) and a bond portfolio manager should be hired as soon as possible. They should be professionals with significant experience in the investment world, either in a bank or an investment counseling firm. Salaries will probably at least have to match the salaries being paid at the local banks.

When the costs can be afforded, it would be wise to add a security analyst to wade through the research material provided by brokers seeking business and to select the primary research organizations that the fund should patronize, for the quality and usefulness of research varies significantly.

It is best to provide the investment management team with whatever backup systems can be afforded. With a large fund it may make sense to index part of the equity portfolio and actively manage that part, that is, to construct a portion of the portfolio that closely resembles a market index in performance. This is the approach being taken by some large corporate funds. For a reasonable one-time cost (about $14,000) it is possible to buy a computer software package that enables the in-house manager to keep an index fund tracking with the Standard & Poor's 500. Indexing a segment of the fund reduces the overall volatility of the fund relative to the market as a whole. That is, the whole equity portion will underperform the market less in bad times than it would if it had been actively managed by most managers, and in good markets it will outperform the market less than it would if it had been completely actively managed.

If the equity portion of the fund is large enough, it might be desirable to use a portfolio optimization system, provided by outside firms. In Chapter 9, an officer of Wells Fargo describes how he uses his firm's system to aid his clients.

7.11 External Management: Small Funds

The fund with $1 million or less in assets, whether it chooses internal or external management, cannot afford all the options open to larger funds. The very small fund has a limited number of alternatives. Most very small corporate funds choose to buy annuities from insurance companies, But annuities, while they solve administrative problems, are generally not a good investment bargain. They are somewhat similar to whole-life insurance policies, and the investment return assumption in their pricing is generally low, sometimes below even bank passbook rates. Further, they limit flexibility; they can be costly to get out of if the sponsor wishes to change to different forms of investment.

A more sophisticated form of annuity contract is the guaranteed investment contract (GIC) offered by some insurance companies. These offer a higher rate of return than the standard annuity, and they are generally for a specific period, say ten years, rather than for the working life of an employee. A GIC may make sense for a fund with limited need of liquidity and a low tolerance for risk. However, some argue that it makes more sense to buy high-quality bonds than to buy a GIC. A high-quality bond carries little risk of default and a high interest rate. Further, with a high-quality bond the sponsor will benefit from the capital gain if interest rates fall. With a GIC the insurance company reaps the benefits of the capital gain.

Both annuities and GIC's are passive strategies for the small fund. Small funds can also put their money to work through bank and insurance company pooled funds. Here the banks and the insurance companies pool the assets of many small pension and profit-sharing plans to achieve economies of scale in management of the assets. They offer a wide range of pooled funds, including the standard stock and bond funds. Morgan Guaranty Trust, for example, offers several separate common stock funds—one invests in S&P 500 type stocks, another invests in smaller companies, a third invests in new and emerging companies, a fourth invests in the foreign stock markets. Morgan also offers bond funds and a real estate fund that invests largely in mortgages and mortgage certificates. Other banks and insurance companies offer varieties of commingled funds.

Some investment management firms offer separate management funds as small as $500,000. Small investment management firms may be willing to manage small funds, and they often have innovative investment approaches. But even larger, well-established firms, such as David L. Babson, take smaller funds.

Finally, the mutual fund is an option. Some investment managers have set themselves up as small fund specialists and use mutual funds as a way of getting economies of scale. Instead of trying to select portfolios of stocks that will produce the best results, these firms try to select portfolios of mutual funds. Instead of having to buy thirty to fifty stocks to get adequate diversification, they buy half a dozen mutual funds with good investment records.

External Management: Medium Funds 7.12

Once again, a fund in the $1 million to $25 million range has more options open to it. It has all the options of the smaller fund and a wider selection of management firms willing to offer individual management. While the very small fund would be hard put to hire anyone but a balanced manager (one who uses both common stocks and bonds), the medium-sized fund can hire specialist managers. It can hire a management firm that invests only in stocks and another that invests only in bonds. Alternatively, the sponsor can split the money among several commingled funds that offer diversity of management style. The sponsor of the larger fund might even be able to adopt a strategy that is becoming more common among corporate pension sponsors. This is the active-passive approach pioneered by Honeywell. In this approach, part of the assets are passively held in an index fund, and a group of specialized managers all with different investment strategies is placed around the passive core. This could be done with commingled funds by the medium-sized sponsor.

External Management: Large Funds 7.13

Large funds, with over $25 million in assets, have a virtually unlimited range of investment approaches. With $25 million, a sponsor could give $5 million each to five different managers. The sponsor could select one active fixed-income manager, one passive fixed-income manager, one index fund manager, one investment manager specializing in smaller stocks, and one who invests in the larger growth stocks, or some other combination. The large fund sponsor has all the options for both external management and internal management.

Investment Approaches—Equities 7.14

When interviewing the prospective investment officers for internal management or investment firms for outside management, the trustees must be clear about the investment approach they want for both equity and fixed-income investments. For equity investments the basic choices are between the fundamental, technical, and modern portfolio theory approaches.

7.14.1 Fundamental Approach

The fundamental approach, as its name implies, attempts to look at the fundamentals of individual companies to determine whether the values of the companies are fully reflected in their prices. It attempts to determine whether companies are undervalued or overvalued at their current market prices. One approach to fundamental investing, the top-down approach, starts by looking at the economy and where it seems to be going, assessing which industries are likely to fare best in that economic scenario, and then analyzing the companies within those industries that seem likely to fare best and to be underpriced.

A bottom-up approach starts by looking for companies whose market prices appear to be below their realistic value. There are several methods of determining whether a stock is underpriced. The classical method is the Graham and Dodd method first expounded by Benjamin Graham in the 1930s and described in detail in the classic book *Security Analysis*. The Graham approach consists of five basic steps. First, determine the company's average earnings per share over the last ten years. Second, determine the average growth of the company's earnings per share over the last ten years. Third, establish an appropriate price-earnings ratio for this company by looking at the price-earnings ratios of companies with similar growth or earnings rates. Fourth, multiply the p/e by the company's average earnings to get an appropriate selling price for the stock. Fifth, buy the stock if its current price is at least 33% below the selling price established in the first four steps.

Another bottom-up approach, with many variations, attempts to project corporate earnings or dividends for a number of years, usually one to five years. These projections are based on intensive study of the management of the company, its product line, its historic growth rate, and the outlook for the economy. Then these projections are discounted back to a present value by an appropriate interest rate. If the present value of the earnings or dividends is greater than the current market price of the stock, then the stock is a buy candidate. If the present value is less than the market price, it is a sell candidate.

7.14.2 Technical Approach

Technical analysis is an approach based on historical stock or market trends. Technical analysts, in general, attempt to determine the emotional state of the stock market, or the direction and momentum of the market, from market statistics. They do not attempt to analyze the investment outlook for individual stocks based on intrinsic value or earnings projections.

The pure technical analyst believes that fundamental analysis is of little value to the investor because all the relevant information about a stock is already reflected in the price. In this the technical analysts find themselves in agreement with the proponents of modern capital market theory. The technician believes that the market as a whole, and even individual stocks, move in regular cycles and that the problem is to determine where in the cycle the market is. To this end they chart aspects of the market and the stocks, hoping to be able to determine the state of the market of particular stocks. However, in the past two decades, academic research has thrown perhaps more doubt on the validity and usefulness of technical research than on fundamental research.

Modern Portfolio Theory Approach 7.14.3

Modern portfolio theory forms the basis of the investment styles of several investment management organizations and of several products, for example, the index fund concept. (See chapter 9 for a more detailed description of applied modern portfolio theory.) The theory holds that the stock market (and perhaps the bond market) is very efficient at digesting information and that it is therefore difficult for the individual investor to consistently have unique information about individual stocks or about the market in general. Information that will affect the price of a stock spreads quickly enough that the price will adjust before the individual can gain a significant advantage.

Numerous academic research projects have shown that the market is indeed very efficient, though perhaps not perfectly efficient as some scholars would have it. The research has been supported by the relative lack of consistent investment success by professional investment managers. Few investment managers have been able to produce investment results superior to those that would have been achieved by investing in a random selection of stocks. Indeed, fewer than 20% of professional managers have been able to equal the market indexes over recent ten-year periods.

Ironically, this very failure suggests that the market is not perfectly efficient. If it were perfectly efficient, it would be as difficult to underperform consistently as to outperform it, once results have been adjusted for transactions costs. That is, if all stocks are efficiently priced, it should be as difficult to select stocks that will lose money as it is to select those that will be winners.

Many investors now believe that the market is relatively efficient, but not perfectly so. That is, they recognize that it is far more difficult to beat the market than most people have believed and that most stocks are correctly priced most of the time. But they believe that there are some inefficiencies that can be exploited. This is so, they believe, because market efficiency is based largely on the work of security analysts who research stocks and spread their information. There are so many stocks available that the analysts cannot turn their full attention to all of them at once. For this reason the smaller stocks, those outside the well-researched Standard & Poor's 500, may be inefficiently priced at times. Some investment managers have had better-than-market returns in the past decade because they recognized that smaller companies, those outside the S&P 500, were often inefficiently priced, and they concentrated their research and buying activities among these stocks.

Investment Approaches—Bonds 7.15

Fixed-income investing can be broken down into two basic approaches, active and passive, each with a number of variations. Active fixed-income managers attempt to anticipate changes in the fixed-income market and to vary the structure of their portfolios accordingly. For example, if they believe that interest rates are likely to rise, they sell their long-term bonds and buy short-term ones. If they think interest rates are near a peak, they do the opposite. This is because bond prices are affected by changes in interest rates. If interest rates rise, the market value of outstanding bonds declines. A bond that has a face value of $1,000 and pays 7% should bring a price near $1,000 if interest rates on similar bonds are 7%. If interest rates on similar new issue bonds rose to 8%, the bond would bring less than $1,000, because an investor would buy the 7% bond only if its price fell far enough for his effective yield to be 8%. That is, only if the price is no more than $875. In that case the seller would suffer a capital loss. Of course, the investor could hold the bond until interest rates decline or until the bond matures, and some bond managers do this. They structure their portfolios to achieve a certain long-range return and restructure only by very careful buying of issues with new cash flow. These are passive managers.

Some active managers go beyond attempting to anticipate changes in the fixed-income markets and look for inefficiencies in those markets. They look for bonds whose current prices might be lower than the prices of bonds with a similar quality rating, coupon (interest rates), and maturity (time to redemption). When they find such bonds, they sell and buy bonds to modify their portfolio. This kind of active bond manager is sometimes called a trader because he trades in bonds, constantly seeking a price advantage.

Socially Oriented Investing 8

Pools of state and local public funds have always held a special temptation to their sponsors. Looking at money accumulating in pension funds, the general fund and other accounts, trustees, legislators and executives visualize a host of worthwhile investments. As pension funds and general fund bank balances have grown, particularly in the economically troubled 1970s, so have the proposals for socially useful investments. Private, state, and local government pension funds now have assets approaching $500 billion. State and local government pension funds alone have assets in excess of $200 billion. Each year state and local government bodies pour an additional $20 billion to $25 billion into the funds. Bank deposits of general funds and other state and local public accounts comprise close to one-tenth of all commercial bank deposits. What if these billions were poured into low-income housing, child care centers, rehabilitation of sewer systems, or local economic development projects? Why the tattered infrastructure of the northern industrial states, or the immature infrastructure of the industrializing southern states, could be dramatically improved. That is the argument being advanced by a number of advocates today.

This concept is called "socially oriented investing," or simply "social investing" by some observers. But social investing is actually two separate concepts. There is an active concept of social investing—changing society by actively making investments that change the social environment in some way. But there is also a passive concept of social investing, which attempts to change some aspect of the environment by avoiding certain investments: for example, by selling or not buying the stock of companies that pollute the atmosphere or the water or do business with South Africa.

Active social investing of pension funds is the deliberate use of such funds to spark the development of some part of the social or economic fabric, for example, construction of needed housing. In the short term, active social investing often seeks to promote economic development or to provide jobs to specific sectors of the economy such as the building trades. In the long term, the active approach seeks to provide a long-term asset for the society—a needed hospital, housing, or the like.

Several avenues are available to those pursuing active social investing. The most mundane is through the use of targeted long-term pension fund investments in stocks, bonds, and mortgages. For example, the funds might be invested in the stocks or bonds of local companies to promote their growth and keep them healthy. The funds could also be used to provide housing money in a state or locality by buying pools of Ginnie Maes (Government National Mortgage Association) mortgages. (See below for a description of these and other instruments.) Pools of such mortgages can be bought from a specific geographic area. It should be possible for the banks originating the mortgages to make new mortgages, thus stimulating local housing construction.

The working capital balances of pension funds, general funds, and other accounts could be deposited in particular banks (as demand and savings accounts and CDs) with the understanding that the money will be used for local mortgages. This "link deposit" approach has recently been adopted by several public investors. It is based on the belief that financial institutions will change their lending practices to obtain attractive deposits from government agencies.

In all these approaches the objective is to achieve a market rate of return while at the same time promoting some social benefit. Some advocates, however, suggest using pension fund assets to pursue social aims even when market rates of return cannot be achieved for projects such as low-income housing. They argue that the indirect or *secondary* return in increased tax revenues and lower unemployment benefits coupled with the nonmonetary value of providing a valued social service justifies the lower direct or *primary* return on investment. (See Exhibit 8.A.)

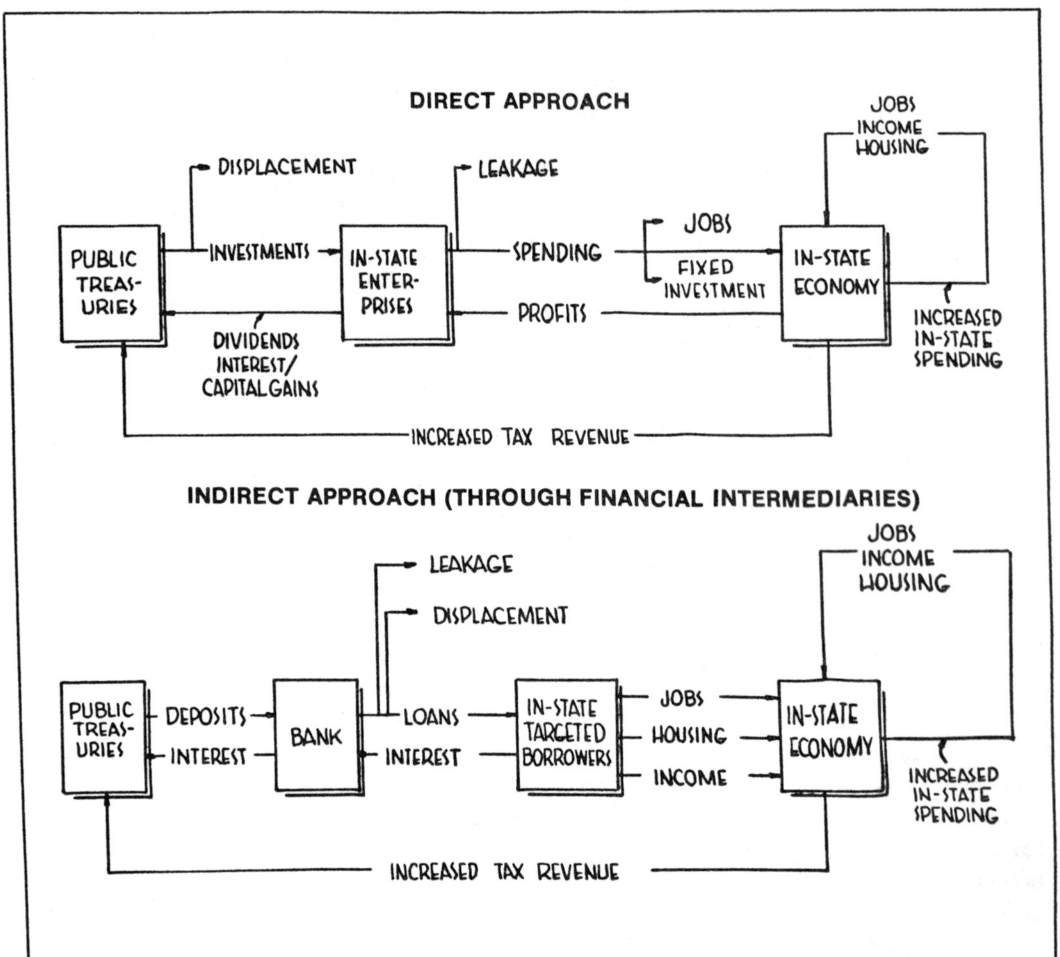

EXHIBIT 8.A / Active Social Investing

Critics of active social investing are numerous. Conventional economists continue to favor an analytic perspective that weighs only monetarily quantifiable risks and yields of the primary investment. They note the difficulties of identifying and measuring secondary benefits and costs. Existing techniques of estimating secondary impacts, they argue, are either too expensive (such as elaborate input-output models) or are too simple to trace all the benefits and costs.

Conventional economists contend in addition that the capital markets of the United States are "efficient," that is, private sector investors will naturally seek out investment opportunities that offer adequate yields for the risks involved. If low-income housing promised sufficiently attractive rates of return, they argue, there would be no shortage of investment capital and no need to use pension funds. The same applies to hospitals, child care centers and senior citizen centers. Critics have argued against using pension fund assets to rescue declining industries to preserve jobs. If a declining industry cannot attract enough capital to revitalize itself in conventional capital markets, most prudent fund managers may regard the expected return from the investment as too small to offset the risk.

With passive social investing certain investments are avoided in an attempt to change the behavior of those enterprises. The most familiar example is the campaign of some college endowments to sell their securities holdings of American companies doing business with South Africa in an attempt to force them either to modify their behavior in South Africa, so as to weaken apartheid, or to halt operations in South Africa.

A variant of passive social investing involves putting pressure on the targeted companies through their underwriters or other intermediaries. A successful example of the use of this approach was the campaign of the Amalgamated Clothing and Textile Workers' Union (ACTWU) to force executives off the board of directors of J.P. Stevens, Inc. Other unions, responding to broad hints from the ACTWU, threatened to fire Manufacturers Hanover Trust as manager of their pension funds if a bank officer did not leave Stevens' board and a Stevens executive did not leave the bank's board. Both executives resigned.

Another interesting example is the decision of a group of nuns and priests in Kentucky to buy the stock of a company whose behavior they wished to influence. The stock was not broadly held, and the group hoped to be able to use proxy votes at annual meetings to bring about the desired behavior, perhaps even to win a seat on the board. But this was a special situation; most companies are too broadly held for this tactic to work.

Some labor organizations are now refusing to invest in firms with anti-union records. A few activists even suggest that pension fund managers refuse to invest in the securities of persistent violators of federal employment or environmental standards.

Methods of Active Social Investing 8.1

There are many methods of active social investing. The most obvious applications of long-term pension fund investing to achieve social objectives are outlined below.

8.1.1 Common Stocks

Advantages. If the stock is newly issued, then the proceeds flow directly to the company, strengthening its financial base and financing expansion. If the company uses the money to expand locally, the desired effect of the investment has been achieved. Even if it expands elsewhere, local jobs may have been made more secure because the company is stronger. If the stock is not a new issue, then the effect is much less direct. There is no advantage to a local company unless the increased demand for the stock lowers the cost of raising capital for the company. That is, if the price of the stock moves substantially, say from \$10 a share to \$15 a share, then it costs the company less to raise additional external funds because it has to issue relatively fewer shares to obtain a given amount of funds.

Much high-quality research is available for measuring a company's prospects, thus reducing risk. Among the factors considered are the dividend yield, which if average, would be about 5% per year at present; a chance for substantial appreciation of the investment; and a liquid market for disposal of the investment should the need arise. Total returns from common stock investments have far surpassed the returns available on all other types of investment (with the possible exception of real estate) over the past fifty years.

Disadvantages. There is always a chance of capital loss if the company should fall on hard times or if the market should be negative when the trustees wish to sell the investment. The greatest drawback as far as social investing is concerned is the difficulty of measuring the impact of the investment. This is, of course, a problem that afflicts virtually all social investing programs. How much has investment in a particular stock helped the company or strengthened employment in the area? The causal relationship between the actions of a single investor or a group of investors and the long-run price of a company's stock is tenuous. In addition, attempting to boost stock prices in the short run may expose the leaders of the campaign to legal liability in view of federal laws prohibiting unfair investment practices.

The related problems of displacement and leakage must also be considered. These problems plague virtually all aspects of social investing. Displacement occurs when the public pension fund merely substitutes for other investors who would have purchased the shares. Leakage occurs when the proceeds of a new stock issuance are used by the company to expand outside the pension fund's target area. In both cases, the pension fund's objective of increasing local investment is frustrated.

8.1.2 Corporate Bonds

Advantages. Many of the advantages of common stocks also apply to publicly traded corporate bonds. Like common stocks, they are highly liquid because there is a highly developed secondary market in which the bonds may be resold. There is also much research available, with the rating companies evaluating the quality of many bonds. Almost any amount of money can be put into the bond market, though specific corporate issues are of limited size. The historic returns on corporate bonds have trailed those of common stocks, but they are still superior to the returns on government securities.

Disadvantages. As with common stocks, funds invested in new bonds accrue to the company directly. But also like buying stocks, purchasing previously issued bonds has only an indirect effect on the corporation. Displacement and leakage problems must also be considered.

Locally Issued Municipal Bonds 8.1.3

Advantages. The primary advantage of investing in locally issued municipal bonds is the promise of a double dividend: a market for local issues is found, and income for the pension fund is secured.

Disadvantages. Income from municipal bonds is exempt from taxation and therefore carries a far lower yield (two-thirds to one-half) than AAA to A rated taxable corporate bonds; their yield is even lower than Treasury obligations. Public pension funds, which are tax exempt, lower their investment income significantly by purchasing municipal bonds. To compensate for reduced investment income, a pension fund would have to increase contributions and/or reduce benefits.

Pension fund purchases of municipal bonds may simply displace purchases that private investors would have made. But what if the locality cannot sell its bonds to private investors? New York City faced the prospect of bankruptcy in the late 1970s when it failed to attract private investors for its bonds. The city's pension funds were induced to purchase huge sums of city bonds, thus staving off financial collapse. (The legal ramifications of these purchases are analyzed in section 8.9.)

New York City's case was exceptional. Only in rare cases is pension fund purchase of locally issued bonds a viable solution to municipal financial crisis. Other solutions, such as a state loan (Boston), a state aid advance (Philadelphia), and limited state guarantee of local debt service (Newark), are politically and judicially more attractive.

State and State Agency Bonds 8.1.4

Advantages. By investing in state bonds, a pension fund is helping the state in its general operations. Pension funds can also invest in the bonds of agencies that apply bond proceeds to narrowly defined areas of need, for example, housing. State housing finance authorities issue bonds to create moderate and low-income housing.

Disadvantages. These bonds are exempt from taxation and therefore have the same drawbacks as local municipal bonds.

Private Placements 8.1.5

Advantages. A private placement of corporate bonds allows the pension fund to purchase bonds directly from the issuer, thereby eliminating underwriting costs and the costs of registering the securities with the Securities and Exchange Commission. The yield to the pension fund should accordingly be somewhat higher than the yield on publicly issued bonds of the same corporation. Another advantage is the ability of the pension fund to propose to the issuer how the bond proceeds should be applied.

Disadvantages. In exchange for higher yield, the investor in private placements gives up some liquidity, as the secondary market for the bonds may be poor. And the pension fund's ability to bargain with the issuer about how the proceeds are applied may be in reality quite limited: the issuer can threaten to place its bonds elsewhere.

8.1.6 Ginnie Maes

Ginnie Maes are Government National Mortgage Association (GNMA) mortgage-backed passthrough securities. The association issues certificates, similar to bonds, which are backed by pools of FHA and VA insured mortgages initiated by mortgage bankers, brokers, or savings and loan associations. Principal and interest payments are passed through to the investor monthly.

Advantages. Ginnie Maes have several positive features for the social investor. Pools of mortgages can be tailored to the needs of the investor, so a particular state or local pension fund can specify that its pool be made up of mortgages on local properties. Ginnie Maes generally carry yields slightly higher than high-grade corporate bonds. Timely payment of interest and principal is guaranteed by the federal government. While Ginnie Maes are traded as if they have twelve-year average lives, the actual life is often far shorter, eight or nine years. This results in a relatively high yield for the actual term of the investment.

Disadvantages. There are very few drawbacks to Ginnie Maes. Perhaps most important from the viewpoint of the socially concerned investor is that Ginnie Mae mortgage pools are generally not made up of low-income housing mortgages. For the most part, they consist of pools of mortgages made to the lower levels of the middle class. Banks still originate the mortgages, and even with FHA and VA assistance most low-income families find house prices beyond their reach in most areas of the country. Another disadvantage is that the secondary market for Ginnie Maes, and their cousins, Fannie Maes, is still developing. Thus there may be a problem with liquidity. Some people find the monthly payments of interest and principal amortization to be a disadvantage because of the administrative chore of reinvesting them.

Overall, Ginnie Maes are among the best social investments. One advantage—the premium over corporate interest rates—and one disadvantage—the underdeveloped secondary market—may both disappear as more investors become familiar with them.

Freddie Macs 8.1.7

Freddie Macs are similar to Ginnie Maes in that the Federal Home Loan Mortgage Corporation (FHLMC) buys and pools conventional mortgages and sells them in the secondary market. Interest and principal are paid monthly. The advantages and disadvantages are generally similar to Ginnie Maes. However, Freddie Macs carry a slightly higher rate of interest than Ginnie Maes because the principal and interest are not government guaranteed. No security of the FHLMC has ever defaulted, and the underlying mortgages serve as collateral. A major drawback is that targeting is difficult since most Freddie Mac packages are geographically diverse mortgage pools.

Farmers Home Administration Participation Certificates 8.1.8

The Farmers Home Administration (FmHA) makes loans for a variety of purposes including improvements to family farms, business development projects in towns with populations of less than 50,000, and refinancing of farm debt. The FmHA allows the lending institution to sell the portion of the loans it guarantees.

Advantages. The guaranteed portion of the loans is backed by the full faith and credit of the U.S. government. The yields on these loan packages usually range between 0.25% and 0.75% over those of U.S. government agency securities of comparable maturity and quality. Further, an investor can specify desired loan characteristcs, making it possible to target funds for specific purposes, for example, to stimulate business development and thus employment.

Disadvantages. Many eligible farmers and small businessmen fail to take advantage of FmHA loans due to lack of knowledge of the program. Without additional demand, it may be difficult to justify a program to increase investment in these instruments.

SBA Participation Certificates 8.1.9

The Small Business Administration guarantees parts of loans made by commercial banks to small businesses. The banks may then sell the guaranteed portion of the loans to third parties.

Advantages. Since the loans are made to small manufacturers, wholesalers, and retailers, the socially conscious investor can stimulate a particular kind of development. Further, the investor can target the assistance by buying loans from commercial banks in a particular area. The yields to maturity of these loans are generally 0.25% to 0.75% higher than the yields on U.S. government agency securities.

Disadvantages. The maximum size of an SBA loan is only $500,000. An investor may have to purchase many of them to have a significant impact on the targeted area, raising administrative costs. In addition, SBA loan yields are less than those of high quality corporate bonds. Liquidity is also limited.

8.1.10 Other Guaranteed Loan Investments

Other guaranteed loan programs sponsored by the federal government allow investors to buy the guaranteed portion of the loan from the sponsoring bank, thereby freeing the bank's funds for additional loans. These programs include the Federal Vessel Loans, Coal Loan Guarantees, Business Development Guaranteed Loans, Aircraft Guarantee Loans and Coal Conversion Guarantee Loans. Most are similar to the other investments described here, and have similar advantages and disadvantages.

8.1.11 Real Estate Leasebacks

Direct investment in real estate is unusual for public pension funds in the United States but very common in Great Britain and other European countries. Where used in this country, the most popular form is the purchase and leaseback of real estate. The pension fund buys the real estate and may build on it. It then leases the property to an operator, such as a franchise chain of a manufacturing concern. If it is an office building, it can be leased to a management company or to a large corporation. If the property is a retail outlet, say a supermarket or a fast-food franchise, the owner receives a guaranteed minimum or a fixed percentage of sales.

Advantages. These investments can be targeted to help well-defined geographical areas and the yield can be much higher than common stocks or bonds. In addition, the public treasury may quickly benefit from increased sales, income, and property taxation generated by the project. Real estate investments are available in a range of sizes, from a few hundred thousand dollars to millions of dollars.

Disadvantages. Real estate investments can be very illiquid. While returns in the past have been high, returns in the late 1970s were depressed because of competition for good opportunities from foreign and domestic investors able to take full advantage of the liberal depreciation allowance and low capital gains taxes associated with real estate investment. Tax exempt investors such as public pension funds, cannot take advantage of these tax benefits. In addition, to evaluate real estate opportunities requires expertise not generally available to state and municipal pension funds.

8.1.12 Summary

These major avenues for socially oriented investing will leave some social activists unsatisfied because they do not reach the poor and underprivileged. But they may be acceptable to those who argue that pension funds should be invested in the sole interest of the beneficiaries and who interpret that to mean invested to earn the highest return compatible with an appropriate level of risk. Few will argue against investing pension funds in government-guaranteed securities which incidentally may be targeted to help local housing and employment, since these investments are easy to make and carry competitive yields.

Investments other than government guaranteed securities and high quality, publicly traded corporate stocks and bonds generally embody greater risk and less liquidity and must be examined carefully by professionally qualified analysts. In a proposal made to one union pension fund, a builder asked the fund to invest $1.5 million, almost half of its assets, in a construction project that the builder said would provide employment for the union's members. However, the union found that the project would provide only about two weeks of work for half a dozen men. Needless to say, it decided that the investment was an inefficient way to use its funds; the employment opportunities offered to the members were not sufficient to offset the lower return and the higher level of risk. An examination of many socially oriented investment opportunities would probably show the same—that the social benefits, as prudently forecasted, are insufficient to justify the investment.

If a board of trustees decides to make such an investment, the decision should be made within the context of carefully drafted investment guidelines. Exhibit 8.B furnishes some sources for social investment guidelines. Subsequent exhibits present other guidelines proposed or in use by governments, unions, and institutions of higher education.

Plan beneficiaries are justified in asking why they should be responsible for the sponsoring of the social investment. Should not the federal, state, or local government sponsor social investments directly from general revenues? There is no doubt that the pension beneficiaries are in effect subsidizing the general public in such a situation, for if the investment return is less than a market return, then the costs of the pension plan to the sponsor have increased.

The trustees might ask the beneficiaries to approve such an investment. They might find, for example, that retired beneficiaries favor investments in health care facilities for the aged because they are old, and because their benefits are not likely to be increased in any event. If the plan is well funded, then the low investment return poses no threat to the benefits of those already retired. But those still working might see no direct benefit in these investments. Lower investment yields today might mean lower benefits in the future.

Another example of this dichotomy of interests might be a proposal to use pension funds to promote employment in a state. This use of funds might be beneficial to retirees still living in the state but would not help those who have moved elsewhere. Many New York State retirement checks, for example, are mailed to Florida. Are the interests of those retirees helped by investments that spur employment in the private sector in New York State or build health care or child care centers in the state?

These organizations monitor activity in social investing. Some have taken formal positions advocating or opposing social investing programs.

California Alternative Investment Task Force, 616 25 St., Sacramento, CA 95814 (415) 548–1320)

California Public Policy Center, Bradbury Building, 304 South Broadway, Room 224, Los Angeles, CA 90013 (213) 628–8888)

Center for Economic Studies, 475 Kingsley Ave., Palo Alto, CA 93401 (415) 328–1039

Conference of Alternative State and Local Policies, 2000 Florida Ave., NW, Washington, DC 20003 (202) 387–6030

Community Economics, Inc., 6529 Telegraph Ave., Oakland, CA 94609 (415) 653–5555

Corporate Data Exchange, Inc., 198 Broadway, Room 706, New York, NY 10038 (212) 962–2980

Council on Economic Priorities, 84 Fifth Ave., New York, NY 10011 (212) 691–8550

Interfaith Center on Corporate Responsibility, Room 556, 475 Riverside Drive, New York, NY 10027 (212) 870–2936

Investor Responsibility Research Center, 1522 K St. NW, Washington, DC (202) 833–3727

National Association of State Retirement Administrators, 302 Public Safety Building, Montgomery, AL 36100

National Conference of State Legislators, 1405 Curtis St., Denver, CO 80200

Pensions & Investment Age, 740 N. Rush St., Chicago, IL 60611
P & I, a leading journal on institutional investing, reports frequently on social investing.

People's Business Commission, 1346 Connecticut Ave. NW, Washington, DC 20009 (202) 466–2823

Strategic Investment Advisors, 1320 Campus Drive, Berkeley, CA 94708 (916) 443–6281

Wisconsin Center for Public Policy, 315 W. Gorham St., Madison, WI 52703 (608) 257–4414

EXHIBIT 8.B / Further Information on Social Investing

8.2 Investing for Employment

Jeremy Rifkin and Randy Barber's book, *The North Shall Rise Again: Pension Power and Politics in the 1980's* (Beacon Press, Boston, 1978) has focused national attention on social investing. Its main thesis is that state, municipal, and union pension funds together have enough economic clout to reverse the flow of industry from the old northern industrial states to the Sunbelt. Rifkin and Barber argue that such funds should be invested to support companies remaining in the northern states, to buy out and renovate failing companies, perhaps even to start new companies in the North to preserve industries and jobs.

However, G. J. Borjas of the University of California, Santa Barbara, has examined the Barber-Rifkin thesis and finds it wrong on several counts. In his monograph, *Union Control of Pension Funds,* he contends that jobs are following the workers. People are moving South and West for the life-style, not for jobs, and industry is following the population shift. He argues that the companies the pension funds were likely to buy were "losers." Why, he asks would any employee want his pension fund assets invested in companies that were likely ultimately to fail?

The Wisconsin Center for Public Policy and the A. G. Becker Company, an investment management consulting firm, recently studied the effect of concentrating more of the fund's investments in Wisconsin, as is called for by the Rifkin-Barber strategy. The study found that the controlling factor in the degree of risk was the financial condition of the fund. The greater the unfunded liability of the fund, the greater the risk added by increasing the amount of the fund invested within the state.

A. G. Becker found that for the Wisconsin fund there was a 2% greater risk to the pension beneficiary if 30% of the state fund's assets were concentrated in Wisconsin. The risk increases by 4% if 70% of the assets are concentrated in the state. These figures assume that the investments would provide returns equivalent to those achievable outside the state. The risks would be even higher if the increased availability of funds for investment in the state lowered intrastate investment yields.

On the other hand, the Wisconsin study did conclude that the investment of $50 million in the state's manufacturing sector would, at the very least, create 3,000 more non-agricultural jobs and increase personal income by $60 million to $70 million per year. In turn, state personal tax revenues would rise $5 to $6 million annually.

Rifkin and Barber also suggest that pension funds be used to prevent corporate operations from moving out of state, by making a private placement loan on favorable terms to the business. If the company is moving because of high operating costs, then the lower cost of money might be enough to offset the lower operating costs of the other state.

But Richard Ennis, a vice-president with A. G. Becker, has argued that this thinking is flawed. Ennis, in a recent issue of ***Pensions & Investment Age,*** cited a hypothetical case in which Widget Enterprises, Inc., is selling its widgets at $3 each (it cannot raise prices because of competition). In state A its costs are $1 for labor, $1 for raw materials, and $1 for debt service. If it moves to state B, its costs will be $0.75 per widget for labor (because of lower, non-unionized labor costs), $1 per widget for raw materials, and $1 for debt service. Thus it can make a profit of $0.25 per widget by moving to state B. But union and political forces urge the state employees pension fund to make a loan at three-fourths the going market rate to the company to keep it in the state. The fund agrees and the loan is offered. The company thinks that is a good offer and is on the verge of accepting when state B counters with an offer of its own. It can offer a similar loan from its state pension funds, and once again it has undercut state A.

Ennis reasons that if states begin to offer such loans backed by their pension funds, the rational corporate strategy is to encourage a bidding war. If the investment subsidies or tax concessions offered by the states are competitive, the company is likely to accept the subsidies of, and locate in, the same state that it would have located in without the offers of subsidy. Only the company and the federal tax collectors gain, and at the expense of the public pension funds that grant the subsidies.

8.3 Examples of Active Social Investing

Active social investing of state and local public pension funds has probably gone on since these funds began to emerge at the end of the 19th century as major pools for long-term investment. And without doubt many pension fund investments over the past three generations have been made with real or purported social objectives in mind. But examples of major active social investing programs in the 1970s are relatively few. If social investing is narrowly defined to include only investments with a lower return or a higher than normal risk, then it is hard to find *bona fide* examples among public pension funds today.

Universities, colleges, church groups, and private sector unions experimented with active and passive social investing in the 1970s. Trustees of public pension funds and managers of the investable assets of general and other government funds have been in general very cautious. Exhibits 8.C, 8.D, and 8.E profile several social investing programs undertaken in the 1970s.

Perhaps the most historic social investments by pension funds in recent history were those involving Chrysler Corporation, the United Auto Workers, and the State of Michigan. The auto manufacturer and the union signed a unique contract in 1979. The agreement called for 10% of the company's net pension contributions to be put into social investments such as mortgages on low and average cost homes for union members, nursing homes, health maintenance organizations, day care centers, and other nonprofit institutions. Chrysler accepted these provisions when the union agreed to allow the company to defer up to $200 million in pension contributions to help it out of its financial crisis.

There is little problem with justifying these mortgages as investments. A return near the market rate is likely, unless the union members receive special considerations. But the other investments are harder to justify. What kind of return can be expected from an investment in a nonprofit institution? These types of investments may conflict with the prudent investment provisions of ERISA, the Employee Retirement Income Security Act of 1974. ERISA regulates UAW pensions but does not apply to state and local public pension funds. (See Chapter 7 for more on fiduciary responsibilities of fund trustees.) Health maintenance organizations and day care centers may serve the pension plan beneficiaries now, but the beneficiaries may be trading current benefits for future penury if the investments strain Chrysler's ability to make future pension payments.

In early 1980 Chrysler signed another agreement with the State of Michigan. The governor, acting on powers granted him by P.L. 30 of 1980, authorized a $150 million, 15-year loan at a fixed rate of 15.5% to be extended to Chrylser. The loan was

. . . A university must weigh the ethical consequences of its investments. It should make an independent ethical judgment on issues presented to shareholders of companies in which it holds stocks. And it should, in extraordinary circumstances and after assuring itself that the University's primary mission would not be impaired, refuse to hold shares in enterprises whose activities, even though legal, would lead to social consequences that in its opinion are ethically unacceptable. . . .

. . . The separationist racial policies—apartheid—of the government of South Africa, and the repressive steps employed by that regime to maintain total political control of the country, are an intolerable assault upon human decency. . . . The Corporation has earlier stated publicly its abhorrence of the policies of the present government of South Africa and hereby reaffirms that statement, unanimously without qualification. . . . We believe that the University has an ethical duty to contribute to the process of peaceful change rather than see that process deferred so long that change can only come about through massive racial and civil warfare. We know that social injustice exists in many nations. And we do not presume to infringe upon the proper responsibilities of the United States government. But apartheid in South Africa is so distinctive in degree as to require special attention. . . .

. . . About $175 million of Yale's approximately $540 million of endowment (as of 12/31/77) was invested in U.S. based companies doing business in South Africa. . . . We believe that U.S. based companies in South Africa should act as responsible agents of change in that society. And we believe that it would be unwise to adopt a general policy of disposing of securities from the University's portfolio as an instrumentality for effecting that change. There are however, as we note below, measures which can be taken. If a company proves to be unwilling to consider or implement such measures, we will then assess the company's total response and begin a process that may lead to a range of actions, among them the possibility of ultimate disinvestment. . . .

. . . Yale should use its position as a shareholder in such companies to encourage them toward ethically responsible ends. A significant start has been made in this direction through the so-called Sullivan Principles, developed by Reverend Leon Sullivan. A number of U.S. companies with operations in South Africa have agreed to abide by these Principles, which commit an employer to:

1. eliminate segregation of the races in all eating, comfort and work facilities;
2. institute equal and fair employment practices for all employees;
3. provide equal pay for all employees doing equal or comparable work for the same period of time;
4. initiate and develop training programs that will prepare, in substantial numbers, blacks and other nonwhites for supervisory, administrative, clerical and technical jobs;
5. increase the number of blacks and other nonwhites in management and supervisory positions;
6. improve the quality of employees' lives outside the work environment in such areas as housing, transportation, schooling, recreation and health facilities.

. . . We believe . . . that there should be a seventh principle: U.S. based companies should strive to assure workers of all races equal opportunity to organize unions. This opportunity should also include the organization of racially mixed unions and the willingness of companies to negotiate with them in good faith. . . .

. . . If any U.S. based company operating in South Africa in which Yale is a stockholder refuses to commit itself to these six Sullivan principles or has not used its best efforts to fulfill that commtment within a reasonable period of time, the University will then consider alternative action which could include disposing of its shares in that company. At that time, we will take into account the question whether the contemplated action is likely to impair the capacity of the University to carry out its primary educational mission. . . .

. . . Even where a U.S. based company has followed the principles listed above, the particular activities of the company may be of a special character that provide major assistance to the South African government . . . banks at present hold 20% of the outstanding foreign bank debt of the South African government. As a general proposition, a U.S. bank that makes loans to the South African government contributes much more directly to the support of the government itself than do Africans. . . . The appropriate officer of the University will communicate to the officers of each bank of which Yale owns stock that Yale will henceforth use its voice and vote as a shareholder to urge banks whose stock is held by Yale to make no new or increased loans to the South African government or its agencies. . . . Where such efforts do not succeed, Yale will consider alternatives including the disposition of its stock.

. . . We will also consider . . . whether Yale should also decline thereafter to hold any bonds or certificates of deposit of that institution. . . .

EXHIBIT 8.C / Yale University's Policy on South Africa (Excerpts from June 30, 1978 Policy Statement)

drawn out of the State's Common Cash Fund, a pool of cash and short-term investments of 69 separate funds; 35% to 40% of the pool's balance belonged to the state pension funds.

The Alabama State Retirement Systems have a program to invest in *mortgage pools*. Part of the Systems' $1.9 billion in assets is invested in local mortgages by buying Ginnie Mae pools of Alabama mortgages. According to David Bronner, secretary and treasurer of the Alabama State Retirement Systems, the mortgage bankers initially offered them mortgage pools with yields 0.2% below the general market rate. However, Bronner said, "we decided we could not purchase them unless the yield was the same as that of comparable securities. Eventually the mortgage bankers offered them on the market." More than $100 million of the funds' assets are in Ginnie Maes, 75% to 80% of which are Alabama pools.

One reason that the rates on specific pools of mortgages may be lower than those on general pools is the additional administrative costs of purchasing and registering mortgages for a targeted area.

West Virginia is another state whose pension funds have invested in FHA and VA guaranteed mortgages. About 15% of the West Virginia Public Employees' Retirement System and Teachers' Retirement System assets are invested in these mortgages.

Four western states have invested significant amounts in mortgages. California has invested by far the largest amount—$1.6 billion to $1.7 billion from the State Employees' fund and the Teachers Retirement System fund. California uses both conventional mortgages and Ginnie Maes. Most of the conventional mortgages are FHA or VA guaranteed. Some 35% of Hawaii's pension fund assets are invested in mortgages. The largest amount is in home mortgages, with a small amount in commercial mortgages. Alaska and Oregon also buy mortgage instruments to stimulate housing construction.

Some states have used *commercial loans* as investments. Alabama has lent about $10 million to two Alabama banks that do a substantial part of their business within the state. In addition, the pension funds have also bought private placements ranging in size from $10 million to $50 million from the Alabama-based businesses—two paper companies and a chemical company.

In December, 1977, the AFL-CIO Convention passed a resolution calling for union pension funds to be invested in a manner that better serves working people, and urged an investigation into the feasibility of legislation which would achieve the intent of this resolution.

The resolution urged pension fund fiduciaries of the AFL-CIO and its affiliated unions to consider participation in guaranteed mortgage funds designed to stimulate union construction of houses, schools, hospitals, stores, and factories in the United States and Canada. They were also urged to allocate at least 10% of available monies for investment in appropriate guaranteed mortgage investment portfolios.

EXHIBIT 8.D / AFL-CIO Social Investing Policy

Oregon has recently initiated a program to make commercial loans of $5 to $10 million to Oregon companies to stem the outflow of investment funds. Wyoming has had a somewhat similar program for several years. The Wyoming system has been buying the guaranteed portion of in-state Small Business Administration loans. About $14 million of that system's $200 million in assets is so invested. The program was started when the local banks were unable to find secondary market buyers for the loans they originated. According to state fund officials, the management costs associated with servicing the loans made them unattractive investments, and the system suspended its program. Costs were high in part because loans were not pooled.

The Kansas Public Employees Retirement System has also invested in SBA-guaranteed loans to local businesses packaged by the Kansas Development Credit Corporation. So far the fund has invested less than $10 million. However, it has also invested about $15 million in privately placed debt of Kansas corporations and about $21 million in the common stock of companies with substantial operations in Kansas. The object, apparently, is to help support the stocks of these companies, thus making it cheaper and easier for them to raise new capital. The Milwaukee Employees' Retirement System has begun investing up to $6 million in SBA loans.

Direct equity ownership of *commercial real estate* is one of the most difficult of investment avenues to pursue successfully, partly because it requires an expertise not generally found within a state investment organization, and partly because of the tremendous competition for good projects. Real estate is a particularly attractive field for taxable investors because of liberal tax benefits. Nonetheless, the Minneapolis Teachers Retirement System has been able to invest $10 million of the fund's $130 million in assets in commercial real estate in an area around the city. It follows a policy of working with national and regional franchise businesses. The fund buys the land and building in which a franchise intends to locate and leases the property to the franchise operator at either a percentage of the investment or a percentage of the sales.

Thus a number of states have taken steps to implement active social investing for the benefit of their economies. For the most part these steps have been small ones, and the results appear to be mixed and very difficult to measure. However, these states

> The University of Wisconsin is subject to a 1973 Wisconsin law that prohibits it from holding investments in any company "which practices or condones through its actions, discrimination on the basis of race, religion, color, creed or sex." The Regent's Business and Finance Committee of the University determines whether the laws apply to particular investments held by the University. It has decided that employers in South Africa fall into the proscribed category. In May, 1977, the State Attorney General advised the Board of Regents that all securities in firms with operations in South Africa should be sold. As a result, the university sold about $10 million in stock, one half the equity portfolio and one third of the university's total endowment.
>
> *Source:* Council on Economic Priorities

EXHIBIT 8.E / Example of State Guideline

have shown that there are ways to target the investment of pension assets to help the local economy without significantly increasing risk or reducing investment return.

These programs are relatively modest in size. How many more funds can be applied to these programs before investment yields decline remains to be seen. And the intended benefits of these programs may be diminished by displacement, leakage, or possibly some unperceived flaw in design or execution. In addition, it is difficult to determine with confidence whether an investment program, such as those described above, is in fact generating the intended secondary return of social benefits.

8.4 Passive Social Investing

Passive social investing attempts to influence corporate behavior by boycotting the securities of specified companies and by using stockholder voting rights at annual stockholders' meetings. The outstanding social issue currently being addressed through passive social investing is American business ties with South Africa. Some fund trustees believe they should show disapproval of South Africa's racial policies by voting to sell the stock of companies doing business there. They also expect that sale of the stock will pressure the companies to pull out of South Africa, and that in turn will encourage South Africa to change its policies.

The publication of Rifkin and Barber's book has brought other passive investment issues to the fore. Why, they asked, should union employees and retirees own the securities of companies with poor union relations? Rifkin and Barber urged Taft-Hartley and other union-sponsored pension funds to sell their investments in such companies. They also called for the sale of investments in companies that have been found guilty of Occupational Safety and Health Act (OSHA) or Equal Opportunity Commission (EEOC) violations, or in companies that are polluters of the environment.

Those who support the use of pension funds to register disapproval of these actions argue that pension fund beneficiaries have an interest in promoting good corporate behavior since the beneficiaries will ultimately be affected. For example, all workers are affected by a company that is antiunion, or even nonunion, because the strength of the whole labor movement is reduced by the existence of such companies. Similarly, all workers are adversely affected by the actions of companies that violate OSHA and EEOC laws and regulations. Finally, all beneficiaries, both current and retired, are affected by companies that pollute the water and atmosphere.

Critics of passive social investing argue that these are larger social concerns, not just concerns of pension fund beneficiaries and that they are thus more properly addressed by political or judicial means. Further, they argue, individual pension funds can have only a minor influence on the price of a company's securities since few pension funds own even as much as 5% of the outstanding stock of any one company. Indeed, even a major bank's total investment in the stock of one of the nation's largest companies is usually less than 5%. If a violating company is also a particularly successful company, the pension funds may be surrendering superior investment returns and thus compromise the performance of the fund's portfolio.

Critics also question the right of trustees to make value judgments for the beneficiaries, especially if those value judgments may affect pensions in the future. Not all beneficiaries (or trustees, for that matter) embrace identical social and economic values. Liberals may wish to boycott South Africa and encourage solar energy development; conservatives may wish to support South Africa and boycott birth control manufacturers.

The South Africa Question 8.4.1

The divestment of the stocks of companies doing business in South Africa first became an issue on college campuses. Relatively few public pension funds have yet taken a stand. Even among the colleges the verdict is not unanimous. Ohio State University's trustees reversed a decision to divest of stocks of companies involved in South Africa when they found that they were selling the shares of companies which were among the largest corporate donors to the school.

One of the first universities to take action against companies doing business in South Africa was the University of Wisconsin, which adopted a resolution requiring divestiture of any company, corporation, or subsidiary or affiliate that "practices or condones through its actions, discrimination on the basis of race, religion, color, creed or sex." As a result, the unversity's investment counsel was required to divest the endowment of all stocks having any connection with South Africa. The counsel, Heritage Investment Advisers of Milwaukee, had to do considerable research to identify every company doing any level of business with South Africa. Earlier studies had identified only the companies with major business interests in the country.

Neither Heritage nor the Wisconsin trustees suspected how many companies had some involvement with South Africa. The investment manager found that 116 of the largest of the 500 stocks in the Standard & Poor's index had to be sold. These amounted to almost half of the fund's equity portfolio of about $10 million.

The president of Heritage, John Windsor, told *Pensions & Investment Age* that restrictions on investment in South Africa-connected stocks meant that a portfolio lost "every significant multinational company." However, he noted that the costs of divesting the fund of the South Africa stocks will not be known for some time. "We are unsure of the long-term penalties," he said, "and we won't know for four or five years."

In the first several years following divestiture, the performance of the University of Wisconsin fund was actually better than average, according to Windsor. That was because the stock market had favored small companies in the two or three years after divestiture. By sheer coincidence, the fund shifted its investments from large multinational companies to small companies (typically with no ties to South Africa) in time to benefit from this temporary trend.

Stocks of small companies are traditionally more volatile in price than stocks of large companies. Thus a pension fund avoiding companies with South African ties—that is, large companies—may well find its common stock portfolio declining more than the market when the market declines and rising more than the market when the market rises. However, its volatility will be a significant concern only if the fund has a large number of retired workers depending upon current performance or if benefits are related to the value of the portfolio on the date of retirement.

Nevertheless, a number of public and private institutions have decided that their assets should not be invested in the stocks of companies having significant connections with South Africa. The United Auto Workers, for example, won the right in its 1979 contract negotiations with the Chrysler Corporation to name five stocks each year that the company would sell from its UAW pension plan portfolio. The union has indicated that South African related stocks would be chosen at least for the first year. In 1978 the National Union of Hospital and Health Care Employees banned from its $236 million pension fund investments that would "financially assist or aid or support the present government or economy of South Africa."

Brandeis University's board of trustees in 1979 voted to drop a $350,000 investment in Ford Motor Company bonds because of the company's activities in South Africa. The trustees concluded that Ford's sale of vehicles to the police and military in South Africa "constitutes severe social injury in support of apartheid."

The board of trustees of Boston University voted to divest holdings "in any company which is not constructively seeking to maximize black opportunities and pay, and to support an end to apartheid." They voted to dispose of some $6.6 million in bank deposits, bonds, and nonvoting stock. The nonvoting stock was sold because it offered the university no opportunity to influence corporate behavior.

The University of Oregon instructed its investment managers to dispose of all endowment investments in the twenty-seven companies indentified by the vice-chancellor for administration as being engaged in substantial activity in South Africa. Further, the managers were instructed to refrain from acquiring investments in any company that employs more than fifty persons in South Africa, earns more than $500,000 from business operations in South Africa, or has investments in excess of $500,000 in fixed assets or loan portfolios in South Africa.

In March 1978 voters in Davis, California, approved a proposal recommending that funds invested by the city, the University of California, the state treasurer and the State Public Employees Retirement System be withdrawn from private banks and corporations doing business in South Africa, and that the funds be invested to solve the problems of unemployment, hunger, housing, crime, education, energy, and the environment. Cambridge, Massachusetts, recently took a similar stance on divestment.

However, some unions oppose this trend. Even if they are against apartheid, they may feel that American companies can do more to overcome South Africa's racial policies by remaining there and working for change than by leaving and surrendering any possible influence. The strategic issues are very complex. Ford Motor Company, for example, has led the way in improving the plight of black South African workers by raising wages and providing loans for workers' housing. Yet, at the same time, Ford sells vehicles to the South African policy and army.

In Sacramento, California, three public employee unions and an organization of retired public employees opposed a proposal by two members of the city retirement board to divest the city's $100 million pension fund of the stocks of all companies doing business in South Africa. These organizations expressed "strong objection to the practice of 'social' investment in any form."

"No man can serve two masters," their letter said. "It is impossible for one in a fiduciary relationship to serve his own philosophical interests and properly discharge the duties of his trust. Moreover, true social justice would require the awkward and unacceptable system of polling all current and retired city employees in the matter of each investment in order to determine whose social and political interests are to be served." The letter added, "We sincerely trust the Board will continue in the sound investment practices" that had produced an excellent record of investment performance.

Other Social Issues 8.4.2

Rifkin and Barber, among others, have suggested that pension funds should look at criteria other than South African investment practices. They suggested that companies that were antiunion, OSHA or EEOC violators, or significant polluters of the environment ought to be boycotted. So far, however, there has been more talk than action about boycotting the stocks of these companies.

In one of the first significant steps in this area, the investment management firm of Drexel Burnham Lambert in Philadelphia announced a program to screen out stocks of antiunion companies for its union clients. The firm developed a screen that eliminated antiunion companies from stocks that passed through Drexel's other investment screens. As of late 1979, Drexel had three announced clients for the program—the International Association of Machinists, the International Molders and Allied Workers Union, and the Carpenters and Joiners of America. Officials of Drexel Burnham said they expected that eventually billions of dollars will be invested after review of social criteria.

Unions have successfully used their pension fund muscle in the J. P. Stevens case, as noted in the introduction to this chapter. By threatening to rescind their pension fund investment management agreement with Manufacturers Hanover Trust, the unions forced the president of J. P. Stevens, Inc., to resign from the Manufacturers Hanover board of directors, and a Manufacturers Hanover executive to resign from the Stevens board.

Identifying the Violators 8.5

One major problem with passive social investing is targeting the stocks to be boycotted. As Heritage Investment Advisers discovered, it is not even easy to identify companies doing business in or with South Africa. The number of companies that had to be excluded far exceeded Heritage's expectations. Other organizations are not as rigid in their criteria. Some wish to exclude only companies that appear to be helping preserve apartheid in some way or those that discriminate against black Africans.

Some activist groups have risen to the challenge and attempted to identify the

Four influential nonprofit organizations that monitor the social performance of American corporations are described below. Information was compiled by a Massachusetts Task Force on Public Pension Investments.

Corporate Data Exchange (CDE)
198 Broadway, Room 706, New York, NY 10038 (212) 962-2980)

CDE was founded in 1975 to study economic concentration and the ownership and control of major corporations in the United States. Although the heart of CDE's research has been ownership, rather than company practices, it reports regularly on issues such as redlining, job discrimination, and political influence. CDE's publications include:

- Stock Ownership Directories: ownership profiles and operating data about major corporations in specific economic sectors
- Special Handbooks: data on loans by American banks in South Africa and on the holdings of public and private pension funds in companies that have been criticized for certain practices or repeatedly found in violation of federal regulations.
- Company Profiles: data profiling the ownership and operating practices of specific firms, either from the CDE's computerized data bank or on special request

Council on Economic Priorities (CEP)
84 Fifth Ave., New York, NY 10011 (212) 691-8550

CEP was founded in 1969. It publishes reports comparing the social performance of companies within industries, such as minority hiring among banks and pollution control among steel manufacturers. CEP's publications include:

- Portfolio Review Service: initial reports on the social performance of each company chosen by the subscriber with follow-up reports
- Research publications: including CEP studies, CEP reports and CEP newsletters
- Briefings: occasional meetings at which investors can meet with researchers and company officials

Investor Responsibility Research Center (IRRC)
1522 K Street NW, Washington, DC 20005 (202) 833-3727

The IRRC was founded in 1972 by a group of universities and philanthropic foundations to provide them with impartial research on social and environmental questions raised in shareholder resolutions. IRRC has since expanded its activities to include general studies of public policy questions, corporate governance issues, SEC regulation of shareholder action, and analyses of the response by major institutional investors to all of these matters. The IRRC's publications and other services include:

- Proxy Issue Service: analyses of issues raised in shareholder resolutions and corporate proxy materials
- Newsletter Service: a monthly publication reviewing developments relating to social responsibility and investor action
- In-Depth Research Service: detailed reports on issues relating to corporate and investor responsibility

The IRRC is registered with the SEC as an investment advisor under the Investment Advisers Act of 1940.

Interfaith Center on Corporate Responsibility (ICCR)
475 Riverside Drive, Room 556, New York, NY 10027 (212) 870-2936

The ICCR is a membership organization which includes 15 Protestant denominations and 150 Roman Catholic bodies. The ICCR's publications and services include a monthly newsletter highlighting advance information about church-sponsored shareholder resolutions.

EXHIBIT 8.F / Monitors of Corporate Social Performance

companies that should be avoided by the socially conscious investor. The best known monitors of corporate social performance are described in Exhibit 8.F. Perhaps the senior of these is the Corporate Data Exchange, which identified ninety-nine "target" companies, companies that had failed at least four criteria. The companies were "predominantly nonunionized," had been found guilty of OSHA or EEOC violations, or were major lenders or investors in South Africa. Among the companies found not to meet the criteria were AT&T, Sears Roebuck, Procter and Gamble, Ford, and Control Data Corporation.

Measurement of the social performance of corporations is both costly and subject to many errors of fact and judgment. Unfortunately, organizations monitoring corporate social performance are generally underfinanced and are dominated by researchers with strong ideological points of view. It is no surprise that their reports are frequently criticized. Professor Roy Shortland of Georgetown University Law School, for example, cited CDE for inconsistent application of standards, disregard for investment returns, and use of criteria that discriminated against larger firms. For example, CDE labelled as an EEOC violator any company that signed a consent decree in which the monetary settlement was $100,000 or more, regardless of the firm's size of payroll, age, or turnover of work force. Also, a firm was considered an OSHA violator if it was subject to a penalty of $25,000 or more.

Do "Socially Desirable" Investments Underperform the Market? 8.6

CDA, a consulting and research firm in Silver Spring, Maryland, examined the ninety-nine top institutional holdings as of September 30, 1974, to see how many were on CDE's list of socially undesirable stocks and how those that were had performed relative to socially acceptable stocks. CDA found that thirty-nine of the ninety-nine largest holdings were on the "socially undesirable" list and had outperformed the acceptable stocks over the five years from September 1974 through September 1979. According to Robert A. Levy, president of CDA, the undesirable stocks had an average appreciation over the five years of 83.5%. The sixty desirable stocks, on the other hand, produced an average appreciation of only 76.8%. Mr. Levy also compared the returns from all ninety-five companies in the CDE undesirable list with those of the Standard & Poor's 500 index. He found that the ninety-five undesirable stocks had an average price appreciation of 109.2% while the S&P 500 was up only 72.0% in the same period. This occurred even though the undesirable stocks are generally among the largest stocks, and the stock market has been unkind to these large stocks in the past five years. Indeed, Mr. Levy found that the thirty-nine socially undesirable stocks among the ninety-nine largest institutional holdings had been 51.3% of the market value of all ninety-nine stocks.

Thus returns may be lowered if pension funds use CDE's list to avoid socially undesirable stocks. However, further research over longer periods will be needed to determine whether socially acceptable stocks generally underperform the undesirable stocks.

8.7 Proxy Voting

Another avenue open to socially conscious investors is the use of proxies to try to influence the behavior of company managements. There has been limited success with this tool, since winning a proxy fight is a difficult process. Rarely can those opposed to management's behavior accumulate enough proxies to change the board of directors or to pass a resolution. But if the dissidents manage to accumulate a significant number of proxies for a year or two, management usually takes notice and makes changes. If the dissidents can accumulate proxies representing 5%, or sometimes substantially less, managements can be swayed. Even accumulating 5% of the proxies against management is a difficult task. Management has the economic and clerical resources of the corporation, and it knows who its shareholders are. The dissidents often cannot find out in time to take action.

In one proxy campaign, the Minnesota State Board of Investments recently voted its 135,000 shares against Northwest Airlines' board of directors because of the company's poor labor and customer relations. The action pleased employee unions attempting to persuade other institutional stockholders to take similar action. The State Board of Investments argued that it had an economic as well as social motive for its action. It claimed that the value of the stock and dividend income would fall if there was another strike against the airline. "Sometimes issues that appear to be social and moral can affect earnings down the road," said Jim Lord, Minnesota State Treasurer and trustee of the state funds.

Proxy voting is a legal right of every shareholder, and boards of directors do not like to see significant votes against their proposals. The effect of negative votes by large numbers of shareholders, even if they represent only small percentages of outstanding shares, is often slow to be seen but can be effective if the vote is consistent over a number of years.

8.8 Link Deposit Programs

Government money managers can use idle cash and short-term investments to leverage socially productive investments from depository banks. A *link deposit program* "links" the placement of a demand or savings account or a Certificate of Deposit with explicit commitments from the depository bank, such as expansion of student, housing, or commercial loans within a target area or to a target population. Link deposit programs are predicated on the assumption that financial institutions will alter their lending behavior in order to obtain government funds on deposit.

Link deposit programs deserve special attention because any government with bank deposits can implement one. Idle cash from virtually any source—pension funds, general fund, or other accounts—can be used. Link deposit programs are generally no riskier than conventional deposits and produce yields equal to or only slightly lower than conventional deposits.

It is likely that most local government treasurers leave funds in local banks with the implicit expectation that these deposits increase the amount of funds available for local loans. An informal link deposit program of this kind, however, is impossible to monitor properly. The intended benefits of tacit link deposit programs can be dissipated by undetected displacement and leakage. Formal guidelines for awarding deposits and evaluating performance should be used.

The State of Illinois' link deposit program, introduced in 1967 by then-Treasurer Adlai Stevenson, contains key features of other programs. The Treasurer awarded one-year time deposits to banks that proposed to pay at least a minimum interest rate and, as well, furnished their communities with student, SBA, and other loans and consumer services. Participating banks were required to sign the following pledge:

> . . . This bank pledges not to reject arbitrarily mortgage loans for residential properties with any specific part of the community served by the bank because of the location of the property. The bank also pledges to make loans available on low and moderate income property throughout the community within the limits of its legal restrictions and prudent financial practices.

The State of Colorado introduced a link deposit program in 1975 under the direction of then-Treasurer Sam Brown. One- and two-year time deposits were awarded to banks on the basis of a ranking system that added to a bidding bank's proposed interest rates bonus points for past performance in loaning to farms, students, small businesses, and sponsors of "low-cost and older" housing.

One of the drawbacks of link deposit programs is the substantial effort required to define award criteria, analyze bank bids, and monitor bank loan performance after the awards are made. A study conducted for the Massachusetts Social and Economic Opportunity Council concluded that indifferent management could gut an otherwise well conceived program. The study's authors urged that the structure and operation of the system should be established as clearly and definitely as possible in advance of the bidding process.

The Legality of Social Investing 8.9

While corporate pension funds have to be concerned about the legality of social investing under ERISA, state and municipal pension funds have to meet only statutory restrictions on permissible investments and the more general standards of the common law prudent man rule. This rule requires that the assets be invested as a prudent man, acting in his own behalf, would invest his own funds. Some may have laws that add burdens to trustees, and these should be examined before a course of social investing is taken. The proposed Public Employees Retirement Income Security Act could add new requirements.

These laws and the general prudent man doctrine should be examined to determine the extent to which objectives other than direct financial benefits from an investment influence the selection of an investment.

A partial answer to this problem was provided in *Withers v. Teachers Retirement System of the City of New York.* In this case a group of retired teachers sued the trustees who had invested assets of the fund in New York City bonds to aid the city in its financial crisis. Although the bonds carried a respectable coupon rate of 9%, they were virtually unmarketable. There was also a chance that the city would go bankrupt, making the bonds virtually worthless. The retired teachers also argued that the trustees had breached their duty of loyalty because the investment was made to help the city government and to preserve the jobs of active members of the system rather than to benefit retired members.

The court ruled, however, that the purchase was a prudent one in the circumstances because ''the importance of the solvency of the city to the retirement system lay not only in its role as the major contributor of the funds, but also as the ultimate guarantor of the payment of pension benefits to participants.'' The court found that the trustees' interest in the city's solvency was solely related to this pension-related role, and to neither the protection of jobs nor the general public welfare. It also found that the trustees had treated all pension beneficiaries impartially, since in the event of a bankruptcy, the retired teachers might have fared well while those still employed would have been severely disadvantaged.

Although the Withers case worked out well for the trustees of the New York Teachers fund, it highlights the kinds of questions that may be raised if pension assets are used for social purposes. Trustees should be cautious. Special enabling legislation may be required to launch a social investing program.

Managing the Retirement Funds: An Integrated Process 9

Over the past ten years or so, the financial press has increasingly focused upon a family of ideas (and their applications) which is now somewhat loosely referred to as Modern Capital Market and Portfolio Theory, or, for short, MPT. The main ideas of MPT, at first popular in academic circles, are now widely accepted. When one inspects any controversy associated with them, one finds that disagreements are largely semantic rather than substantive. Where substantive controversy does occur is in the practical applications of the ideas to the real world problem of successfully managing investment portfolios.

The purpose of this chapter is to review the essential concepts embodied in MPT, to provide some helpful definitions of its more widely used and misused terminology, to remind the reader of certain basic facts of life related to economics, traditional investing concepts, and the nature of risk or uncertainty, and then to pull all of these elements together in a practical context. The author's objectives are to leave the reader with a foundation of MPT—an understanding which will be helpful in making informed judgments, judgments which will lead to the increasingly effective management of the ongoing pension asset investment problem.

MPT, in its larger definition, provides two basic ideas: a concept of *risk* and how the risks of individual assets interrelate to produce portfolio risk, and a concept of *efficient* portfolios. An efficient portfolio is that unique combination of investments which, at a given point in time, provides the highest possible expected return at a chosen level of total portfolio risk.

In some applications, classical notions of value are employed together with MPT-derived tools. These value estimates rely upon analyst calculations of expected rates of return. Thus, value equals the present worth of the cash flows (interest, dividends, return of principal, etc.) promised to or expected to be received by the holders of financial instruments.

The value of a financial instrument today is based upon the pricing of expectations; inside every price is an implied discount rate, or expected rate of return. Since the expected rates of return are based on estimates of cash flows to be received over some time period which lies in the future, uncertainty (or risk) becomes part of the "risk-to-return" equation.

Underlying each component of this chapter is the classical concept of the risk/return trade-off. MPT provides valuable insights on the risk element, and traditional investing concepts can effectively deal with return. MPT-derived tools, when appropriately linked and operated by investors, provide a powerful advance over the traditional methods associated with portfolio management. Before demonstrating this, however, some bricks and mortar are required.

9.1 Definitions

9.1.1 Primary and Secondary Markets

The Primary Market. This is "Corporate America": the sum of all business enterprise where, in combination, capital, labor and management produce real wealth in the form of goods and services, thereby providing the means to compensate labor, pay taxes and reward management and capital. Corporate America *is* our economic system to a large degree. Gross National Product contains the sum of its achievements. When Corporate America needs capital in excess of internally generated funds, it frequently borrows or raises equity capital by offering to sell securities. These securities, once distributed to investors, trade in the secondary markets.

The Secondary Markets. These are composed of all traded securities. Taken together, all securities comprise what is known as the *market portfolio*. The market portfolio is, of course, made up of components: the stock market component, the bond market component, second deeds of trust, and so on. These components are, in turn, comprised of individual security issues, each with its unique weight relative to all other issues. (E.g., the market value of all IBM shares makes this issue the one with the largest weight in our stock market.)

The secondary market as a whole, together with its component asset classes, are largely "closed systems." While the ownership of individual shares or bonds changes through time, there remains a market portfolio: the combination of all securities held by investors, generating a total market return. No investor or group of investors can control or manage the market portfolio's behavior. When the return that the total market portfolio produces over a given period is netted, market investing is a zero-sum game. That is, to the extent that some investors "win" relative to the market as a whole, some combination of others must "lose" by an equal amount, and since all investors pay transaction costs and many pay investment management fees, there are *always* more investor dollars losing than winning, relative to the total market, even though in absolute numbers most investors may be "winners."

From time to time, reliable performance measurement data indicate that the average of all pension portfolios outperforms the market, and/or that more portfolios outperform the average portfolio than underperform it. What explains this apparent contradiction with the earlier assertion that there are always more losers than winners? There's an apples and oranges problem here. Firstly, the popular market averages do not capture the entire market portfolio. The S&P 500, for example, captures about two-thirds of the total market value of all stocks, while the Salomon Bros. bond index covers perhaps 15% of all *debt* instruments. Secondly, the earlier assertion refers to the total of dollars invested, and the latter to the number of players investing those dollars. While more investors (or managers) may win in a given measurement period, more invested *dollars* lose than win. The winning investors cannot be managing more than half the market's dollar-value. If they did, and they won, then the "market's" return would have to be higher than reported!

In essence, Corporate America (The Primary Market) creates real wealth. Real wealth is neither created nor destroyed in the secondary markets. Part of the primary market's wealth is reinvested in projects which replace and/or increase wealth-producing plants and equipment. Another part is distributed to investors in the secondary capital markets as dividends and interest payments, while the third part is consumed. When corporations need capital beyond their own ability to generate it from existing plant and equipment investment, they issue securities which are subsequently held by or traded among investors. The trading is accomplished via the secondary market mechanism. Prices, whether for individual securities or total market components, are set by the consensus of investors by combining an often instinctive assessment of the present worth of future cash flows with a perception of the risk or uncertainty that those cash flows may not be generated or paid as expected (see *Risk,* below).

As shall be developed later in this chapter, a prudent investor is in a better position to make judgments on what to buy, hold, or sell when he has a clear view of how the present worth of expected cash flows is being established by the sum of all who hold and trade securities. In addition, he is even better off if his assessments of present value are rigorously integrated with a quantifiable notion of risk.

Risk and Return 9.1.2

Risk. The notion of risk is one we all deal with in every facet of our lives all of the time. Risk is the chance that what actually happens tomorrow will differ to some degree from what we expect today. At some level of consciousness, we are each continually dealing with risk-to-expected return trade-offs. How we individually elect to manage our diet, our friendships, our dental hygiene, our budget, etc. . . . all involve such trade-offs. To complicate matters, the risk management decisions we make in one area of our lives are integrated with, and have an effect upon, the risk management decisions we make in all other aspects of our lives. Constructing and managing portfolios of secondary market securities is a similarly dynamic and complex risk-to-expected return trade-off problem.

Until the early 1970s, portfolio managers managed this multi-faceted trade-off problem with a combination of experience, traditional wisdom, and instinct, much as we manage our personal lives. The first and third were critical because the second, as it turns out, wasn't always very helpful or reliable. Over the past decade, some management organizations, with a strong conceptual assist from prominent university schools of business, brought the quantification of investment risk and security valuation out of the closet, put them in the center of the table and began to learn how to manage them explicitly in portfolios. The conceptual assist emanating from academia has long since been labeled MPT. Wells Fargo Investment Advisors was the first investment management firm to commit itself totally, philosophically and organizationally, to this body of new knowledge.

Every practitioner of capital budgeting applies the classical definition of investment value. In essence, "value is the present worth of all future payments." This concept of valuing promised or prospective cash flows is old hat to corporate financial officers who, for example, evaluate line-officer recommendations that this plant be built or that one expanded. However, it was not until the early 1970s that the discounted cash flow approach to common stock evaluation was employed *exclusively* and systematically at a major investment management firm.

In 1971, Wells Fargo integrated the MPT concept of systematic (or market-related) risk with discount rates generated by a dividend discount model supplied with analyst forecasts. Today, many organizations use similar approaches. What Wells Fargo did was really quite simple. They adopted and modified an already well-known model which took analysts' forecasts of dividends (future cash flows) and a stock's current price, and then solved for the discount rate or *expected return (ER)*. The price is, in effect, a statement of the present value of future dividend flows. A good analogy here is the bond portfolio manager who asks a broker "What's the bond selling for?" The answer, typically, is not a price. Nor is it a description of coupon flows and return of principal. Rather, the answer is "It's selling to yield (return) 11.5%." This is an expected rate of return on the bond given its price, coupon rate, and maturity. You might well say, "That's easy in the case of a bond, but stocks are different. Stocks don't *mature* and dividend flows are uncertain. How can I have any confidence at all in a stock valuation process which, at least in some form, requires dividend forecasts to perpetuity? What possible use is a valuation process that is so clearly based on forecasts which (except by chance) will prove inaccurate?" Good questions, all. However, the success of the approach does not rely upon analysts accurately forecasting future events. Investors price *expectations* of future reality, not what reality turns out to be. It is important for the reader to understand and identify with this basic fact of life because it obviates the concerns conveyed in the above questions.

9.1.3 Variability, or Sigma

Let's return to bonds for a demonstration of MPT's notion of *risk* as it applies to the bond market portfolio. For this example, assume that a market-like portfolio of fixed income securities has a weighted average yield to maturity (expected return) of 11.5%. This means that one year from now, we expect to have realized a return of 11.5%. When we actually look back over our shoulders 12 months hence, we are likely to find that a higher or lower return has been delivered. It is the *range of probable outcomes* around what we expect before-the-fact that is the reflector of risk. Thus, in the case of our assumption, if you asked Wells Fargo or another MPT-oriented firm for its 12-month bond market return forecast, they would tell you "11.5%," because that's what the bond market portfolio is promising when you put the question. The firm would quickly add, however, that "with two-thirds confidence, the return will be 11.5%, give-or-take six percentage points." Here, the six percentage points represent an estimate of the *standard deviation* of returns around the return judged most likely. In the jargon of MPT, standard deviation is called *sigma*. If you wanted a stronger response, they would say that "with 95% confidence, the return will be 11.5%, give-or-take twelve percentage points," that is, two sigmas.

Note that, as in this example, MPT employs conventional statistics as a means of specifying uncertainty (risk).

Thus the definition for the risk of the bond market is appropriately expressed in terms of estimates of future ranges about a central expectation of, in this case, 11.5%. (Note that tomorrow, the then-in-place bond market return expectation may be higher or lower than 11.5%. Whatever the new expected return is, it will have changed because in the interval a revised set of market expectations, based on additional information and altered perceptions, must be accommodated.) The same approach is taken to express the expected return and risk associated with all other asset classes for which there are representative prices, cash-flow forecasts (and thus expected returns), and an estimate of the range of probable outcomes (sigma) around the return currently expected.

Stocks, for example, always promise a higher expected return than bonds. Clearly, however, they are riskier and, thus, ought to promise more than bonds in order to induce investors to buy or hold. Historically, stocks have actually delivered more return than bonds. On a year-by-year basis, however, because stocks as a class *are* riskier, annual returns from them tend to swing about their realized long-term average return a good deal more than bond returns tend to swing to either side of *their* realized average return. Thus, each asset class's expected risk, or expected sigma, is unique and unavoidable.

Investors can't avoid this risk. For example, if cash is invested in a stock index fund, a fund that all but perfectly mirrors the market, the portfolio will experience the variability (sigma) of the market as a whole. Available, historical data indicates that, for example, the stock market portfolio for the 1926–1978 period produced a geometric mean return of 8.9% with a standard deviation of 22.2%. This simply means that if one had put a dollar in at the beginning of the period and left it there (accumulating and reinvesting dividends on a tax free, no-transactions-cost basis) until year-end, 1978, the realized, compound annual rate of total return would have been 8.9%. The standard deviation of 22.2% means that if you picked a single calendar year's return at random, you had a two-thirds chance of finding a realized return (for that year) of 8.9%, give or take 22.2% points.

Wells Fargo's position in 1979 on *prospective* standard deviation for equities was that it would be 18% points. This expectation is, in large part, derived from the observed stock market standard deviation for the post-World War II period.

So, MPT tells us about asset class risk in sigma terms, while classical financial theory of discounted cash flows helps in estimating the return side of the equation. Exhibit 9.A may serve as a review of the progress we've made so far.

The 16% represents the expected return for stocks. In the example, we assume the following components of expected return, derived from observation of the primary and secondary markets.

7.5%	Long-term inflation expectation*
3.0	GNP real growth expectation*
+5.5	Current one-year dividend yield on the market portfolio
16.0%	Total expected return

*To the year 2000, for example.

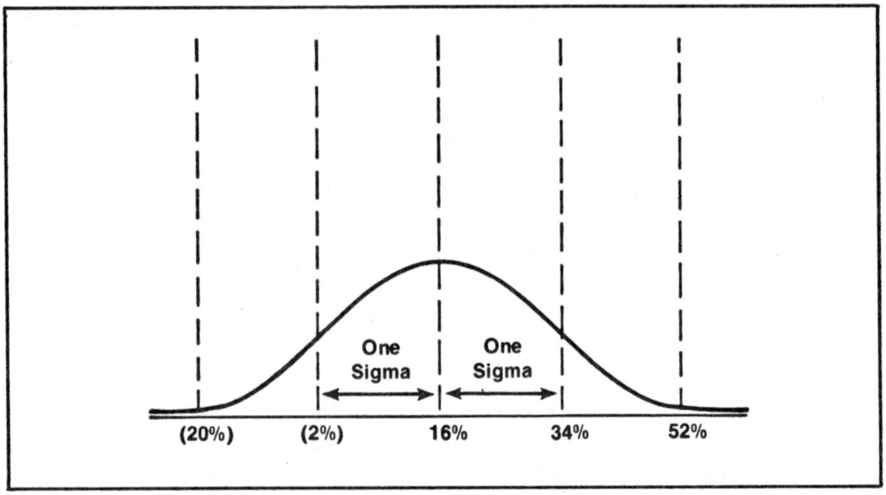

EXHIBIT 9.A / Expected Return and Risk for Stocks (One Year Horizon)

We don't know what the stock market will actually return over the next 12 months, but we can be two-thirds confident that the realized return will be 16%, plus or minus 18 percentage points (one sigma, or one standard deviation). Double the range, and we can expect the market return to be lower than −20% or higher than +52% in only one of twenty cases. No matter how much we would all prefer more certainty, it simply cannot be had.

For bonds, lower the 16% expected return to 11.5%, and tighten the distribution of potential outcomes to reflect less risk. Use 6% points for sigma instead of 18% points, and Exhibit 9.B comes into focus.

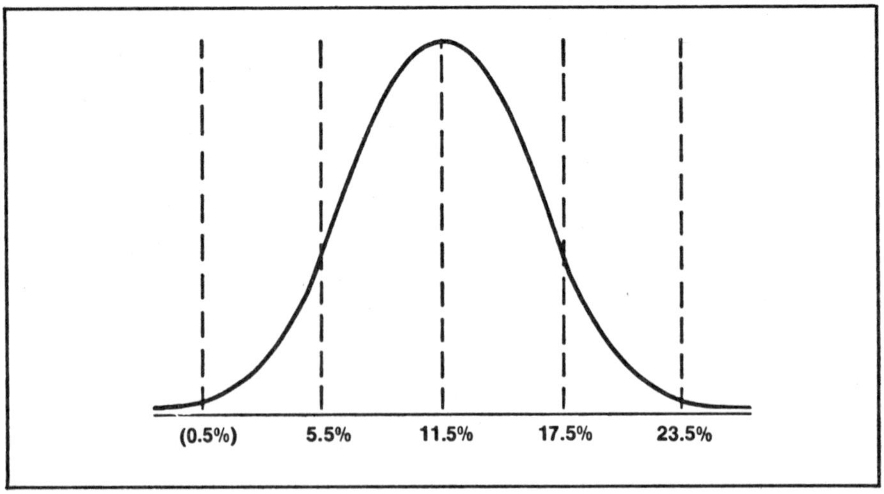

EXHIBIT 9.B / Expected Return and Risk for Bonds (One Year Horizon)

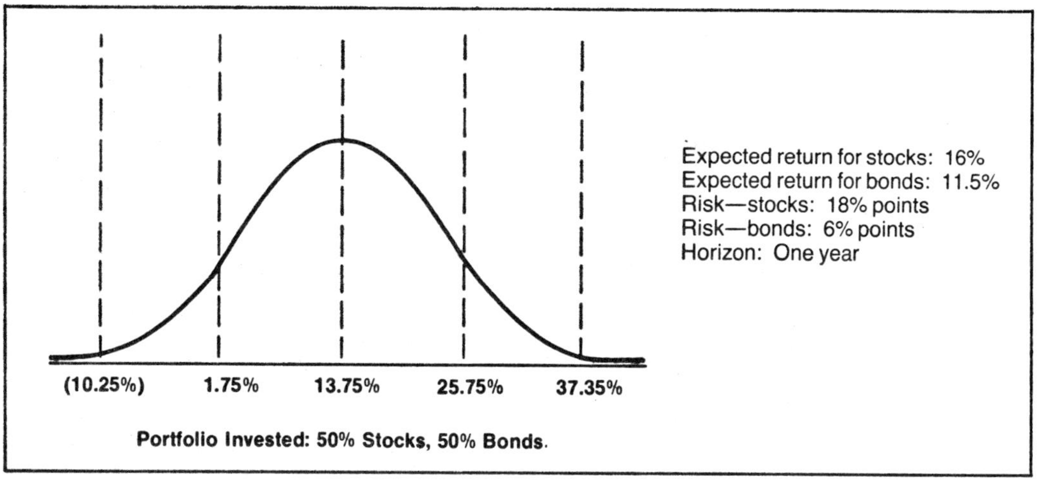

EXHIBIT 9.C / Expected Return and Risk for a Mixed Portfolio

Here again, it's worth pausing to repeat that the very large range of potential outcomes around the best estimate is an unavoidable fact of life. If by some magic, managers always "knew" what returns would be, then management organizations would disband, the employees would manage their personal portfolios, and we would all be living in an unreal world.

By implication, MPT provides other, related insights concerning the notion of risk. For example, by combining asset classes in a portfolio, one can explicitly regulate the risk-to-expected-return trade-off.

Exhibit 9.C demonstrates that if you put half your money in stocks and the other half in bonds, the result is a portfolio with an expected return about midway between that of stocks and bonds, and a sigma risk that is greater than bonds but less than stocks; another classic (and rather self-evident) quantified example of the risk-to-expected-return investment-world reality.

Correlation 9.1.4

Probably MPT's most important contribution to professional investment management practice is the concept of *correlation,* which profoundly affects the way in which risks combine. Why is this so? Why is it important? We'll address the latter question. In so doing, the answer to the former will become obvious.

Friend A makes the following proposition: give him a dollar, and the friend will invest it to return an average of 10% per year over four years. The promise involves delivering annual returns of two zeros and two 20% returns. Whatever the sequence, this investment program will return 44¢, plus the original dollar. Friend B makes the same offer, with the single exception that when A delivers a zero return in one year, B will deliver a 20% return in that year, and vice versa. Whether you choose A or B is of no consequence. In either case, the result will be payment of $1.44 at the end of four years. But observe what happens if you put half of your dollar with A and half with B! The return over the four-year period is smoothed to 10% in each year. The total return over the four-year period happens to be $1.46. The higher return is a function of the period of time selected for the example. The important point is that return variability *is* risk (or an acceptable proxy for risk) and that this risk can be reduced without impairing return if investors successfully combine assets/securities possessing differing cross-correlation characteristics.

Thus, how asset classes (and individual investments within asset classes) correlate is of critical importance in constructing and managing portfolios. As imperfectly correlated assets of similar risk and expected return are combined, risk can be reduced while expected return is maintained. MPT's explicit recognition of this reality is the primary driving force behind the theory's growing acceptance as well as the proliferation of sophisticated computer programming to assist managers in dealing with the mass of data that must be processed if this correlation phenomenon is to be successfully and explicitly captured and then managed in portfolios. (Why are some major pension plan sponsors so interested in foreign equity components as a complement to existing domestic equity exposure? Because foreign stock markets are not highly correlated with ours.)

9.1.5 Beta

What about the risk of each stock in the market portfolio? This is much harder to cope with. Better to try to cope, however, than to simply sweep the problem under the rug. This is where *beta* joins sigma and correlation.

The most simple and yet intellectually correct definition of ***beta,*** as it applies to a given company, is the future business and financial risk of that company, relative to the future business and financial risk of all other companies in the economic system.

A stock's beta, as estimated by securities analysts, is a measure of the future relative price variability of a stock compared to the market portfolio. The market's beta is 1.0 by definition. A stock with a beta of 1.2 is expected to be more variable in price changes than the market. A beta of 0.8 signifies an expected variability less than that of the market. Beta forecasts for individual stocks are rather crude, despite over a decade of research. For example, a stock may be assigned an expected beta of 1.2, but subsequent tracking of the stock's performance could indicate a much higher or lower realized beta. Thus, in selecting individual stocks, beta is not a reliable tool. On the other hand, the usefulness of even crude beta estimates improves very significantly when employed in a portfolio context. A randomly diversified, 25-stock, equal dollar weighted portfolio with an average beta of 1.2 will probably exhibit a realized beta of between about 1.16 and 1.24 (in other words, the portfolio's beta estimate carries a sigma of about 4 basis points).

Assume we have an index fund—one that mirrors the market and therefore has a beta of 1.0. What if we sell IBM from the portfolio and reinvest in Envirotech shares? Since the former's beta is assumed to be relatively low and the latter's relatively high, the portfolio's beta will have increased slightly and it will no longer track the market with its former precision. As one skews a portfolio away from the mirror image of the market portfolio, *portfolio sigma* is introduced to and combined with the sigma risk already imbedded in the market as a whole.

Alpha 9.1.6

The last of MPT's greek lexicon to be discussed in this chapter is *alpha*. The concept is quite simple. It concerns a portfolio's historical and prospective performance relative to the average performance of all portfolios which have the same beta. An example followed by some discussion is probably the most direct and effective means of communicating the concept of alpha.

Portfolio A contains 30 stock holdings. Adjusting for the varying dollar-sizes of the holdings, its beta is 1.00, the same as for the market. Thus, looking at beta alone, one would say that portfolio A's expected return is the same as that for the stock market as a whole.

Enter portfolio A's sigma. Clearly it is greater than the sigma of the much more diversified market portfolio. Thus, portfolio A's range of probable returns is greater than the range of probable returns for the market, even though they both exhibit identical expected returns.

When the given performance measurement period is completed, let's say that portfolio A outperformed the market by 2 percentage points. In MPT terms, a 2 percentage point positive alpha has been achieved by portfolio A. Another portfolio, B, began the measurement period with the same beta and sigma characteristics as exhibited by A. B, however, delivered a return of 3 percentage points below the market's return. Thus, portfolio B is said to have delivered a 3% negative alpha.

In this rear-view-mirror context, alpha is a measure of a particular portfolio's realized return relative to the average return of all other portfolios managed at the same level of beta risk. This average rate of return has, by definition, an alpha of zero. Thus, for example, an index fund always produces an alpha of zero, and the alpha of the average return of all portfolios managed, say, at a beta level of 1.20, is likewise zero.

What about prospective alpha? Here the ice gets perilously thin. Nonetheless, one must deal with the hazards of taking the risk of realizing a negative alpha if one reaches for a positive alpha. Here again, an example will be helpful.

Investors who employ the discounted-future-cash-flow approach to stock evaluation can determine the range of expected returns offered by each component of the stock universe being dealt with. The more market-like this universe is, the better the entire exercise will reflect the range of expected returns offered at any point across the market's spectrum of beta risk. For example, the investor can observe that some stocks offer more return than the average of all stocks of similar risk. Likewise with portfolios of stocks. Each exhibits a prospective alpha. Employing modern investment management techniques, investors can construct and manage portfolios to specified beta and sigma targets and, within these risk management constraints, maximize prospective alpha.

9.1.7 Integration of Concepts

Let's take a look at the linkage between alpha, beta, and sigma. Every portfolio has produced returns in the past that can be analyzed and attributed quite confidently to some explicit combination of alpha, beta, and sigma. On an expectational basis, all portfolios can be examined to determine what alpha, beta, and sigma are in place. Furthermore, each characteristic can be managed. Remember, the only item of concern in the total portfolio equation which cannot be managed is what the market portfolio actually does. What the secondary markets do over the long term will be mostly attributable to the degree to which the primary market delivers cash flows to investors. In the short run, the volatility of the secondary markets will be most attributable to investors' changing levels of confidence that the primary market will in fact deliver as expected over the longer term.

For the sake of discussion, let's accept the capitalization-weighted S&P 500 Index as a stock market proxy (it's far from perfect). The mirror-image Index Fund then becomes a "market portfolio" which, day-by-day, year-in and year-out, will deliver the market rate of return. What is this portfolio's alpha? It is zero, by definition. The market will return whatever it will return, and that's all there is to that. What is the portfolio's sigma risk? It is the annual variability of return around the annual average return of the market. What is its beta risk? By definition, it is 1.0. What happens to this index fund portfolio's alpha, beta, and sigma if the manager sells IBM and adds the proceeds to other holdings? The beta of the "new" portfolio may or may not change, depending upon what combination of issues and issue-weightings are purchased. What will happen to the portfolio's total sigma risk? It will *increase!* The investor/manager, by moving the portfolio's diversification away from the market-mirror-image, has introduced the risk that the new portfolio will under- or over-perform the market. Note that a one-stock portfolio with a beta of 1.0 will have a large sigma. Note also that if an investor sets out to achieve a higher-than-market return, his portfolio will have to have more sigma risk than is imbedded in the market portfolio.

Why accept a portfolio sigma that is above that of the market? There would be no point whatever in doing so unless one thought that one would be compensated for the additional risk by receiving a positive alpha. Reaching for positive expected alpha carries with it the risk of realizing a negative alpha. Note the relationship to sigma. In short, to employ a useful analogy for the first of several times in this chapter, portfolio alpha, beta, and sigma comprise a three-dimensional spider web: pull on one strand and the others move.

One last word on correlation, a fourth dimension of our spider web (others will be added when we discuss investor needs, tax status, risk-taking attitudes, planning horizons, etc.). Observe Exhibit 9.D.

At a point in time, bonds offer a given expected return at a given level of risk. Likewise for stocks; more expected return, more risk. The curved line linking the A-to-B extremes represents an infinite number of combinations of bonds and stocks. Point C represents a portfolio that is mostly invested in bonds, but has some (say 10%) stocks. While stocks and bonds are positively correlated, they are not perfectly

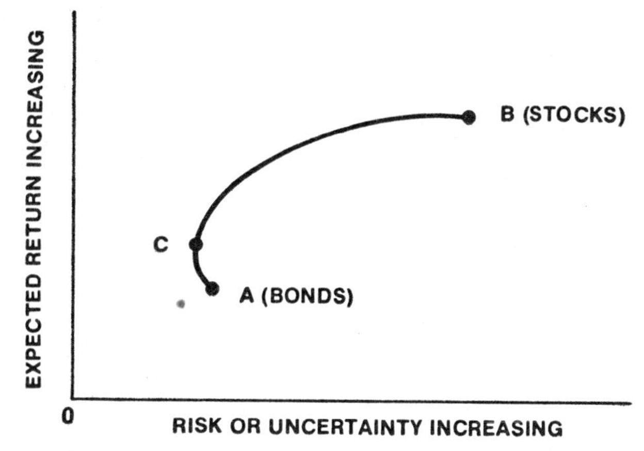

EXHIBIT 9.D / Asset Allocation Tradeoff

correlated. Thus a porftolio that is 100% bonds (point A), promises a lower expected return at a higher level of risk than a portfolio invested 10% stocks/90% bonds! Recall the earlier example involving the one dollar and the four returns of two zeros and two 20%'s? The correlation phenomenon applies not only to asset classes, but to the individual securities comprising each asset class. Thus an index fund, for example (at least one which is a true mirror image of the S&P 500 Index), contains 500 securities, each of which has cross-correlation coefficients with the other (499) stocks: 12,250 correlation coefficients in total! (Is it clear why a computer is essential in a modern approach to portfolio management?)

So, now the reader has an overview of the ABC's of modern portfolio management concepts: alpha, beta, sigma, and correlation. When they are explicitly and imaginatively taken into consideration by experienced professionals, and when those professionals possess the necessary computer hardware and well-conceived and designed software, many advantages accrue to their investor-clients. In short, prospective risk and return can be explicitly managed to suit a client's need for return and financial and attitudinal ability to assume risk.

Application of MPT 9.2

With the foregoing as background, the following fictional episode will be helpful in structuring a framework for managing a public retirement (or any pension fund) system's investment portfolio. We assume in this case study that a Wells Fargo portfolio manager has been retained by a municipal pension system. The author suggests that a priority-sequence of major issues be established and routinely addressed through time, preferably with a strong assist from well-conceived and constructed analytical tools.

- Establishment of rate-of-return objectives. This will lead to . . .
- Identification of permitted asset classes which, in turn, leads to . . .
- A statement of appropriate asset allocation policy. Once ranges of permitted asset class exposure have been established for each selected secondary market component . . .
- Then risk management policies (beta ranges and sigma ranges) should be set for each asset class, the combination of which will cause the portfolio to fall within a stated range of total portfolio risk management limits.
- The strategic asset allocation decision comes next. Within policy ranges, what is the optimal mix now? Also, within each asset class, how much should be passively managed and how much actively? (E.g., what portion of the equity exposure should be in an index or other passively managed portfolio, and how much under specialty management intended to result in above-market return [positive alpha]?)
- Within the actively managed portion of each asset class, what strategic alpha, beta, and sigma should be sought in the current capital markets' risk-to-expected return environment?
- What combination of what investments *within* each asset class is optimal?
- What are the cost-to-benefit trade-offs associated with moving the portfolio's structure from its current position to the desired position?
- Evaluation of past activity.

June 6, 1979. This particular meeting takes place once a year; soon after Gotham City's retirement system board's actuarial firm delivers and defends revised estimates of future pension plan costs. Those attending are: an outside portfolio manager, two members of the retirement system board's investment policy and management subcommittee, a senior retirement system administration officer, and a member of the city's legal department who acts as legal advisor to the board.

With the actuary's revised estimates in hand, the group will spend the better part of the morning reviewing existing asset allocation policy and, possibly, formulating a proposed revision. A revision may be called for because cost projections have increased, altering the required rate of average annual return from the portfolio. Permitted asset classes are U.S. cash/cash-equivalents, stocks, bonds, and first mortgages on buildings within the city.

Once a recommendation on the asset allocation policy issue has been hammered out, related, subsidiary issues will be addressed.

- Within the to-be-proposed policy for asset-mix ranges, what is the optimal strategic mix now? On what basis should the strategic mix be re-examined over the next 12 months?
- Once the strategic mix question is settled, what portion of each asset class should be passively managed versus actively managed?
- What risk-management guidelines (beta and sigma, again) should the manager operate within for handling the active stock and bond portfolios?
- Within the proposed asset class management guidelines for active management, what are the optimal risk-management strategies now?
- What risk-management strategies are imbedded in the current stock and bond portfolios?
- What minimum turnover (and estimated turnover costs) would be required in order to move the stock and bond portfolios from their current, suboptimal strategy positions to optimal positions? Can such move simultaneously and efficiently accommodate a (presumed) preferred change in strategic asset mix?
- What political and attitudinal considerations should be explicitly recognized and, thus, accommodated in the processes employed to reach and implement all of these policy and strategy decisions?

If the board retains more than one outside portfolio manager, it may wish to retain a consultant to address other issues, such as:

- What risk strategies are currently imbedded in each manager's portfolio?
- What are the weighted, combined risk strategies of each asset class, and for the aggregate portfolio?
- What returns can be expected from these portfolios (and the combined portfolio) over three-, five-, eight-, and ten-year horizons.
- What is the distribution of possible return and impact-on-contribution-rate outcomes around the most likely one for each horizon?
- If these are unacceptable, how should investment policy guidelines be modified for each manager? What would be the implications for allocations of cash flow contributions? Given the new constraints (broadened or tightened) on manager discretion, what average annual return can reasonably be expected from each at what total portfolio sigma?

While there are indeed many interrelated issues requiring attention, everyone at the table recognizes that the asset allocation policy and strategy issues dwarf all others combined in terms of their long-term effect on the system's ability to meet benefit obligations. The board has long since moved away from such futile practices as second-guessing the manager's inevitable, occasional failures in security purchase/sale judgments, etc., a position which correctly recognizes that well over 90% of a diversified portfolio's future health, or lack thereof, is due entirely to policy decisions that, ultimately, the board itself must stipulate in beta and sigma terms.

Available to the group is a sophisticated pension simulator, accessible by video terminal and a printer linked to a remote computer. Its function is to process a variety of planning variables (planning periods, ranges of liability and capital market risk, return and correlation assumptions, etc.) and to indicate the implied impact of multiple asset mix combinations on future contribution rates.

9.3 Setting Asset Class Range Policy

The group proceeds to develop basic investment goals with the simulation program, employing the following liability assumptions for the 1979–1988 period:

5/31/79	Benefit Payments	Normal Costs	Accrued Liabilities	
1979	$ 385,694	$1,731,661	$14,939,152	
1980	423,912	1,865,314	17,460,052	
1981	467,508	2,039,328	20,545,436	
1982	546,774	2,221,269	24,005,834	
1983	694,764	2,421,877	28,211,268	
1984	876,221	2,611,637	32,303,100	
1985	1,071,991	2,800,881	36,880,087	
1986	1,267,144	3,019,368	41,790,946	
1987	1,497,341	3,257,462	47,069,595	
1988	1,743,635	3,524,210	53,074,620	
Other:	• Vested accrued liabilities		$57,815,008	(1988)
	• Payroll		$33,751,732	(1988)
	• Interest rate assumption (Required rate of return)			9.0%*

*This is 0.5% higher than the return number employed one year ago because projected payroll has, in the interim, been unexpectedly enlarged.

The retirement system's future contributions and their variability are highly sensitive to the risk and return assumptions on stocks and bonds. One distinct set of capital market risk and expected return assumptions and related estimates is selected as the most likely:

Expected return—stocks : 16.00%
Expected return—bonds : 11.50%
Sigma stocks : 18.00%

Sigma bonds : 6.00%
Correlation stocks with bonds : 0.50*

*On a scale of minus one-to-plus one where plus one equals perfect positive correlation.

The risk and return assumptions for stocks and bonds in this scenario are, as it happens, close to the June 1979 Wells Fargo forecasts. They are long-term in nature and the group agrees to use them after considering others provided by several sources.

The selected capital market scenario, in conjunction with the pension liability projections, are used to construct a probability distribution for the retirement system's contributions as a percent of payroll, which are graphically displayed in Exhibit 9.E.

The vertical axis of the graph measures contributions as a percent of payroll and the horizontal axis measures the percent of pension assets in equities (versus bonds). Each of the five lines in the graph represents a given percentile, and together they illustrate how the distribution of contributions (as a percent of payroll) changes with alternative asset mixes.

As an example, Exhibit 9.E shows that the median (50th percentile) contribution level as a percent of payroll is 4.75% for a 0% equity/100% bond mix. This implies that one half of the possible contribution levels in 1988 will be greater than 4.75% and one half will be less than 4.75%. For the same asset mix, the 90th percentile outcome is 5.75%. This suggests that there is a 10% chance that the retirement system's contribution in 1988 will be at, or more than, 5.75% of the payroll. In the 100% equity asset mix there is a 50% chance that the contribution level will be no more than 2.50% of payroll (50th percentile); a 25% chance that the contribution level will be more than 6.00% of payroll (75th percentile); and a 10% chance that the contribution level will be greater than 7.75% of payroll (90th percentile).

Exhibit 9.E illustrates the distribution of contributions using the selected forecasts for the capital markets. This produces distributions suggesting that significant reduction in contributions can be achieved by permitting the retirement system's equity exposure to reach at least 60% from time to time. The expected (median) contribution level drops from 3.00% of payroll to close to 2.75% as equity exposure is increased from 40% to 60%. Also note that the risk of relatively high contributions in the year 1988 increases only nominally. There remains only a 10% chance that contributions will exceed the 5.50%–5.75% range (90th percentile) of payroll for any combination of stocks and bonds where stocks are at most 60% and at least 40%.

The city's financial planners are assuming that the retirement system's contribution will be 5.00% in 1988, down from its current 7.20% level. Their worst-case assumption is that it will be maintained at the current rate. Relating these expectations to the board's own goal of a 3.00% rate in 1988 and the simulator probability distributions, the group recognizes that a policy permitting at least a 40% exposure to stocks is essential. Because of interim strategic asset mix decisions, a minimum permitted equity exposure of 40% will not, in all likelihood, be in place over the full

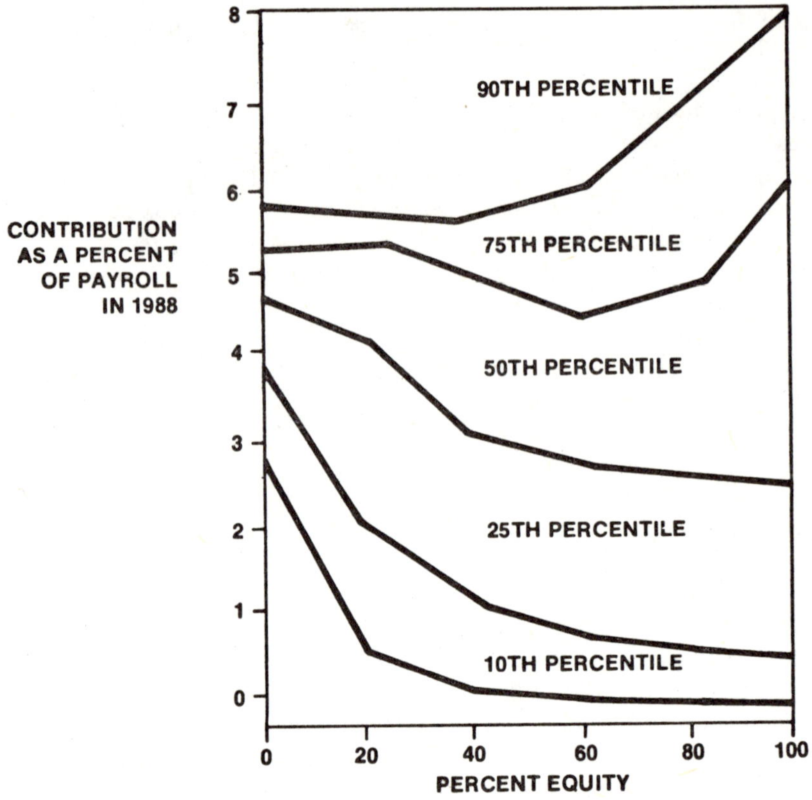

EXHIBIT 9.E / Forecast of Pension Contribution Level

8-year period. It is estimated that these strategic asset mix moves, coupled with slightly above-market annual returns from actively managed segments of the portfolio, will push the odds to approximately a 3-to-1 relationship, that the planners' 5.00% contribution rate level will be achieved, and that the board's own 3.00% objective is about a 50-50 proposition.

9.4 Allocating Among Asset Classes

The question of maximum equity exposure policy is then addressed, and the group decides that no matter how competitive stocks may be vis-à-vis bonds from time to time, the board should not bet on stocks drastically at any point. Inspection of simulator output leads to a consensus conclusion that the maximum equity exposure limit should be 60%.

Here is a summary of what the simulation's output suggests. The author appreciates that Exhibit 9.E may be difficult to grasp at first. However, with some study of the graph, along with the following data, a clear picture of the simulation's implications will emerge.

Distribution of Probable Contribution Rate
(at 8th year)

Stocks	Bonds	10th%	25th%	50th%	75th%	90th%
0	100%	2.75%	3.80%	4.75%	5.25%	5.75%
20	80	0.50	2.00	4.00	5.25	5.70
40	60	0.00	1.10	3.00	4.80	5.65
60	40	0.00	0.75	2.75	4.30	5.90
80	20	0.00	0.60	2.60	4.66	6.85
100	0	0.00	0.33	2.40	5.95	7.80

The entire process of analyzing, inspecting, and discussing plan cost and capital market return, risk, and correlation assumptions has taken some three hours. The effort has been well worthwhile, because the board's representatives and the portfolio manager are agreed that the asset allocation policy issue has been dealt with intelligently, employing the best relevant approaches currently available, rigorously coupled with economically supportable forecast assumptions and reasonable measures of uncertainty pertaining to each. All involved realize that they are dealing with expectations, not reality as it will turn out to be. The problems being dealt with by the group are dynamic in nature. As time passes, new information will flow in, and new expectations and estimates of uncertainty will take form. There is some comfort, however, in knowing that this information and expectation stream is being dealt with in the most intelligent (and defensible) manner currently possible. Additional comfort derives from the likelihood that ongoing research at investment management firms, university campuses, and elsewhere is likely to yield improved insights into the pension management problem in general, and the policy-setting issue in particular.

After a short lunch, the group goes further into the strategic asset allocation issue. What should equity exposure be now within the currently proposed equity policy range of 40–60%? The matter of asset allocation policy can be reviewed effectively only as frequently as the plan's actuary provides explicit cost-revision estimates, normally once a year. In the interim, however, capital market risk-to-expected-return conditions are in constant flux. The spreads between the expected returns from the permitted asset classes are changing daily as investors adjust and readjust their return requirements (and, much less frequently, their cash flow forecasts) from the various asset classes.

The current spread relationships between asset classes is a critical factor to be explicitly dealt with in reaching strategic asset allocation decisions. Expected, risk-adjusted return spreads *within* asset classes bear on a lower priority issue already touched upon, and to be discussed at greater length later. For example, within equities, what should the strategic beta management decision be? Should lower risk stocks be favored over higher risk stocks, etc.?

The input assumptions required by the strategic asset allocation decision-making process are:

1. Expected return—stocks 16.00%
2. Sigma—stocks 18.00%
3. Expected return—bonds 11.50%
4. Sigma—bonds 6.00%
5. Correlation—stocks with bonds (1.0 is perfect, positive correlation) ...... .50
6. Investment horizon .... 8 years (1988)
7. Required rate of return 9.00%
8. Risk ratio 6-to-1

1. *Expected Return (ER)—Stocks (16%).* This is the capitalization-weighted ER for a robust proxy for the entire universe of U.S. stocks. The universe used by Wells Fargo in 1979 contained 367 stocks. By design, the firm constructed it to be market-like in all substantive respects. In effect, this universe's weighted ER is a "spot rate" for equities; it is a function of the firm's analyst forecasts of future dividend cash flows to investors and of current prices. This "bottom-up"-derived estimate of future return for the stock market (16% in this case) is chosen because it has a good, confirming "fit" with the group's then-current forecast constructed from the "top-down," or macroeconomic approach (7.5% long-term, realized inflation, plus 3% real growth in GNP, plus the one-year, forward yield on the S&P 500 of 5.5%). The 16% "forward rate" for stocks is much higher than has been realized historically. The reason for this is that current expectations for inflation are much higher today than realized (historical) inflation has been.

2. *Sigma—Stocks (18% points).* This is Wells' expectation for the annual variability (sigma) of returns around its current "best estimate" of 16%. Sigma is a probabilistic statement of the range of returns around the most likely return.

3. *ER—Bonds (11.5%).* Current, weighted yield-to-maturity for the retirement system's existing fixed-income portfolio. As of 1979, 11.5% is close to the ER promised by new 20-year, high-quality corporates.

4. *Sigma—Bonds (6% points).* Bonds are assumed to be about one-third as risky as stocks.

5. *Correlation—Stocks with Bonds (positive 0.5 on a scale of −1.0 to +1.0).* Because inflation expectations are such a large component of Wells Fargo's total ER estimates for each asset class, stocks and bonds are expected to be correlated positively, but not perfectly. In other words, bonds and stocks will tend to move

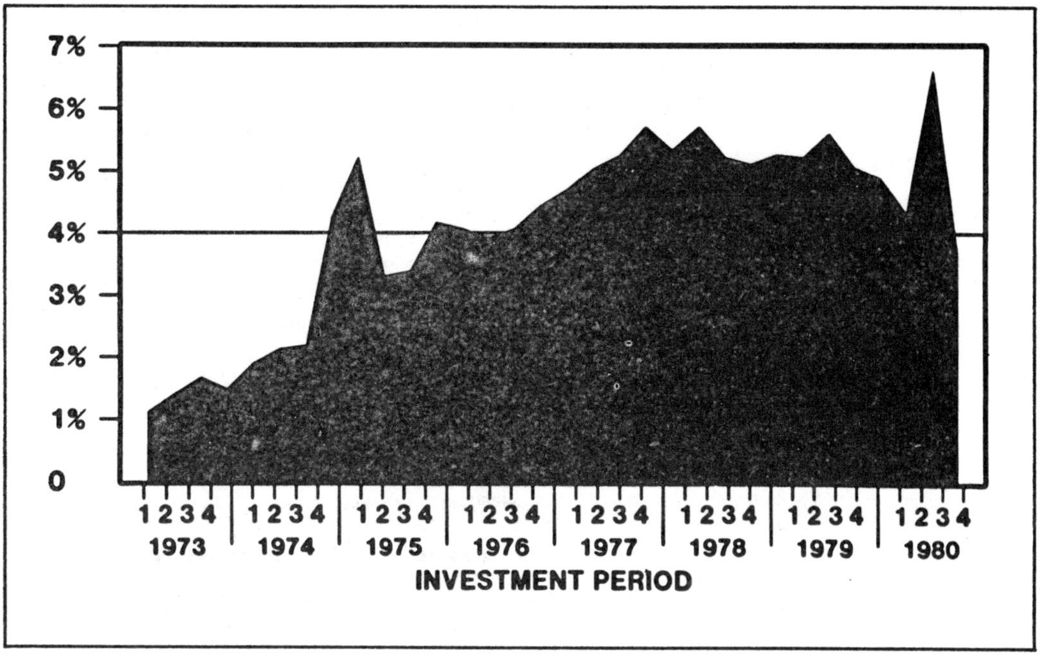

Stock/Bond Expected Return Spread

up and down more or less in concert over longer time periods, but not necessarily to the same degrees.

6. *Investment Horizon (8 years).* The policy simulation exercise described earlier keyed off the year 1988. Thus eight years is appropriate. The board understands that if one-to-three-year horizons are employed, the portfolio will very likely be at or near its minimum permitted equity exposure most of the time. If this were to occur through time, the odds would be poor that lower contribution rate objectives would be met.

7. *Required Rate of Return (9%).* That return which, if achieved on average each year through 1988, will drive the contribution rate down from the current 7.20% to the 3.00% objective.

8. *Risk Ratio.* This is a measure of the board's attitudes. It expresses how the board trades off risk with expected return. Reducing attitudes to a mathematical measure is a hazardous business at best. Wells Fargo uses an iterative process which helps the board make the 6-to-1 ratio statement about itself. In very gross terms, 6-to-1 utility says that the board considers a chance of a 6%-point return above its required rate in a given 12-month period can be balanced with a chance of a 1% shortfall. The firm has found that the inevitable imperfection of these measures is not critical to the usefulness of the information derived from its asset allocation process. What is critical, however, is that the client not vary the measure through

TWO ASSET ALLOCATION PROGRAM

GOTHAM CITY RETIREMENT SYSTEM 6/ 6/79

PROGRAM INPUTS

INVESTMENT HORIZON	8 YEARS
MINIMUM REQUIRED RETURN	9.00% PER ANNUM
RISK RATIO	6/1
EXPECTED RETURN-EQUITY PORTFOLIO	16.00% PER ANNUM
RISK - EQUITY PORTFOLIO	18.00% POINTS PER ANNUM
EXPECTED RETURN-FIXED INCOME PORTFOLIO	11.50% PER ANNUM
RISK - FIXED INCOME PORTFOLIO	6.00% POINTS PER ANNUM
CORRELATION-EQUITY AND FIXED INCOME	0.5

PROGRAM RESULTS-THE HIGHEST LEVEL OF CLIENT SATISFACTION (UTILITY RANKING=1) OCCURS AT AN EQUITY-FIXED INCOME MIX OF 60% EQUITY AND 40 % FIXED INCOME.

8-YEAR HORIZON

DISTRIBUTION OF RETURNS
ANNUAL RATE OF RETURN COMPOUNDED ANNUALLY (%)

ASSET MIX				PROBABILITY					UTILITY	PROBABILITY
EQUITY	FIXED	MEAN	S.D.	95	75	50	25	5	RANKING	OF 9.00%
100	0	16.0	6.3	4.8	10.5	14.6	18.9	25.4	7	82.12
90	10	15.5	5.8	5.3	10.6	14.4	18.3	24.2	5	83.15
80	20	15.1	5.3	5.8	10.6	14.1	17.7	23.1	3	84.13
70	30	14.6	4.8	6.3	10.7	13.9	17.1	21.9	2	85.08
* 60	40	14.2	4.3	6.7	10.7	13.6	16.5	20.8	* 1	86.21
50	50	13.8	3.8	7.2	10.7	13.2	15.8	19.7	4	87.29
40	60	13.3	3.4	7.5	10.7	12.9	15.2	18.5	6	88.30
30	70	12.8	2.9	7.8	10.6	12.5	14.5	17.5	8	89.07
20	80	12.4	2.6	8.0	10.4	12.2	13.9	16.5	9	89.44
10	90	11.9	2.3	8.1	10.2	11.8	13.3	15.6	10	88.88
0	100	11.[illegible]	2.1	7.9	9.9	11.3	12.8	14.9	11	86.86

DISTRIBUTION OF ANNUALIZED RATES OF RETURN

```
5.0%          10.0%          15.0%          20.0%          25.0%          30.0%
95%-----------75%---------50%--------25%---------------5%
 95%----------75%--------50%--------25%-------------5%
   95%---------75%------50%-------25%-----------5%
    95%--------75%------50%------25%----------5%
     95%-------75%----50%----25%---------5%
      95%------75%---50%----25%------5%
       95%-----75%--50%---25%-----5%
        95%---75%--50%--25%-----5%
        95%---75%-50%--25%---5%
        95%---75%50%-25%---5%
        95%--75%50%-25%--5%
```

The top third of Exhibit 9.F is devoted to a summary of program inputs and the resultant "solution"; i.e., given the inputs on the one hand, and the construct of the asset allocation model on the other, the "right" thing for the board to do at the moment is to expose the capital to the risk of stocks to the maximum degree permitted by equity range policy (60%).

The center section gives us some interesting details. Reading from left to right:

Asset Mix. These columns contain 11 mix strategies, from 100% stocks to 100% fixed income. The program will, upon request, deal with a larger number of mix alternatives.

(continued on next page)

EXHIBIT 9.F / Two Asset Allocation Program

Mean. This is the most likely annual return which will be realized from the given strategy over the stipulated eight-year period. With 100% stocks and 0% bonds, the most likely return is 16%.

SD. Standard deviation, or the firm's estimate of the range of actual return outcomes at the two-thirds confidence level *for the full 8-year period.* Note that the number is 6.3% points rather than 18.0. Why is this? Basically, because we're looking at 8 years, not one. It's true that risk (sigma) expands with time (more precisely, by the square root of time). In this case, the square root of 8 years is 2.83. Multiply this times 18.0 and you get 50.91% as the 8-year sigma. The *annualized* standard deviation for 8 years is, thus, 6.3%, the number at the top of the fourth column from the left.

Return also expands with time, and does so at a greater rate than risk. If one compounds a 16% annual return over eight years, the result is a return of 228%. Thus, the firm would say that the 100%/0% stock-bond mix promises 16%, and that the 8-year ER is 228%, give-or-take 51%, with two-thirds confidence (one sigma).

Probability. These five columns exhibit probability distributions of annual, realized returns around the most likely return of each mix (see 50th percentile probability column). Here, for the 100%/0% stock-bond mix, the most likely outcome is 14.6%, compounded annually. Why isn't it 16%? The reason is as follows: Looking forward, the spot rate (ER) for stocks is in fact 16%. However, while an average of 16% is the most likely outcome, it is extremely unlikely that exactly 16% will be delivered each year. In fact, the most likely median return will be 14.6%. Variability of return decays the effect of compounding.

Now look at the column labeled 95. The 100%/0% stock-bond mix carries with it a one-in-20 chance (5% probability) that the strategy will produce a compound return of 4.8% per year, or less. The 75-column indicates a one-in-four chance of compounding at 10.5% or less, etc., until we find that there's a 5% chance that the strategy will produce a 25.4% compound rate of return or more.

Utility. See Risk Ratio below.

Probability (of attaining 9% or more). Note that over the 8-year period, none of the mixes available offers 100% certainty that the minimum required rate of return (9%) will be achieved. The range of probability is 82.12% for the 100%/0% stock-bond mix to 89.94% at 20% stocks, 80% bonds. Why isn't the 20%/80% mix preferred? Now we come back to the notion of utility or risk ratio, or how the city's retirement system board trades off units of increased ER with units of additional risk.

Risk Ratio. The 6/1 risk ratio (utility) input is an expression of the board's aversion to risk. All 6/1 means is that the board feels that it must be promised, for example, 6% points of additional ER for each additional 1% point of sigma risk it assumes. Without some measure of risk aversion, the usefulness of the program is diminished. With the measure, however, the 60/40 mix is highlighted as being optimal for this particular client, given the requirement/expectation inputs.

Sometimes a retirement board might look at Exhibit 9.F and say, "I really prefer the 40/60 mix. After all, my probability of achieving 9% increases, and the 5% chance of compounding at 6.7% or less is improved." That is, the number in the column headed 95 increases from 6.7% to (at 40/60) 7.5%.

This is a critically important observation for the client to make to the portfolio manager. All of the *other* inputs are then carefully reviewed. If both sides of the table are still satisfied that they are of the highest possible quality, then the focus reverts to the risk ratio input: 6/1.

The problem resides here, and the group decides to run the asset allocation program several more times, holding all other inputs stable, but varying the risk ratio until the utility ranking 1 (second column from the left, presently indicating 60/40 as being optimal) moves to the 40/60 strategy! As it turns out, a 7/1 risk ratio does the trick. Both sides sign off on 7/1.

Distribution of Annualized Rates of Return. This is simply a graphic display of the probability columns in the center of Exhibit 9.F. Try turning the distribution of annualized rate of return graph upside down, and then visualize a skewed but almost bell-shaped distribution curve "describing" the array of distributions. See how it is skewed to the left? The reason it is not perfectly bell-shaped (normal) is that the worst case for any non-leveraged strategy is that one loses all (100%) of one's money. The other side of the coin is, however, that one can experience returns of more than 100%.

We suggest that investors identify their unique level of risk aversion by observing the alternative return distributions based on the "best" capital market inputs available, and then choosing that one which displeases them the least! There is no free lunch.

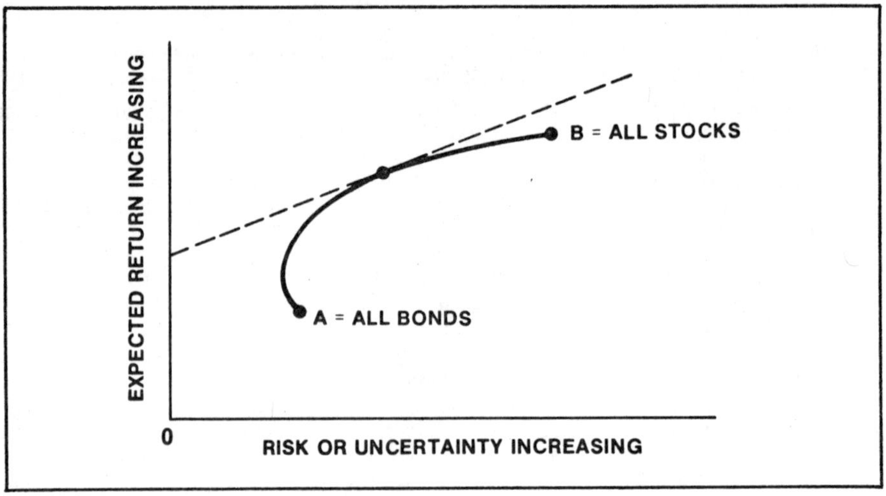

EXHIBIT 9.G / The Risk Ratio Line

time except for valid, rational considerations (e.g., the organization acquires another, the nature or composition of the labor force is substantively changed, and, perhaps, the business and financial risk of the "new" organization is altered). Clients are prone to want to make such changes for irrational reasons. It is only natural that desire for risk increases when risk has been rewarding investors recently, and decreases when risk has produced pain.

The printed output of the asset allocation program is shown in Exhibit 9.F.

Sometimes it's easier to look at a picture rather than at a bunch of numbers. Exhibit 9.G is designed to convey the essence of Exhibit 9.F.

The curved line we've seen before (Exhibit 9.D). It is an expression of the current stock/bond, risk/return trade-off; a representation of an infinite number of possible combinations of stocks and bonds, each with its unique risk-to-expected return trade-off characteristics. The dashed, sloping line is, in effect, a mathematical statement of the board's risk ratio or utility function, describing how the board trades off units of increased risk with units of expected return.

It is critically important that the board not vary the slope of this risk ratio line, except to rationally reflect substantive changes in plan circumstances. Re-examine Exhibit 9.G. Note that there is a spread of ER between stocks and bonds (vertical axis). Now look at what happens when price levels for bonds increase, while stock prices increase even more! In Exhibit 9.H, ERs decline for both asset classes, but correlation is not perfect. Expected returns have declined for both stocks and bonds. The spread of ER has become smaller, meaning that stocks are now relatively less attractive vis-à-vis bonds than was the case in the prior exhibit. By holding the risk ratio steady, the asset allocation process calls for a *decrease* in exposure to stocks. And, as we all know, most investors would want to *increase* stocks after a period when stocks have greatly outperformed bonds.

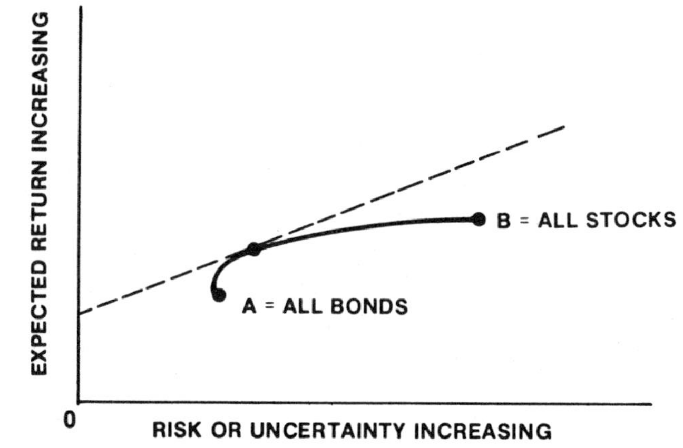

EXHIBIT 9.H / The Risk Ratio Line

The group then varies the capital market input assumptions for the asset allocation program but keeps returning to the earlier conclusion that the original set is most supportable from intellectual, economic, financial-need, and attitudinal viewpoints. The strategic asset allocation recommendation to be conveyed to the board is 60% stocks, 40% bonds. No rear-view-mirror-derived return expectations have been employed. All are as they should be: prospective.

The reader has probably noticed that only two of the four permitted asset classes (stocks, bonds, cash/cash equivalents, first mortgages on public buildings) have been employed in the foregoing policy and strategic asset allocation decision-making examples. The author has taken the liberty of simplifying the problem by working with stocks and bonds alone. The hypothetical board's problem really requires ERs, sigma risk, and cross-correlation estimates on all asset classes. Wells Fargo's model accommodates such requirements for up to 20 distinct asset classes and/or for each manager in a given pension system (e.g., three separate bond managers, one real estate manager, four equity managers, etc.). For the following discussions, we will continue to deal with only the stock and/or bond components of a portfolio.

Active/Passive Mix 9.5

The next step in the integrated decision-making (recommendation) process is to solve what can be called the "active-passive" question. For example, how much of the strategic equity exposure should be in an S&P 500 Index Fund or another fund or some combination of similar funds and how much should be exposed to manager judgments intended to produce a positive alpha relative to the stock and other asset class market portfolios? To help the group deal with these decisions here are new inputs. In this case, we deal only with common stocks.

- Assumed positive alpha from active equity management, net of fees and assumed transaction costs: +1.75%
- Sigma risk statement which describes the degree of board uncertainty that the 1.75% alpha will actually be produced each year: 2% points. (That is, actual alpha will likely be between −0.75% and 3.75%.)

We already have an ER for the passive component (index) of 16% and a sigma of 18% points, so the active equity management is expected to have an ER of 16.00% plus a net of 1.75%, or 17.75%, with a sigma of 2% points, to express a measure of the board's uncertainty that the manager will actually deliver as expected relative to whatever the market portfolio returns. The computer analyzes these inputs within the context of an eight-year time horizon, to determine the most appropriate mix. The optimal mix turns out to be 70% active/30% passive.

Intuitively, the group isn't satisfied with this suggested solution. They really want the manager to be more aggressive in seeking positive alpha. They ask the program to raise the required positive, net alpha from Wells' stock-selection process to 3.0% and, concurrently, to widen their uncertainty measure to the appropriate corresponding degree: 5% points. The recommended solution is now 30% active/70% passive. Total expected return and risk for equities haven't changed, but the board's implied fees for management have dropped significantly, since passive management fee costs are much less than those for active management.

The group then turns to setting management guidelines for the actively managed portions of the bond and stock portfolios: beta range, sigma maximum, minimum required positive alpha. Here again, simulation programs are available, permitting the group to observe "what if" return-outcomes and distributions of potential returns (around the most likely) as capital market return and ER-spread relationship assumptions are varied. These activities lead, for example, to the conclusion that the active equity portion should be managed within the following stock portfolio beta and sigma constraints.

Beta maximum	:	1.40
Beta minimum	:	1.10
Sigma maximum	:	12% points
Required positive alpha	:	3% points

9.6 Evaluating a Portfolio

A stock portfolio should be evaluated in light of prevailing assessments of its expected return and risk. Wells Fargo has attempted to define rigorously the relationships among stock yields, stock betas, and expected returns. These relationships, when analyzed, suggest which stocks to favor and which to avoid. In today's market, how much extra beta must the investor incur in order to select stocks with highest ER? Would selection of stocks with very high yields significantly or only marginally improve ER?

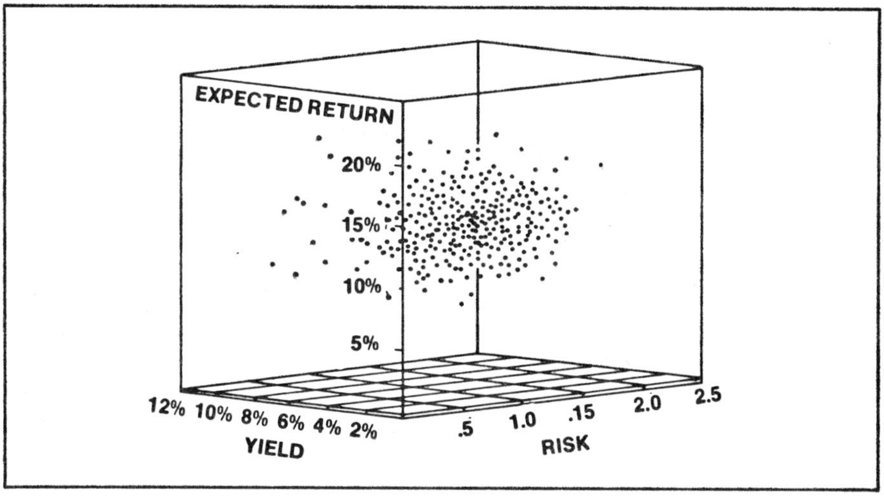

EXHIBIT 9.I / Beta, Yield, and Expected Return

Exhibit 9.I graphically interrelates beta, yield, and ER.

Each stock in Wells' 367-stock universe has a beta risk (forecasted by Wells Fargo's analysts), an ER (derived from analyst dividend cash-flow forecasts), and a current yield. Wells Fargo's equity evaluation process takes the 367 risk/return/yield coordinates in its market-like universe of stocks and "finds" a plane of best fit (Exhibits 9.J and 9.K). The plane describes the average risk-to-ER–to yield trade-off resident in the price structure of the equity market at a moment in time.

At a given level of beta risk, ER, and yield, securities are either fairly valued, overvalued, or undervalued relative to the Market Plane. This is a *prospective* view,

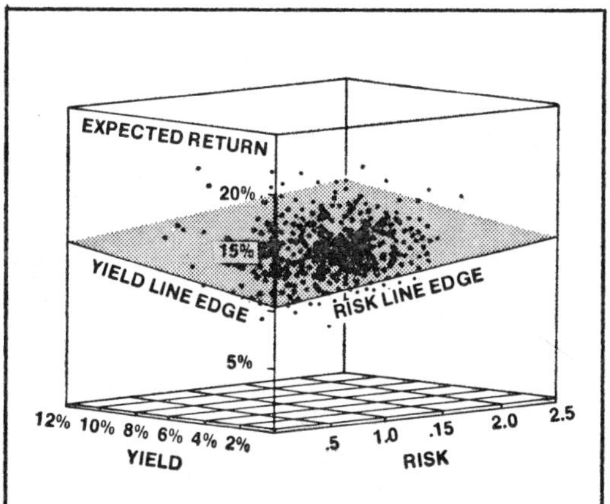

EXHIBIT 9.J / The Market Plane (1)

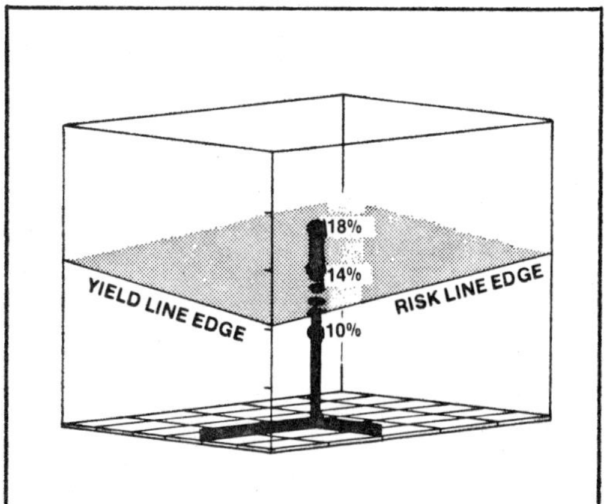

EXHIBIT 9.K / The Market Plane (2)

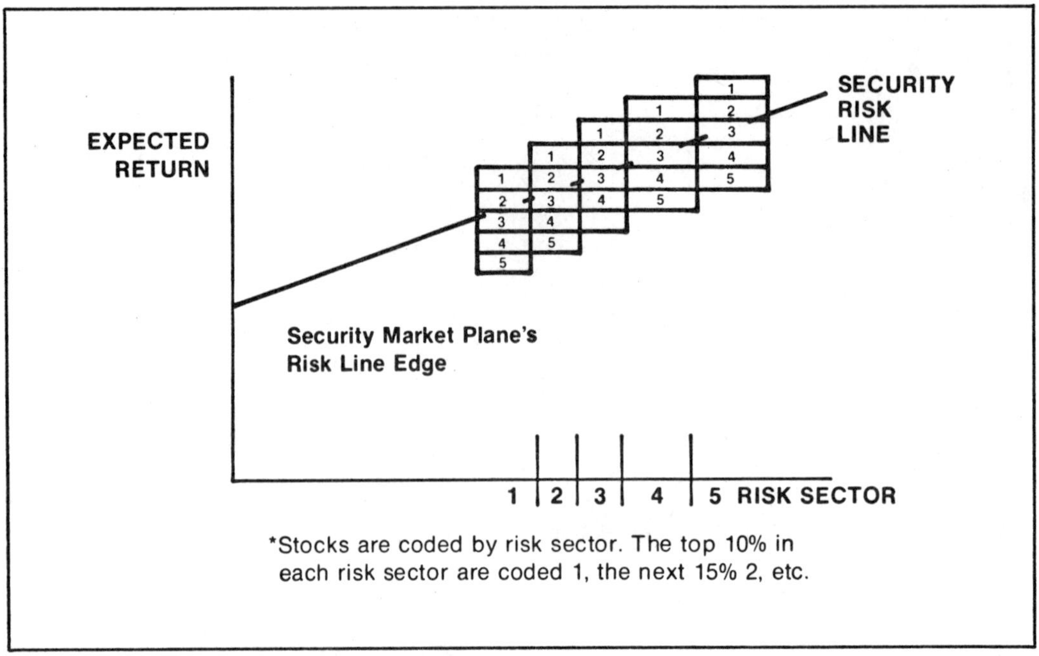

EXHIBIT 9.L / Wells Fargo Stock Coding Process*

given the existing yield, beta risk assignment, and ER, which emanates from the dividend cash flow forecasts and current price. Whether or not a given security is *actually* over-, under-, or fairly priced, only time will tell.

From the process, a "security selection" mechanism is derived. Exhibit 9.L shows how it operates.

Looking at the beta risk-to-expected return side of the earlier cube, we find that the risk dimension of the Market Plane, called the Security Risk Line, always has a positive slope. That is, expectationally, equities are priced to return a higher ER as beta risk increases. The slope of the Security Risk Line varies in inclination through time as investors price and reprice beta risk in accordance with their collective changing inclination for bearing risk. Also, the Line's position changes: when stocks decline and cash flow forecasts haven't changed, then ERs rise, and the entire Market Plane moves to a higher position.

Every stock, with its given ER and beta, falls at, under, or over the Security Risk Line. Stocks which plot on (or near) it are considered fairly valued. Other stocks plot above or below it to varying degrees and are, respectively, under- and overvalued. Wells Fargo takes the Security Risk Line and arbitrarily divides it into five risk sectors: 1–5, with 1 being "low risk." Stocks such as AT&T, Exxon, etc., reside in risk sector 1, while risk sector 5 contains securities of companies which are, generally speaking, illiquid, of smaller capitalization, and which tend to be "early" on their expected growth-in-earnings curves.

Within each risk sector, there are underpriced, overpriced, and fairly priced stocks. Wells Fargo takes the 10% most-above the Market Plane and codes them 1, "most attractive" relative to other stocks in the same risk sector. The stock selection structure is, therefore, as follows.

Within Risk Sector	Code	
Top 10% :	1	
Next 15% :	2	
Next 30% :	3	(fairly valued: at or near the Security Market Plane)
Next 25% :	4	
Bottom 20% :	5	

Thus, Exxon might be coded 2 in risk sector 1, while Envirotech might be a 3 in sector 5, even though the latter may offer a *higher* ER than the former! This is an example of what is referred to as *risk-adjusted* expected return.

Exhibit 9.M shows how Wells Fargo's stock selection process has behaved. It indicates a significantly powerful ability to discriminate, before the fact, among undervalued, overvalued, and fairly valued securities.

Lest we forget, we are attempting here to help the board understand why the portfolio manager wants the active equity portfolio to currently carry a particular beta within the permitted 1.10–1.40 beta range. As it happens, on June 6, 1979, the slope of the Security Risk Line is quite modest (Exhibit 9.N). The stock market is offering on June 6, 1979, about as much nominal expected return as it did at the market bottom in the fourth quarter of 1974, but high risk stocks are offering less return, and lower risk stocks are offering more than was then the case. Since the slope of the Security

Wells Universe* Percent of Stock Rated	Price Appreciation 1975	1976	1977	1978	1/1/79 6/26/79	Total Period
10 most attractive	+104%	+56%	+4%	+17%	+19%	+359%
15 next most attractive	+65	+29	+1	+8	+13	+161
30 next most attractive	+54	+23	−7	+3	+10	+101
25 next most attractive	+40	+13	−11	+5	+8	+59
20 least attractive	+29	+6	−15	+3	+7	+29
All stocks (S&P 500)**	+46	+28	−6	+3	+11	+100

*Equal-dollar-weighted
**Returns do not include transactions costs or dividend income

EXHIBIT 9.M / Performance of Stock Valuation Model

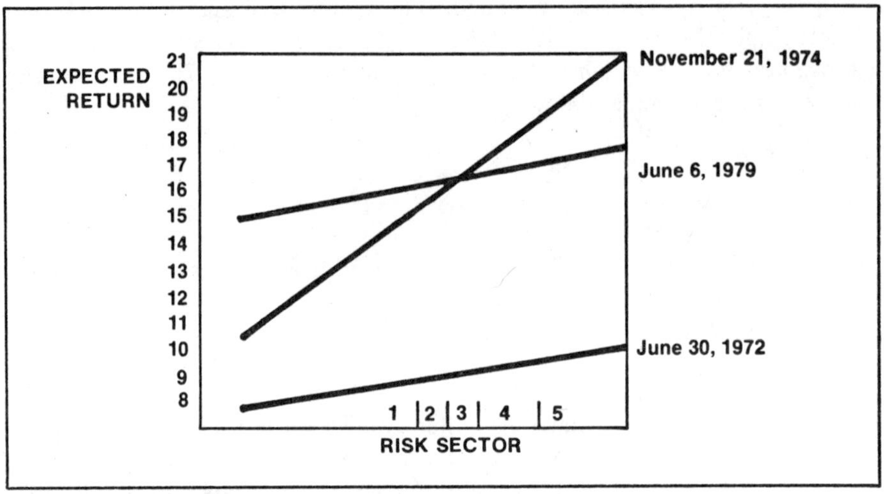

EXHIBIT 9.N / Security Risk Lines (At Market Yield)

Risk Line is so slight (high risk stocks are offering a very small ER premium vis-à-vis low risk stocks; observe that this is in great contrast to the ER-to-risk trade-off offered in late 1974!), it makes sense to avoid a much heavier-than-market weighting in high risk stocks, at least for the time being. This means a stock portfolio biased towards the lower end of the permitted 1.10–1.40 beta range should be selected on a strategic basis. Thus, at least until there's a steeper slope to the Risk Line, the portfolio manager should manage the active equity exposure to reflect a low beta (close to 1.10 minimum guideline). To provide the positive, risk adjusted alpha, the manager must concentrate on 1s and 2s to the extent that total sigma risk will be near but not above a strategically chosen level (up to 12 percentage points in this case).

Let's assume that the current, active equity portfolio has the following essential characteristics:

Weighted stock portfolio beta	1.18
Portfolio sigma	8.92%
Total risk (square root of beta^2 times sigma of market^2 plus portfolio sigma^2	21.32%
Prospective alpha	+2.62%
Prospective yield	4.93%

The portfolio contains mostly 1s and 2s, along with some securities coded 3 and a sprinkling of 4s. Also, the portfolio's below-market yield should be considered. Yield is very important. On a prospective basis, the slope of the Market Plane's yield edge, in a pre-tax context, is always positive, just as the Risk Line always has a positive slope. This means that, at a given level of beta risk, higher yielding stocks always offer more ER than lower yielding stocks. On average, tax-exempt investors should bias their equity portfolios towards above-market yield rather than towards below-market yield.

The portfolio is then submitted to an optimization program which links the portfolio's characteristics and detailed holding descriptions, economic, industry, and other weights, to the Market Plane analysis and coding process. In addition, the group stipulates that a trading program be provided that will reduce the beta from 1.18 to 1.10, and raise the prospective alpha to the maximum permitted by the 12% point portfolio sigma constraint.

The result is as desired. The "new" portfolio, with stock holdings selected from the firm's data base, has a beta of 1.10. Its sigma is 11.82%. Its prospective alpha is now 4.02% and its yield has risen to 6.4%. The problem is that to move the existing portfolio to the new structure requires 62% sales turnover. How much "improvement" can be achieved with 10%, 20%, and 30% sales turnover constraints? In addition, the transaction cost assumption is to be raised from 1% to 1.5% of capital turned over.

The optimizer is put to work on these inputs and produces the following improvement on the current +2.62% alpha.

Turnover	Alpha Improvement
10%	0.39%
20%	0.86
30%	1.32

The portfolio manager recommends the second option since portfolio alpha will be raised to slightly above the 3.0% requirement, and turnover is likely to be acceptable to the board. Yield will be raised to 6.11%

Note that if active equity is being expanded or contracted as a percent of overall portfolio value, the optimization procedures operate unhindered. In fact, the optimization of asset allocation, bond, stock, and other asset classes is totally accommodated by integrated, simultaneous programs.

The reader has probably noted that much space has been devoted to the asset mix policy and strategic asset allocation issues, and much less to subsidiary matters (albeit security valuation is a critical input to the paramount mix policy and strategy decisions). To repeat an earlier assertion, the point is that well over 90% of the relative investment success of a pension system will, in the longer term, emanate from how well the asset mix policy and strategy matters are handled through time. They are dynamic issues, in addition to being by far the most important elements of the overall portfolio management equation. Indeed, they bulk so large that whether or not active management of asset class components "succeeds" or "fails" is of relatively nominal consequence.

Most pension plan sponsors and investment managers are imbued with too large a quotient of what the author calls the Horatio Alger Syndrome. They want to "win." This is natural. In fact, the urge to win is a very productive attitude. What's important, however, is to understand as precisely as possible just what constitutes "winning" in each client case, and identifying winning in explicit, measurable terms. Once this is accomplished, and then viewed and addressed as a dynamic issue through time, it is important to have a manager (or managers) who knows how to integrate return goals and reasonable constraints with the current and prospective capital market risk-to-expected return environment. Only then are a retirement system's needs most likely to be met.

References

General A

Organizational Resources A.1

American Institute of Certified Public Accountants, 1211 Avenue of the Americas, New York, N.Y. 10036, *Accounting and Auditing Guides*

Corporate Data Exchange, 198 Broadway, Room 706, New York, N.Y. 10038, *Social Performance Reports*

Council on Economic Priorities, 84 Fifth Ave., New York, N.Y. 10011, *Social Performance Reports*

William E. Donoghue, Cash Management Institute, P.O. Box 540, Holliston, Mass. 01746, *Technical Assistance*

General Accounting Office, 441 G Street, N.W., Washington, D.C., *Audits of Federal Operations*

Government Finance Research Center, Municipal Finance Officers Association, 1750 K Street, N.W., Suite 650, Washington, D.C. 20006, *Technical Assistance*

Grants Management Advisory Service, 2120 L Street, N.W., Suite 210, Washington, D.C. 20037, *Grant Management Manuals*

Interfaith Center On Corporate Responsibility, 475 Riverside Drive, New York, N.Y. 10027, *Social Performance Reports*

International City Management Association, 1101 Connecticut Avenue, N.W., Washington, D.C. 20036, *Technical Assistance*

International Foundation of Employee Benefit Plans, P.O. Box 69, Brookfield, Wis. 53005, *Technical Assistance*

Municipal Finance Officers Association, 180 North Michigan Ave., Chicago, Ill. 60601, *Technical Assistance*

National League of Cities, 1620 I Street, N.W., Washington, D.C. 20006, *Technical Assistance*

President's Commission on Pension Policy, 736 Jackson Place, N.W., Washington, D.C. 20006, *Policy Analysis*

Rousmaniere Management Associates, Inc., 1330 Beacon Street, Brookline, Mass. 02149, *Technical Assistance*

Marshall D. Sokol Associates, 445 Hamilton Avenue, White Plains, N.Y. 10601, *Technical Assistance*

U.S. Department of Housing and Urban Development, Office of Policy Development and Research, 451 7th Street, S.W., Washington, D.C. 20410, *Technical Assistance*

Books A.2

Aronson, Richard J., and Schwartz, Eli, eds. *Management Policies in Local Government Finance*. Washington, D.C.: International City Management Association, 1975.

Bogen, Jules I., ed. *Financial Handbook*. New York: Ronald Press, 1968.

Friedland, Seymour. *Principles of Financial Management: Corporate Finance Investment and Macro Finance*. Cambridge, Mass.: Winthrop Publishers, Inc., 1978

Max, Lennox L., and Hilhouse, Albert M. *Concepts and Practices in Local Government Finance*. Chicago: Municipal Finance Officers Association, 1975

Rousmaniere Management Associates, Inc. *Automation of Governmental and Nonprofit Treasury Operations: The State of the Art*. Brookline, Mass., 1981.

Smith, Paul F. *Economics of Financial Institutions and Markets*. Homewood, Illinois: Richard D. Irwin, Inc., 1971.

Van Horne, James C. *Fundamentals of Financial Management*. Englewood Cliffs, N.J.: Prentice-Hall, Inc., 1977.

Weston, Fred, J., and Goudzwaard, Maurice B., eds. *The Treasurer's Handbook*. Homewood, Illinois: Dow Jones-Irwin, 1976.

A.3 Periodicals

Federal Reserve Bank of New York: Quarterly Review. New York, N.Y.: Federal Reserve Bank of New York. Published quarterly.

Governmental Finance. Chicago: Municipal Finance Officers Association. Published quarterly.

Hospital Financial Management. Chicago: Hospital Financial Management Associates. Published monthly.

Pensions and Investment Age. Chicago: Crain Communications, Inc. Published bimonthly.

The U.S. Financial Data. St. Louis: St. Louis Federal Reserve Bank. Published weekly.

Wall Street Journal New York: Dow-Jones, Inc. Published weekdays.

B Cash Management

B.1 General & Miscellaneous

Advisory Commission on Intergovernmental Relations. *Understanding State and Local Cash Management*. Washington, D.C., 1977.

American Management Associations Extension Institute. *Managing Corporate Cash*. New York, 1980.

———. *Planning Cash Flow*. New York, 1980.

Bank of America. *Beating the Cash Crisis: Small Business Reporter*. San Francisco, 1975.

Cerrome, R.A. "Cash Flow Checklist." *Hospital Financial Management* 33 (1979): 44-6.

Cingolain, Melodie. *Cash Flow/Cash Management: Small Business Reporter*. San Francisco: Bank of America, 1977.

DePalma, John: Spector, Quentin; and Benway, Bruce. *Cash Management for Small Communities*. Orono, Maine: University of Maine, Bureau of Public Administration, 1977.

DeSalvo, Alfred. "Cash Management Converts Dollars into Working Assets." *Harvard Business Review* 50 (1972): 92-101.

Federal Deposit Insurance Corporation. *Compilation of State Pledging Requirements for the Security of Public Deposits*. Washington, D.C., 1975.

Fisher, David I. *Cash Management*. New York: The Conference Board, 1973.

laag, Leonard H. *Cash Management and Short-Term Investments for Colleges and Universities*. Washington, D.C.: National Association of College and University Business Officers, 1977

Handel, B. "Cash Management: Keeping the Welfare Fund Solvent." *Pension World* 15 (1979): 46-47.

Haskin & Sells. *Implementing Effective Cash Management in Local Government: A Practical Guide*. Chicago: Municipal Finance Officers Association, 1977.

Hill, Roger W., Jr. *Cash Management Techniques*. New York: American Management Association, 1970.

Jump, Bernard, Jr. *Some Thoughts About Teaching State & Local Government Cash and Debt Management*. Boston: Boston University School of Management, 1979.

Lerner, Eugene M. "Stimulating a Cash Budget." *California Management Review* 11 (1968): 79-86.

Lewellen, Wilber G., and Johnson, Robert W. "Better Way to Monitor Accounts Receivable." *Harvard Business Review* 50 (1972): 101-110.

Markstein, David L. "How to Make Short-Term Cash Work at Full-Term Rates." *Modern Business Practices,* January, 1970.

Municipal Finance Officers Association. "Cash Management for Local Government." *Governmental Finance* 4 (1975): 5-10.

National Association of Accountants. *Cash Flow Analysis for Managerial Control*. New York, 1961.

Nauss, R. M., and Markland, R. E. "Solving Lock Box Location Problems." *Financial Management* 8 (1979): 21-31.

The Northern Trust Bank. *Lockbox Services*. Chicago, 1978.

Patitucci, Frank M., and Lichenstein, Michael H. *Improving Cash Management in Local Government: A Comprehensive Approach*. Chicago: Municipal Finance Officers Association, 1977.

Peterson, John E.; Spain, Catherine Lavigne; and Laffey, Matherose, eds. *State and Local Government Finance and Financial Management*. Washington, D.C.: Municipal Finance Officers Assocation, 1978.

Peterson, John E.; Stalling, C.; and Spain, Catherine Lavigne. "Cash Management." In *State Roles in Local Government: A Comparative Analysis*. Washington, D.C.: Municipal Finance Officers Assocation, 1979.

Pflomm, Norman E. *Managing Company Cash*. New York: National Industrial Conference Board, 1961.

Pogue, Gerald A.; Faucett, Russell B.; and Bussard, Ralph N. "Cash Management: A System Approach." *Industrial Management Review* 11 (1970): 15-27.

Rosenborg, Philip, et al. *A Guidebook to Improved Financial Management for Small Cities and Other Governmental Units*. Chicago: Municipal Finance Officers Association, 1978.

Searby, Frederick Wright. "Use Your Hidden Cash Resources." *Harvard Business Review* 46 (1968): 71-81.

U.S. Department of Transportation. *Transit Fare Prepayment*. Washington, D.C., 1976.

Journals

Cash. White Plains, New York: Marshall D. Sokol Assoc. Published monthly.

Cashflow. Glenview, Ill.: Coordinated Capital Resources. Published monthly.

The Cash Manager. Holliston, Mass.: Cash Management Institute. Published monthly.

B.2 Theoretical Studies

Baumol, W. J. "The Transactions Demand for Cash: An Inventory Theoretic Approach." *Quarterly Journal of Economics* 66 (1952): 545-56.

Buck, Randolf F., et al. *Design and Analysis of an Automatic Credit Card Fare Collection System*. Stanford, Calif.: Stanford University, August, 1974.

Maier, S.F., and Vanderweide, J.H. "Unified Location Model for Cash Disbursements and Lock-Box Collections." *Journal of Bank Research* 7 (1976): 166-72.

B.3 Electronic Fund Transfer Systems

American Bankers Association. *Guidelines for the Direct Deposit of Social Security Payments*. Washington, D.C., 1975.

Benton, J.B. "Electronic Funds Transfer: Pitfalls and Payoffs." *Harvard Business Review* 55 (1977): 16-17.

Butel, J. "Consumer Protection and Electronic Fund Transfer." *Computers and People* 27 (1978): 10-11.

"Impact of Corporate EFT." *EDP Analyzer* 15 (1977): 1-13.

U.S. Department of the Treasury. *Electronic Accounting and Cash Management*. Washington, D.C.: Department of the Treasury, 1977.

White, George C. *Cities in The Eighties*. New York: Council on Municipal Performance, 1980.

C Federal Grant Regulations

C.1 Government Regulations

U.S. Department of Treasury. *Notification to States of Grant-in-Aid Information*. Washington, D.C.: Treasury Circular No. 1082.

U.S. Department of Treasury. *Regulation Governing the Withdrawal of Cash from Treasury for Advance Payments Under Federal Grant and Other Programs*. Washington, D.C.: Treasury Circular No. 1075.

U.S. Department of the Treasury. *Treasury Financial Communications System Regulations*. Washington, D.C.: Treasury Circular No. 1083.

U.S. General Accounting Office. *Guidelines for Financial and Compliance Audits of Federally Assisted Programs*. Washington, D.C.

U.S. Office of Management and Budget. *Administration of Office and University Research Grants*. Washington, D.C.: FMC 73-7.

U.S. Office of Management and Budget. *Audit of Federal Operations and Programs*. Washington, D.C.: OMB Circular No. A-73.

U.S. Office of Management and Budget. *Cash Principles Applicable to Grants and Contracts with State and Local Governments*. Washington, D.C.: FMC 74-4.

U.S. Office of Management and Budget. *Cooperation with State and Local Governments to Coordinate and Improve Information Systems*. Washington, DC.: OMB Circular No. A-90.

U.S. Office of Management and Budget. *Cost Principles for Educational Institutions*. Washington, D.C.: OMB Circular No. A-21.

U.S. Office of Management and Budget. *Cost Sharing on Federal Research*. Washington, D.C.: FMC 73-3.

U.S. Office of Management and Budget. *Department of Commerce Directives for the Conduct of Federal Statistical Activities*. Washington, D.C.: Circular No. A-46

U.S. Office of Management and Budget. *Evaluation Review and Coordination of Federal and Federally Assisted Programs and Projects*. Washington, D.C.: OMB Circular No. A-95.

U.S. Office of Management and Budget. *Grants and Agreements with Institutions of Higher Education, Hospitals and Other Nonprofit Organizations*. Washington, D.C.: OMB Circular No. A-110.

U.S. Office of Management and Budget. *Guidelines for Agency Implementation of the Uniform Relocation Assistance and Real Property Acquisition Policies of 1970: Public Law 91-646*. Washington, D.C.: FMC 74-8.

U.S. Office of Management and Budget. *Improving Government Regulations*. Washington, D.C.: Executive Order 12044.

U.S. Office of Management and Budget. *Jointly Funded Assistance to State and Local Governments and Nonprofit Organizations Policies and Procedures*. Washington, D.C.: OMB Circular No. A-111.

U.S. Office of Management and Budget. *Management of Federal Reporting Requirements*. Washington, D.C.: OMB Circular No. A-40.

U.S. Office of Management and Budget. *Uniform Administrative Requirements for Grant-in-Aid to State and Local Governments: Revised*. Washington, D.C.: OMB Circular No. A-102.

Other Government Documents C.2

U.S. Comptroller General of the United States. *Opportunities for Savings in Interest Cost Through Improved Letter-of-Credit Methods in Federal Grant Programs*. Washington, D.C.: Department of the Treasury, 1975.

U.S. Department of the Treasury. *Problems of State and Local Governments with Grant-in-Aid Payments*. Washington, D.C.: Transmittal Letter No. 223.

U.S. General Accounting Office. *Identification of Food Stamp Issues*. Washington, D.C., 1976.

U.S. Office of Management and Budget. *Managing Federal Assistance in the 1980's*. 9 vols. Washington, D.C.: Intergovernmental Affairs Division of Office of Management & Budget, 1979.

U.S. Office of Management and Budget. *Strengthening Federal Cash Management*. Washington, D.C.: President's Reorganization Project, March, 1979.

Non-Government Documents C.3

Cooley, John W. "Is the Federal Cash Management Movement Colliding with Electronic Fund Transfer Initiatives?" *The Government's Accountant Journal* 28 (1979-80): 49-52.

Federal Grants Management Handbook. Washington, D.C.: Grants Management Advisory Service.

Tierney, Cornelius E., and Hoffman, Robert D. *Federal Financial Management: Accounting and Auditing Practices*. New York: American Institute of Certified Public Accountants, 1976.

D Banking Relations

D.1 General and Miscellaneous Periodicals

American Banker. Washington, D.C.: American Bankers Association. Published weekly.

Bank Administration Publications. Park Ridge, Illinois: Bank Administration Institute. Published annually.

Journal of Bank Research. Park Ridge, Illinois: Bank Administration Institute. Published quarterly.

The Magazine of Bank Administration. Park Ridge, Illinois: Bank Administration Institute. Published monthly.

D.2 The Banking System

Federal Reserve Bank of Chicago. *Modern Money Mechanisms: A Workbook on Deposits, Currency, and Bank Reserves*. Chicago, 1975.

Federal Reserve System Steering Committee. "Evolution of the Payments Mechanism." *Federal Reserve Bulletin* 58 (1972): 1009-13.

Hamilton, Earl J. "An Update on the Automated Clearing House." *Federal Reserve Bulletin* 65 (1979): 479-80.

Hoffland, David L. "A Model Bank Investment Policy." *Financial Analysts Journal* Vol. 34, No. 3 (1978): 64-77.

Juncker, George R. "A New Supervisory System for Rating Banks." Federal Reserve Bank of New York: *Quarterly Review* Vol. 3, No. 2 (1978): 47-50.

Levin, W. B. "Check Collection System: Present and Future Status." *Journal of Bank Research* (1978)' 78-81.

Stafeil, Walter. "The Improved Performance of the Check Collection System." *The Magazine of Bank Administration* Vol. 52. No 3 (1976): 40-47.

Stafeil, Walter, and Hess, Catherine. "Check Collection System Performance for 1976." *The Magazine of Bank Administration* Vol. 53, No. 4 (1977): 38-42.

D.3 Banking Services and Costs

American Bankers Association. *A Cost Analysis Procedure for Smaller Banks*. Washington, D.C., 1969.

———. *A Guide for Audit and Control in the Smaller Bank*. Washington, D.C. 1972.

Anderson, Paul S. "Costs and Profitability of Bank Functions." *New England Economic Review* 3 (1979): 43-62.

Buchanan, D. D. "Critical Look at Proposals for Pricing Federal Services." *ABA Banking Journal*, May, 1979.

Functional Cost Analysis. Washington, D.C.: Federal Reserve System. Published annually.

Hathaway, D. D. "Managing Balances in Lock Box Accounts." *Journal of Bank Research* 8 (1977): 59-62.

Knight, Robert E. "Bank Customer Profitability: An Analysis of Alternative Approaches." *The Magazine of Bank Administration* Vol. 52, No. 5 (1977): 12-24.

Looper, C. Eugene. "Effective Employment of a Bank's Human Resources." *The Magazine of Bank Administration* Vol. 53, No. 8 (1977): 27-30.

Lordan, James F. "The Role of the Bank." In *A Profile of Corporate Cash Management*. Park Ridge, Illinois: Bank Administration Institute, 1972.

———. "The Money Mobilization Bank: Criteria for Providing Services." In *A Profile of Corporate Cash Management*. Park Ridge, Illinois: Bank Administration Institute, 1972.

———. *The Banking Side of Corporate Cash Management*. Boston: Financial Publishing Co., 1973.

———. "Bank Compensation." In *A Profile of Corporate Cash Management*. Park Ridge, Illinois: Bank Administration Institute, 1972.

"The Unbundling of Full-Service Banking." *Business Week,* October 27, 1973.

Investing E

General and Miscellaneous E.1

American Management Associations Extension Institute. *Return on Investment*. New York, 1979.

Dougall, Herbert E., and Gaumnitz, Jack E. *Capital Markets and Institutions*. Englewood Cliffs, N.J.: Prentice-Hall, Inc., 1975.

Farrell, Maurice L. *The Dow Jones Investor's Handbook, 1978*. Princeton: Dow Jones Books, 1978.

Goldsmith, Raymond W. *Capital Market Analysis and the Financial Accounts of the Nation*. Morristown, N.J.: General Learning Press, 1972.

———. *The Flow of Capital Funds in the Postwar Economy*. New York: National Bureau of Economic Research, 1965.

Hardy, C. Colburn. *Dun & Bradstreet's Guide to Your Investments*. New York: Thomas Y. Crowall Press, 1979.

Henning, Charles N.; Pigott, William; and Scott, Robert Harvey. *Financial Markets and the Economy*. Englewood Cliffs, N.J.: Prentice-Hall, Inc., 1975.

Homer, Sidney and Liebowitz. *Inside the Yield Book*. Englewood Cliffs, N.J.: Prentice-Hall, Inc., 1972.

Ibbotson, R. G., and Sinquefield, R. A. *Stocks, Bonds, Bills, and Inflation: Historical Review (1926-1978)*. Charlottesville, Virginia: The Financial Analysts Research Foundation, 1979.

Levine, Somner N., et al. *Financial Analyst Handbook*. Homewood, Illinois: Dow Jones-Irwin, Inc., 1975.

Little, Jeffrey B., and Rhodes, Lucien. *Understanding Wall Street*. Cockeysville, Md.: Liberty Publishing Co., 1978.

Mundheim, R., and Werner, W. *Mutual Funds*. New York: Practicing Law Institute, 1970.

National Municipal League. *Model Investment of State Fund Law*. New York, 1972.

Porter, Sylvia. *Sylvia Porter's Money Book*. New York: Avon Books, 1976.

Robinson, Roland I. *Financial Markets*. New York: McGraw-Hill, 1980.

Sharpe, William F. *Investments*. Englewood Cliffs, N.J.: Prentice-Hall, Inc., 1978.

Source Securities Corporation. *Brokerage Commissions and Services for Experienced Investors*. New York, 1978.

Stigum, Marcia. *The Money Market: Myth, Reality, and Practice*. Homewood, Illinois: Dow Jones-Irwin, Inc., 1978.

Tobias, Andrew. *The Only Investment Guide You'll Ever Need*. New York: Harcourt Brace Jovanovich, Inc., 1978.

Van Horne, James C. *Financial Market Rates and Flows*. Englewood Cliffs, N.J.: Prentice-Hall, Inc., 1978.

Woodworth, G. Walter. *The Money Market and Monetary Management*. New York: Harper & Row, 1972.

Journals

Barron's New York: Dow Jones & Co. Published weekly.

Bond Market Roundup. New York: Salomon Brothers. Published weekly.

Credit and Capital Markets. New York: Bankers Trust Company. Published annually.

Institutional Investor. New York: Institutional Investor, Inc. Published monthly.

The Money Manager. New York: The Bond Buyer. Published weekly.

E.2 Short-Term Investing

Advisory Commission on Intergovernmental Relations. "State Sponsored Local Government Investment Pools." *Information Bulletin,* October, 1978.

Arak, M., and McCurdy, C. J. "Interest Rate Futures." Federal Reserve Bank of New York: *Quarterly Review,* 4 (1979-80): 33-46.

Banks, Lois. "The Market for Agency Securities." Federal Reserve Bank of New York: *Quarterly Review* Vol. 3, No. 1 (1978): 7-21.

Berkowitz, William. "Money-Market Instruments: What They Are and How to Choose One." *Practical Accountant,* September, 1978.

Byington, Preston, W. *U.S. Treasury Bills: A Working Handbook*. Culver City, Calif.: PENCO Publishing Co., 1978.

Carrol, McEntee & McGinley, Inc. *Handbook of U.S. Treasury and Federal Agency Securities, Including Other Short-Term Money Market Instruments*. New York: The Street Publishing Co., 1977.

Chicago Mercantile Exchange. *Opportunities in Interest Rates: Treasury Bill Futures*. Chicago: 1977.

Cook, Timothy Q., ed. *Instruments of the Money Market*. Richmond, Virginia: Federal Reserve Bank of Richmond, 1977.

Federal Reserve Bank of Cleveland, Ohio. *Money Market Instruments*. Cleveland, Ohio, 1970.

Federal Reserve Bank of New York. *Guide to the Securities of Federal Agencies, Government-Sponsored Corporations and International Institutions*. New York, 1980.

Haag, Leonard H. *Cash Management Short-Term Investments for Colleges and Universities*. Washington, D.C.: National Association of College and University Business Officers, 1977.

Kirk, James E., and Kresslein, John C. *Options for Developing a Local Government Investing Pool for South Carolina*. Columbia, South Carolina: Bureau of Governmental Research, 1980.

McCurdy, Christopher J. "The Dealer Market for United States Government Securities." Federal Reserve Bank of New York: *Quarterly Review* Vol. 2, No. 4 (1977-78): 35-47.

Melton, William C. "The Market for Large Negotiable CDs." Federal Reserve Bank of New York: *Quarterly Review* Vol. 2, No. 4: 22-34.

Journals

Handbook of Securities of the United States Government and Federal Agencies and Related Money Market Instruments. New York: The First Boston Corporation. Published biannually.

The U.S. Financial Data. St. Louis: St. Louis Federal Reserve Bank. Published weekly.

Pension & Endowment Fund Investing — E.3

A. G. Becker Securities Incorporated. *Measurement Techniques for Evaluating the Performance of Retired and Other Tax-Free Funds*. Chicago, Illinois, 1978.

Advisory Committee on Endowment Management to the Ford Foundation. *Managing Educational Endowments*. New York: Ford Foundation, 1969.

Ahlers, David M. *A New Look at Portfolio Management*. Greenwich, Conn.: JAI Press, 1977.

"Bank Pooled Pension Funds (6th Annual Survey)." *Pension World* 13 (1977): 15-29.

Banks, Lois. "The Market for Agency Securities." Federal Reserve Bank of New York: *Quarterly Review* Vol. 3, No. 1 (1978): 7-21.

Black, Fischer. "The Investment Policy Spectrum: Individuals, Endowment Funds, and Pension Funds." In *Modern Development in Investment Management*, edited by James Lorie and Richard Brealey. Hinsdale, Illinois: Dryden Press, 1978.

Carey, W., and Bright, C. *The Law and The Lore of Endowment Funds*. New York: Ford Foundation, 1969.

Carroll, John B. "Why Not Do it Yourself: Money Manager Selection Checklist," *Pension World* Vol 12, No. 12 (1976): 12-19.

The Conference Board. *Financial Management of Company Pension Plans*. New York, 1973.

Crowell, Richard A. *A Stock Market Strategy*. New York: McGraw-Hill, 1977.

Darst, David M. *The Complete Bond Book*. New York: McGraw-Hill, 1975.

Davey, Patrick J. *Financial Management of Company Pension Plans*. New York: The Conference Board, Inc., 1973.

Federal Reserve Bank of New York. *Guide to the Securities of Federal Agencies, Government-Sponsored Corporations and International Institutions*. New York, 1980.

The Financial Analysts Research Foundation. *Seminar Papers on Portfolio Management Policies, Performance, Measurement, and Evaluation*. 3 vols. Charlottesville, Virginia, 1977.

Graham, Benjamin; Dodd, L. David; and Cottle, Sidney. *Security Analysis: Principles and Techniques*. New York: McGraw-Hill, 1962.

Greenwich Research Associates. *Public Pension Funds: Trustee Report, 1977*. Greenwich, Connecticut, 1977.

Haft, Richard A. *Investing in Securities*. Englewood Cliffs, N.J.: Prentice-Hall, Inc., 1975.

International Foundation of Employee Benefit Plans. *Reading List*. Brookfield, Wisconsin, 1979.

Kohlmer, Louis M. "State and Local Pension Funds Asset Management." In *Abuse on Wall Street: Conflicts of Interest in the Securities Market*, Twentieth Century Fund Report. Westport, Conn.: Quorum Books, 1980.

Lehman Brothers, Kuhn Loeb. *The Lehman Brothers, Kuhn Loeb Bond index*. New York, October, 1978.

Melton, William C. "Corporate Equities and the National Market System." Federal Reserve Bank of New York: *Quarterly Review* Vol. 3, No. 4 (1978-79): 13-25.

National Association of College and University Business Officers. *Bond Valuation for Colleges & Universities*. Washington, D.C., 1977.

National Association of College and University Business Offices. *Reporting on Investments of Endowment Funds*. Washington, D.C., 1975.

Source Securities Corporation. *Directory of SEC Registered Investment Advisers*. New York, 1978.

Train, Richard. *How to Select an Investment Advisor*. New York: Constellation Management, Inc., 1978.

U.S. Comptroller General of the United States. *Investment Decisionmaking in Selected Public Sector Retirement Plans*. Washington, D.C.: U.S. Government Printing Office, May, 1978.

Voorheis, F. L. "How Well Do Banks Manage Pooled Pension Portfolios?" *Financial Analysts Journal* 32 (1976): 35-40.

Wiley, William N. *Pooled Pension Investments: An Option for City Pension Systems*. Frankfort, Ky.: Legislative Research Commission, 1979.

Journals

Fitch Corporate Bond Review. New York: Fitch Investors Service. Published monthly.

Institutional Investor. New York: Institutional Investor Systems, Inc. Published monthly.

International Foundation of Employee Benefit Plans. *Investments Institute Proceedings*. Brookfield, Wisconsin. Published annually.

Moody's Bank & Financial Manual. New York: Moody's Investors Service. Published annually with weekly supplements.

Moody's Bond Survey. New York: Moody's Investors Service, Inc. Published weekly.

Moody's Corporate Index. New York: Moody's Investors Service. Published annually.

Pension World. New York: Communications Channels, Inc. Published monthly.

Standard and Poor's: Corporation Records. New York: Standard and Poor's Corporation. Published quarterly and daily.

Standard and Poor's: Fixed Income Investors. New York: Standard and Poor's Corporation. Published weekly.

Standard and Poor's: Stock Reports. New York: Standard and Poor's Corporation. Published quarterly.

E.4 Professional Standards of Conduct

Bines, Harvey E. *The Law of Investment Management*. Boston: Warren, Gorham & Lamont, Inc., 1978.

Earp, M. H., and Gillis, John G., eds. *Professional Standards of Practice*. Charlottesville, Virginia: The Financial Analysts Research Foundation, 1978.

Loring, A. A. *Trustee's Handbook: Farr Revision*. Boston: Little Brown & Co., 1962.

E.5 Socially Oriented Investing

Abt, Clark C. *The Social Audit for Management*. New York: AMACOM, 1977.

Alexis, M. "Black Banks: An Overview." *Black Enterprise* 7 (1977): 92-95.

Bauer, Raymond A., and Fenn, Dan H. *Social Science Frontiers: The Corporate Social Audit*. New York: Russell Sage Foundation, 1972.

Corporate Data Exchange, Inc. *Pension Investments: A Social Audit*. New York, 1979.

Faux, Jeff, and Lightfoot, Robert. *Community and Capital*. Washington, D.C.: Exploration Project for Economic Alternatives, 1976.

Rifkin, Jeremy, and Barber, Randy. *The North Shall Rise Again: Pensions, Politics, and Power in the 1980s*. Boston: Beacon Press, 1978.

Rousmaniere Management Associates, Inc. *The Audit of Socially-Oriented Investing Programs*. Brookline, Mass., 1980.

———. *Guide to the Design of an Economic Development Bank*. Brookline, Mass., 1980.

Simon, John G., et al. *The Ethical Investor: Universities and Corporate Responsibility*. Hartford: Yale University Press, 1972.

Simonsen, D. G. "Funds Management by State Treasurers: Direct vs. Socio-economic Returns." *Financial Management* 6 (1977): 51-3.

Smart, Donald A. *Investment Targeting: A Wisconsin Case Study*. Madison, Wisconsin: Center for Public Policy, 1979.

Webb, Lee, and Schneke, William, eds. *Public Employee Pension Funds: New Strategies for Investment*. Washington, D.C.: Conference on Alternative State and Local Public Policies, 1979.

Wisconsin Center for Public Policy. *Changing Perspectives for Pension Plans: Is the Prudent Investor Acting in the Public Interest?* Madison, Wisconsin, 1979.

Journals

Conference on Alternative State and Local Public Policies. *Public Policy Reader*. Washington, D.C.: Institute for Policy Studies. Published annually.

Theoretical & Other Research Oriented Studies E.6

Fama, E. F. "Efficient Capital Markets: A Review of Theory and Empirical Work." In *Modern Developments in Investment Management*, edited by James Lorie and Richard Brealey. Hinsdale, Illinois: Dryden Press, 1978. Also in *The Journal of Finance*, May, 1980.

Fisher, L., and Lorie, J. H. "Rates of Return on Investments in Common Stocks: The Year-by-Year Record, 1926-1965." In *Modern Developments in Investment Management*, edited by James Lorie and Richard Brealey. Hinsdale, Illinois: Dryden Press, 1978. Also in *Journal of Business*, July, 1968.

———. "Some Studies of Variability of Returns on Investments in Common Stocks." In *Modern Developments in Investment Management*, edited by James Lorie and Richard Brealey. Hinsdale, Illinois. Dryden Press, 1978. Also in *Journal of Business*, April, 1970.

Hagin, Robert. *The Dow Jones-Irwin Guide to Modern Portfolio Theory*. Homewood, Illinois: Dow Jones-Irwin, Inc. 1979.

Hendershott, Patric H. and Van Horne, James C. "Expected Inflation Implied by Capital Market Rates." *Journal of Finance* 28 (1973): 301-14.

Linter, John. "Security Prices, Risk and Maximal Gains for Diversification." *Journal of Finance* 20 (1965)L 587-615.

Lintner, J., and Glauber, R. "Higgledy Piggledy Growth in America." In *Modern Developments in Investment Management*, edited by James Lorie and Richard Brealey. Hinsdale, Illinois: Dryden Press, 1978.

Lorie, James, and Brealey, Richard. *Modern Developments in Investment Management*. Hinsdale, Illinois: Dryden Press, 1978.

Lorie, James, and Hamilton, Mary. *The Stock Market: Theories and Evidence*. Homewood, Illinois: Dow Jones-Irwin, Inc. 1973.

Malkiel, Burton, *The Term Structure of Interest Rates-Expectations and Behavior Patterns*. Princeton: Princeton University Press, 1966.

———. *The Term Structure of Interest Rates: Theory Empirical Evidence*. New York· McCleb-Seiler, 1970.

Meislman, David. *The Term Structure of Interest Rates*. Englewood Cliffs, N.J.: Prentice-Hall, Inc., 1962.

Pogue, Gerald A., and Modigliani, Franco. "An Introduction to Risk and Return." *Financial Analysts Journal* Vol. 30, No. 2 (1974): 68-85.

Shiskin, J. "Systematic Aspects of Stock Price Fluctuations." In *Modern Developments in Investment Management,* edited by James Lorie and Richard Brealey. Hinsdale, Illinois: Dryden Press, 1968.

"Short Term Interest Rates as Predictors of Inflation." *American Economic Review* 67 (1977): 469-96.

Valentine, Jerome L. *Investment Analysis and Capital Market Theory*. Charlottesville, Virginia: The Financial Analysts Research Foundation, 1975.

Journals

Financial Analysts Journal. New York: Financial Analysts Federation. Published bimonthly.

Journal of Portfolio Management. Published by Institutional Investor System, Inc. New York, N.Y. Published quarterly.

Index